DATE DUE FOR RETURN

FEB 2000

An American Dreamer

An American Dreamer
____A Psychoanalytic Study
of the Fiction
of NORMAN MAILER____

Andrew Gordon

Rutherford · Madison · Teaneck
Fairleigh Dickinson University Press

London and Toronto: Associated University Presses

© 1980 by Associated University Presses, Inc.

Associated University Presses, Inc.
Cranbury, New Jersey 08512

Associated University Presses
Magdalen House
136–148 Tooley Street
London SE1 2TT, England

Associated University Presses
Toronto M5E 1A7, Canada

Library of Congress Cataloging in Publication Data
Gordon, Andrew
  An American dreamer.

  Bibliography: p.
  Includes index.
  1. Mailer, Norman—Criticism and interpretation. I. Title. II. Title: Psycho-
analytic study of the fiction of Norman Mailer.
PS3525.A4152Z66   813'.5'2   77-89778
ISBN 0-8386-2158-9
ISBN O-8386-3066-9 (P)

To my parents, Harry *and* Adele Gordon, *and to the memory of* Edward Arnold Taylor *and* Bela St. George.

Contents

As the years go by and I become a little more possible for Ph.D. mills, graduate students will begin to write about the slapping of my creative rage, of Mailer's vision of his rage as his shield, when what I was trying to say was simply, "The shits are killing us."

Norman Mailer, *Advertisements for Myself*

Key to Abbreviations

All page references within parentheses in the text are to the following editions, which are thus abbreviated:

AD An American Dream (New York: The Dial Press, 1965)

ADV Advertisements for Myself (New York: Putnam's, 1959)

AN The Armies of the Night (New York: New American Library, 1968)

BS Barbary Shore (New York: Rinehart, 1951)

DP The Deer Park (New York: Putnam's, 1955)

ND The Naked and the Dead (New York: Rinehart, 1948)

WV Why Are We in Vietnam? (New York: Putnam's, 1967)

The abbreviations appear only when the cited source changes. Subsequent references to the same source bear only the appropriate page numbers.

Acknowledgments

Every book is the product of many people. I would like to take this opportunity to thank some of them. First, for being there through everything: my wife, Judy Taylor Gordon. Next, for advice and encouragement: Tom Maremaa, Bob Fox, David Walley, Phil Gordon, Mark Shechner, John Cech, Bob Ehrlich, John W. Corrington, Ishmael Reed, and Morton Kaplan. For service above and beyond the call of duty, over the long haul: Professors James E. Breslin and Michael Rogin of the University of California, Berkeley, and the kind editors at Associated University Presses.

I am deeply indebted to Professor Frederick Crews of the University of California, Berkeley for his inspiring teaching and brilliant criticism. This book began as a dissertation under his direction and has benefited over the years from his generous guidance and support.

Special thanks go to the many fine critics of Mailer, too numerous to mention, in whose path I follow. And, finally, to Norman Mailer himself, who once told me, "There's an old Mafia saying: Follow your nose."

The author also wishes to thank the editors of *Literature and Psychology* for permission to reprint material in Chapters 2, 7, and 8 and that was originally in different form in that journal. Material from *The Naked and the Dead, Barbary Shore, The Deer Park, Advertisements for Myself, An American Dream, Why Are We in Vietnam?,* and *The Armies of the Night* by Norman Mailer are used by permission of G.P. Putnam's Sons, the author, and the author's agents, Scott Meredith Literary Agency, Inc., 845 Third Avenue, New York, New York 10022.

Introduction: An American Dreamer

Norman Mailer has always been interested in the power of dreams as an expression of the deepest desires of the individual or of the American culture. Over the years his view of the function of the dream has altered; he sees it first as Freudian wish-fulfillment, later as Jungian manifestation of the collective unconscious, and finally, in *Of a Fire on the Moon*, as a simulation of possible future events, a "dream of the future's face." Despite his shifting conceptions of the nature of the dream, Mailer has remained fascinated by it as the inroad to the unconscious, and tried to approach the unconscious power of the dream in his fiction, as one can see in the title of a novel like *An American Dream*. For America has from the beginning been a country dreamed up out of wishes; "the American dream" of wealth, power, and individual fulfillment is at the center of our self-image. At some point during the twentieth century, Mailer feels, that dream may have changed into a nightmare.

Mailer soon abandoned the tradition of literary naturalism that brought him such enormous early success in *The Naked and the Dead* (1948) because it prevented him from exploring fully the territory that interested him most: that of the psyche. Thus his second novel, *Barbary Shore* (1951), has a Kafkaesque, nightmarish intensity: strange forces have erupted, and the bizarre behavior of the characters has no clear, rational motivation. But at this early stage in his career, Mailer lacked a psychology with which to explain this strange behavior.

Shortly after that novel appeared, Mailer writes:

> I woke up in the morning with the plan for a prologue and an eight-part novel in my mind, the prologue to be the day of a small, frustrated man, a minor artist manqué. The eight novels were to be eight stages of his dream later that night, and the books would revolve around the adventures of a mythical hero, Sergius O'Shaugnessy. . . . (*ADV*, p. 154)

Although the scheme was never completed, it absorbed Mailer's energies as a fiction writer for the remainder of the decade of the fifties. Two sections from that unfinished dream epic are "The Man Who Studied Yoga" and *The Deer Park*. "Yoga," which is narrated by an unnamed narrator who may be Sergius O'Shaugnessy, was to have been the prologue; it begins as the failed artist, Sam Slovoda, awakens one winter morning, and ends that same evening as he drifts into a dream. The dream that is intended to follow evidently will contain the novel that poor Sam cannot write during the day. Next, *The Deer Park* follows the adventures of Sergius, now an apprentice novelist, in Desert D'Or, a resort for wealthy movie people (modeled on Palm Springs). There he discovers through painful experience the mentality of Hollywood, that land of dreams, and learns to distinguish between the false dreams of celluloid, which nourish unreality, and the true dreams of art, which promote growth.

In the sixties, Mailer abandoned the adventures of Sergius in order to plunge even deeper into an exploration of the territory of the dream. There was an urgency about his mission, for he felt that something had gone drastically wrong in American life:

> Since the First World War, Americans have been leading a double life, and our history has moved on two rivers, one visible, the other underground; there has been the history of politics which is concrete, factual, practical and unbelievably dull if not for the consequences of the actions of these men; and there is a subterranean river of untapped, ferocious, lonely and romantic desires, that concentration of ecstasy and violence which is the dream life of the nation.[1]

Mailer wanted to return America to an awareness of its suppressed desires, to tap into the buried dream life of the nation, to reunite the two rivers. Thus he wrote a novel, *An American Dream* (1965), a blend of pop fiction thriller and heroic myth. *An American Dream* is a phantasmagoria of the unconscious in which rationality is thrown out the window (along with the hero's wife). In this novel, what Freud called "the primary process," the workings of the id, rules: the dense imagery and symbols seem formed through the psychic processes of condensation and displacement, and the plot is deliberately riddled with bizarre coincidences and irrational and magical events—all the logic of a dream.

His next novel, *Why Are We in Vietnam?* (1967), is conceived of as a kind of late-night radio show by a Texas teenager named D.J., a mad genius of a disc jockey to America, broadcasting out loud our innermost desires. D.J. too subjects us to primary process thinking—to puns and word play, to scabrous, horrifying visions, and to a cheerful, endless flow of obscenity and scatology—in order to break down our resistance, to force us to confront the violent dream life of the nation, of which we partake every night. For, according to D.J.:

When you go into sleep, that mind of yours leaps, stirs, and sifts itself into the Magnetic-Electro fief of the dream, hereafter known as M.E. or M.E.F., you are part of the spook flux of the night like an iron filing . . . . and it all flows, mind and asshole, anode and cathode, you sending messages and receiving all the night. . . . (*WV*, p. 170)

Mailer hopes through his fiction to tune us into those collective dream messages, to reintegrate our conscious awareness and our unconscious desires, which he feels have diverged to a dangerous extent.

The Armies of the Night (1968) takes its title from Matthew Arnold's famous poem, "Dover Beach,":

> Ah, love, let us be true
> To one another! for the world, which seems
> To lie before us like a land of dreams
>
> . . . .
> Hath really neither joy, nor love, nor light
>
> . . . .
> And we are here as on a darkling plain
>
> . . . .
> Where ignorant armies clash by night.

The America Mailer depicts seems, as in Arnold's poem, to be a land of dreams, but it is actually a battlefield. For example, the army of young people who assemble to march on the Pentagon in protest of the Vietnam War are costumed as if for a masquerade ball: "They were close to being assembled from all the intersections between history and the comic books, between legend and television, the Biblical archetypes and the movies" (*AN*, p. 92). They resemble a vision out of "the collective underworld of the dream" (*AN*, p. 93). Mailer's message, like Arnold's, is that we must be true to one another in the face of the chaos and struggle of modern America: the struggle is ambiguous and the outcome uncertain, but we must be brave and preserve the dream of love. Mailer equates his love for America with his love for his wife, and concludes by saying, "For we must end on the road to that mystery where courage, death, and the dream of love give promise of sleep" (*AN*, p. 288).

Of a Fire on the Moon (1970) also explores the landscape of the dream: "So the Twentieth Century was a century which looked to explain the psychology of the dream, and instead entered the topography of the dream. The real had become more fantastic than the imagined. And might yet possess more of the nightmare."[2]

The moon had been a central symbol in *An American Dream,* and now Mailer sees the flight of the crew of Apollo 11 to the moon as "incisions into the platinum satellite of our lunacy, our love, and our dreams."[3]

In *Of a Fire on the Moon,* Mailer also proposes his own theory of dreams, arguing that they are not, as Freud claimed, simply wish fulfillments, but "a simulation chamber where the possible malfunctions of life tomorrow and life next year could be tested, where the alternate plans could be tried."[4] In that case, "the real substance of a dream was a submersion into dread. One tested the ability of the psyche to bear anxiety as one submerged into deeper and deeper plumbings of the unknowable."[5]

Mailer's poetic theory of dreams may lack scientific validity, but it seems to explain and justify in retrospect what he had been attempting in his fiction, for each of the novels, from *The Naked and the Dead* through *The Armies of the Night,* tests "the ability of the psyche to bear anxiety" as the protagonists plunge deeper into the unknowable. Each of his novels contains some of the features of an anxiety dream.

In his quest for the buried dream life of the nation, Mailer has always pushed to the extremes of experience, to the limits and beyond. In his fiction, Mailer drives himself and the reader as mercilessly as Sergeant Croft drove his platoon up a mountain in *The Naked and the Dead.* If he can penetrate into undiscovered territory in a novel in the face of dread, if he can find out his psychic limits and surpass those limits, then Mailer considers himself a better man for the experience. But his fiction is not simply a wrestling with his private demons. It is a public act, and the agon of a Sergeant Croft or a Stephen Rojack is one in which the reader participates: the terrain that they explore might expand by that much the territory in which the individual American psyche can maneuver. For Mailer conceives of himself as, among other incarnations, the rebel general urging forward the troops. He admits that he will settle for nothing less than "making a revolution in the consciousness of our time" (*ADV,* p. 17).

To achieve his goal of unearthing our buried dreams, Mailer has mined deeply into his own violent fantasy life. His fiction promises to allow us to collaborate in those dreams, to his and our benefit.

II

Let us then consider Mailer's fiction as a series of dream books, simulations of the deep psychic content of the mind of America—

and of the mind of Mailer, for the distinctions between the two have been deliberately blurred in his work. Mailer has a romantic vision of the role of the artist in clarifying a nation's vision of itself; to do that, he must become, like Whitman, a microcosm of the country, and dream for us the American dreams. Mailer has faith in the instinctual wisdom of the unconscious; given the increasing encroachments on the freedom of the individual in a mass, technological society, he feels that the psyche is the one area left that the totalitarian state cannot regulate.[6]

Of course, there are a number of inbuilt limitations in Mailer's approach to the unconscious. How can one distinguish between behavior that is socially influenced and behavior that is presumably "instinctual"? And how can we be certain that the primitive wisdom of the instinctual, unregulated id is always to be trusted and will lead us toward growth and authentic being? Finally, can we ever be sure in his work where Mailer's private fantasies end and America's begin?

Given the limitations of Mailer's approach, his merits as a writer of fiction are nonetheless considerable. He is one of our most adventurous writers, constantly exploring deeper into himself and daring to expose his innermost fantasies. In his attempt to give shape to his experience, he has forged a characteristic rhetoric that at its best is rich, playful, and vigorous (at its worst it is clotted, pretentious, and lumbering) and simultaneously conveys levels of both conscious and unconscious meaning. He has also moved from the naturalism and realism of his early fiction to the mysticism and super-realism of his later work. Novels such as *An American Dream* and *Why Are We in Vietnam?* have the hallucinatory intensity of the dream-vision, and are well suited to his explorations of unconscious meaning in American life.

The central concerns of Mailer's work have always been sex, anality, violence, and power, and the intricate connections between these drives in unconscious thought and conscious behavior. For example, in a critique of the movie *Last Tango in Paris* Mailer is as interested in reviewing the audience as in reviewing the film: "So, too, is the audience of *Tango* an infarct of middle-class anal majesties—if Freud hadn't given us the clue, a reader of faces could decide all on his own that there had to be some social connection between sex, shit, power, violence, and money."[7]

The language of this passage is characteristic late Mailer style, in which the word play advances the explicit themes; it is a style of aggressive desublimation, uniting conscious and unconscious content. The language is pungent and visceral, forcing the reader to confront the anality Mailer is discussing: "infarct," for example, means an area of diseased, necrotic flesh; it suggests decay and clotted rot and the "cancer" of the American spirit to which Mailer constantly refers in his writing. At the same time, the word contains a pun on "fart." For that matter, "a reader of faces" suggests "a reader of feces." How much of this word play is intentional on the author's part is impossible to ascertain, but Mailer's style consistently relies on pungent, overdetermined words with multiple significations.

Is this reading too much into Mailer's language? Let us consider then another example of this poetic style of word association in his prose. Early in *An American Dream*, Rojack recalls his risky assault on two German machine-gun nests during World War II; after flinging grenades into the nests, he had to confront and kill four Nazis face to face. Once he shot the first man, "the next was up, his hole-mate, a hard avenging specter with a pistol in his hand and one arm off, blown off, rectitude like a stringer of saliva across the straight edge of his lip, the straightest lip I ever saw, German-Protestant rectitude" (*AD*, p. 4). That repeated term "rectitude" (a favorite word in Mailer's later fiction) suggests repression, piety, righteousness, hard work, standing up and doing one's duty—all the qualities of the Protestant ethic. At the same time, it puns on the physical characteristics which these qualities connote: *erection* and *rectum*. The term has suggestive force both consciously and unconsciously; it unites phallic and anal characteristics in a single word. On the conscious level, in the action of the novel it is precisely the conventional man, upright and tight-sphinctered, an unconscionable hypocrite who never deviates from society's path, whom the hero Rojack is opposing. The Nazi represents the Christian, puritanical, and totalitarian individual who represses his desires, thereby reinforcing them. With that "stringer of saliva" on his lip he seems like a rabid dog. On the unconscious, fantasy level, he represents authority: the castrated father come to take revenge on Rojack, the rebellious son ("a hard avenging specter with a pistol in his hand and one arm off, blown off"). The reader does not have to work hard to arrive at these conclusions: on the contrary, Mailer seems eager to spell out for us the fantasy meaning of the story, as if he can forestall his anxiety about the unconscious content of this dream through aggressive desublimation, making the latent meaning manifest. This strategy is similar to that of the dreamer who keeps reminding himself, "This is only a dream."

This study will interpret Mailer's fiction in much the same way as Freud analyzed the content of dreams in *The Interpretation of Dreams*—bearing in mind, of course, the fact that the dream, which is a wholly unconscious, involuntary, private, and obscure system of symbology, differs from fiction, which is a consciously willed product intended to have meaning to a wide public. Mailer's novels are not merely a means of working out unconscious psychological problems, of playacting his fantasies. If they were nothing but that, they would be of no interest to the reader. Obviously, his stories are rich and multileveled, involving conflicts that are simultaneously psychological, social, political, and spiritual. These conflicts do not belong solely to the author or to his characters, but are intended to have meaning for all of us, to comment on the situation of contempory Americans. His art is a conscious act by means of which he turns his private fantasies into matters of public concern.

Nevertheless, given these truisms, it is also undeniable that we all work within the boundaries of certain psychological predispositions. An author can change the style or form of his work, but he cannot alter the content or shape of his personality. Instead, he tries through art to make both the strengths and weaknesses of his character yield the maximum dividends: witness for example Ernest Hemingway, who, with his machismo, spoke with "the authority of success"; or Scott Fitzgerald, who, with his frailty, spoke with "the authority of failure" (the judgments are Fitzgerald's on himself and Hemingway).

The dream struggles against the limitations of the self by offering each individual an experience outside the everyday categories; fiction also struggles against the boundaries of the self by offering both writer and reader, through imaginative identification, a temporary transcendence of their ordinary personalities. We read fiction in a state of controlled daydreaming, sharing in someone else's dream. But all dreams end and novels come to the last page; both return us to ourselves and we are left to make the connections between our everyday lives and the knowledge perhaps gained in the transcendent experience. This study is an attempt to add to that knowledge.

Just as our psychological predispositions color our response to fiction, so the psychological predispositions of the author will inevitably affect his creation on all levels, from fundamental decisions concerning structure, point of view, character and situation, to questions of theme and style. Every work of fiction is a compromise solution involving an interplay between conscious artistic decisions and often unspoken needs to resolve and to defend against psychological conflicts. Any successful work tries to balance the tension between private concerns and public meaning, so that the one will reinforce the other; sometimes, however, the most dynamic aspect of a piece of fiction may be a contradiction between its surface concerns and its unconscious content—although too great a contradiction can damage the work, as we see, for example, in Mailer's *Barbary Shore*.

Although unconscious conflicts remain much the same in the course of a lifetime, a worthwhile novelist will vary his attempts at conflict resolution during his career, altering his angle of attack, his form and style, to yield both himself and the reader new knowledge, new perspectives on human emotional experience.

A psychoanalytic study of Mailer's fiction cannot tell us everything about his work, but the selective focus will give us new information about certain underlying emotional continuities in the work and how these affect matters of form, content, and style, and patterns of imagery.

Mailer seems to lend himself to a psychoanalytic approach because of his overt interest in the psyche and his cultivation of the instinctual life and the irrational in both his writing and his career as a celebrity and culture hero. During the fifties, as Mailer despaired of any standard political solution to the psychic plague he saw raging in American society, he turned inward toward an exploration of "the rebellious imperatives of the self" (*ADV*, p. 339). It is impossible to say how much his glorification of the primitive and the instinctual life was a conscious intellectual decision and how much was prompted by impulses that were unconscious and wholly idiosyncratic. Philip Bufithis claims that, "By methods that he himself does not fully understand, for they are in large part subconsciously motivated, he tries. . . . to validate the ideas advanced in his books by eventfully acting them out in the world."[8]

Although psychoanalysis may provide us with an insight into the underlying coherence of Mailer's literary career—a way to look at the man and the work simultaneously, at the fundamental quality of mind he brings to all his work—it is not the primary purpose of this study to analyze the man himself, though of course this may be a byproduct of the investigation. Psychoanalysis is used as a tool to explore some of the problems of the fiction, and there is no simple one-to-one correlation between an author's private life (which is finally unknowable, in any case) and his fiction. The intention here is to aid the reader of Mailer's novels, not to put Mailer on the couch and attempt therapy thirdhand.

Nor should this study be construed as an attack on Norman Mailer as a "neurotic." The value of Freud's discoveries about the workings of the mind lies in their universality; the phenomena Freud describes exist in the development and the structure of all human personality, and can be used to evaluate the behavior of anyone, "sick" or "healthy." Every adult has passed through infancy, childhood, and adolescence, and retains the residue of infantile fantasies as part of the permanent structure of the character. In fact, some of the pleasure of fiction may be due to its sophisticated appeal to primitive instincts; art can be described as "regression in the service of the ego," as Ernst Kris wrote in *Psychoanalytic Explorations in Art*. Nevertheless, it is up to the trained professional therapist to diagnose and prescribe. This study attempts to describe and evaluate critically one segment of a man's art, not to pass judgment on his life or his personality. In this regard, it is worth citing Howard Gardner's observation:

> In his neurosis the artist resembles others. In his ability to objectify it or to achieve distance from it he differs. The artist's genius should be defined in terms of his faculties of perception, representation, making, and feeling. The one part of the artist that is indubitably healthy, whatever may be sick, is that which gives him the power to conceive, plan, and bring his work to fruition. Indeed, his talent is sufficient indication that mental derangement is not dominant.[9]

It may be objected that it is inappropriate to view the works of Mailer through the lens of Freud, since Mailer, at least since 1954, has been more Reichian than Freudian in his psychoanalytic beliefs. Nevertheless, it is possible to interpret through Freud the works of any novelist, whether he be Freudian, Reichian, Jungian in orientation, or none of these. It is also possible to interpret the career and ideas of Reich himself in a Freudian manner; such an interpretation has already been done, to some extent, in the studies of Reich by Charles Rycroft and Paul A. Robinson. It is even possible to interpret Freud in the light of Freud. Whatever the conscious beliefs of the individual, there are unconscious impulses in his behavior; one's psychoanalytic allegiances do not alter the basic structure of the personality. If we are to grant the ideas of Freud any validity at all, we must grant their applicability to everyone.

Thus it is important to distinguish at the outset between the *surface* psychology of a novel, which is compounded of the author's conscious beliefs, and its *depth* psychology, of which he may be totally unaware. As D. H. Lawrence said, "Never trust the artist. Trust the tale."[10] When we look at Mailer's works from a Freudian viewpoint, we can step outside of his Reichian framework and perhaps gain a more objective viewpoint. It may be that the Reich is just protective coloration, a sophisticated intellectual justification for Mailer to gain release for his private fantasies in his fiction. For this reason, the first chapter of this study will outline at length the evolution of Mailer's psychoanalytic allegiances.

Richard Poirier notes that Mailer "has tried to be the literary historian of his own work, and . . . has tended to usurp the interpretive, even quite often the evaluative functions of criticism."[11] In a similar manner, Mailer has tried to anticipate the psychoanalyst by analyzing himself and his own work. But there is no reason to accept his version at face value. A Freudian viewpoint gives us another set of critical terms for evaluating his work than the ones Mailer has provided, such as "existential," "totalitarian," and "hip," words that he and his commentators have already worked to exhaustion.

III

Before proceeding further, it may be useful for the reader to look over the following brief summary of some of the psychoanalytic theories and terminology on which this study will be based.

As stated earlier, the central concerns, both conscious and unconscious, of Mailer's work have always been sex, anality, violence, and power, and the interconnections between these impulses; as his career went on, these concerns became increasingly overt, so that, for example, the implicit anality of *The Naked and the Dead* (in the rot of the jungle and the decay of the body) becomes the explicit anality of *Why Are We in Vietnam?*, whose narrator D.J. indulges in compulsive obscenity and scatology, and even refers to himself as "a shit-oriented late adolescent. . . . marooned on the balmy tropical isle of Anal Referent Metaphor" (*WV*, p. 150). We can take D.J.'s remark as Mailer's ironic comment on himself, as though he had realized at a certain stage in his career that he too was forever marooned on the island of Anal Referent Metaphor. If he could not escape it, he might as well try to enjoy those "balmy tropical" breezes. Thus he made excremental imagery the core of his style and began to interpret all characters in his fiction in an overtly anal way; he incorporated it into his private symbology and cosmology. Some of this activity might be termed counterphobic, for in certain respects he never overcame his anxiety and his ambivalence about anality: he tried instead to make the best of it by incorporating it consciously rather than merely unconsciously in his writing. Of course, great literature does not stand or fall exclusively on anal-sadism or -erotism, but many literary effects do depend on how the author manages his impulses; that is the subject of this study. Therefore, it would be relevant at this point to survey briefly the theories of Freud and the post-Freudians concerning the "anal stage" of human development.

According to Freud, after the first or oral phase of pregenital development of the libido, in which pleasure revolves around the incorporation of nourishment from the breast, comes the second or anal phase, when the infant is toilet-trained:

> The process of defecation affords the first occasion on which the child must decide between a narcissistic and an object-loving attitude. He either parts obediently with his faeces, "offers them up" to his love, or else retains them for purposes of auto-erotic gratification and later as a means of asserting his own will. The latter choice constitutes the development of defiance (obstinacy), a quality which springs, therefore, from a narcissistic clinging to the pleasure of anal erotism. [12]

During this anal stage, writes Freud:

> we find an antithesis of trends with active and passive aims. . . . The active trend is supplied by that general instinct of mastery which when we find it serving the sexual function we call sadism. . . . The passive trend is fed from anal erotism. . . . [13]

He further asserts that the individual can become fixated at this stage and be ambivalently torn between the active impulses of anal-sadism and the passive impulses of anal-erotism:

> This form of sexual organization can persist throughout life and can permanently attract a large portion of sexual activity to itself. The predominance in it of sadism and the cloacal part played by the anal zone give it quite a peculiarly archaic colouring. It is further characterized by the fact that in the opposing pairs of instincts are developed to an approximately equal extent, a state of affairs described by Bleuler's happily chosen term "ambivalence." [14]

As we shall see, the urge toward mastery, anal-sadism and -erotism, a narcissistic overevaluation of the self, defiance, and emotional ambivalence all play a large part in Mailer's writing.

Freud also claimed that in such fixated individuals, even the genitals become associated with anality: "The faecal mass, or as one patient called it, the faecal 'stick,' represents as it were the first

penis, and the stimulated mucous membrane of the rectum represents that of the vagina."[15] We shall also see a symbolic equation
or confusion in Mailer's writing, sometimes unconscious and sometimes deliberate, between anus, phallus, and vagina, leading in his
later fiction to repeated images of anal rape.

Individuals who become fixated at this early stage of development or who regress to the anal-sadistic level due to emotional
stress later in life show a predisposition to develop what is termed
obsessive-compulsive or simply obsession neurosis (obsession is the
thought and compulsion is the act), claimed Freud: they feel forced
to carry out strange, repeated ritualistic procedures, a kind of
private religion. These compulsive acts Freud interpreted as "re-
action-formations against anal-erotic and sadistic impulses."[16]
The anal ambivalence between sadism and erotism, hate and love,
combines with the later oedipal hostility to intensify the ambivalence toward the love object to an intolerable degree: "The impulse
to love must then mask itself under the sadistic impulse. The obsessive thought, 'I should like to murder you,' means . . . nothing else
but 'I should like to enjoy love of you.' "[17] In defense, the obsessional develops a tyrannical superego: "in order to protect object-
love from the hostility which lurks behind it, the obsessional
neurotic is compelled to build up an overconscientious system
of ultra-morality. . . ."[18] This oversevere superego only makes the
conflict more acute.

The bizarre ritual of the obsessional is both a substitute for the
desired sexual act and a means of undoing the desire. If he fails
to carry out the act, he experiences a nameless "feeling of dread"[19];
thus the ritual is necessary to escape anxiety. At the same time, "the
symptoms serve the purpose of sexual gratification . . . they are a
substitute for gratifications which he does not obtain in reality."[20]
Every obsessional symptom is a compromise, offering both an
escape from dread and a covert gratification of the repressed
libidinal impulse. Consequently, obsessive acts can become self-
indulgent, pleasurable in themselves since they are charged with
unconscious sexual meaning.

In characters such as Marion Faye in *The Deer Park* and Stephen
Rojack in *An American Dream* Mailer has, whether deliberately
or not, created personalities who correspond to the classic psychological profile of the obsessional: nameless feelings of dread,
impulses to love that are transformed into impulses to murder, a
tyrannical superego, and compulsive ritual acts.

Do Freud's theories about the anal character and the obsessional
neurotic have any scientific validity, or are they merely interest-

ing speculation or imaginative metaphors? In *Fact and Fantasy in Freudian Theory*, Paul Kline writes:

> Psychoanalytic theory cannot be said to be true, for the data on which it is based are not well established. On the other hand it cannot be said to be false—because no collection of evidence has as yet falsified the entire complex. Finally, there is no acceptable alternative to the theory. . . . theories are not deposed by facts that do not fit them, but by alternative superior theories. In summary . . . psychoanalytic theory [is] a premature empirical synthesis offered in advance of the evidence.[21]

However, Kline considers all the existing psychological studies and finds that sexual symbolism "has been amply demonstrated to occur both within and outside dreams. . . . The fact that sexual symbolism has been verified means that the insights into art and literature offered by psychoanalytic theory need not be dismissed out of hand."[22] Kline also concludes that, from all scientific studies to date, there is "good evidence" for the Oedipus complex and the castration complex, and "firm evidence" for the existence of the anal character.[23]

Post-Freudian psychoanalysts such as Karl Abraham, Otto Fenichel, Melanie Klein, and Erik Erikson modified or added to Freud's observations about the anal phase of human development. Abraham, in "Contributions to the Theory of Anal Character," enumerated many of the pronounced traits of the anal neurotic: from anal sadism came obstinancy, pride, pretention, depreciation of other persons ("Everything that is not in me is dirt"), a need to have everything his own way, resistance to outside interference, and violent hostility to psychoanalysis. On the other hand, there coexists with such vanity a feeling of helplessness; intestinal impotence—constipation—is felt to be as bad as genital impotence.[24] All of these characteristics could be summed up in Mailer's eloquent cry in *Advertisements for Myself:* " 'The shits are killing us' " (ADV, p. 19).

Otto Fenichel added a number of details to the portrait of the obsessive in *The Psychoanalytic Theory of Neurosis*, particularly the split in the neurosis between overdeveloped intellect and a belief in magic and superstition[25]; again, we see the same split in Mailer's writing, though one can never be sure how much he believes, or wants to believe in the superstitions he offers, and how much is playful speculation and metaphor. Robert Solotaroff sees an ambivalence in Mailer's attitude toward magic, as if Mailer wants to have it both ways: "Yeats . . . did not ask us to believe his system . . . but to understand that it offered him images for his poetry. Mailer does ask us to accept his system but to understand that he speaks in metaphors."[26]

Coming after Abraham and Fenichel, the psychoanalyst Melanie Klein put new emphasis on the importance of the earliest months of life to the development of the superego. She treated children between the ages of two and six and allowed them to reveal their fantasy life through play. She found that the child has a primitive morality, believing in outside objects as good or bad depending on whether they give him pleasure or pain. However, this means that the child can both love and hate the same object in rapid succession. It lives in a world peopled by gods and devils. The child's mental states are modeled on the processes of introjection (taking in milk) and projection (defecation), and its aggressive fantasies revolve around oral-sadistic ideas of biting and devouring and anal-sadistic ideas of feces as a weapon. The child may project these ideas upon the mother, who can sometimes be a "bad" object; it then must retaliate against the mother through aggressive fantasies.[27] In Mailer's fiction, we often see this blending of oral-and anal-sadistic fantasies, desires to befoul or to devour cannibalistically, particularly in the behavior toward women of such characters as Hollingsworth in *Barbary Shore*, Sergius in "The Time of Her Time," Rojack in *An American Dream*, and D.J. in *Why Are We in Vietnam?*

Finally, according to Erik Erikson in *Childhood and Society*, when the infant learns sphincter control, he passes through the stage of *autonomy* vs. *shame and doubt*. The child must find a balance between the conflicting physical and psychological modes of retention and elimination, holding on and letting go. Holding on can become either cruel retaining or tender care; letting go can turn into either destructive release or relaxation. If he successfully passes through the anal stage, the child learns autonomy: true self-control. However, if he is overcontrolled at this crucial stage, he may succumb to lifelong shame and doubt. "Powerless in his own body (and often fearing the feces as if they were hostile monsters inhabiting his insides) and powerless outside," the child develops a false autonomy.[28] He may become hostile, using his feces as ammunition, or stubbornly resistant to control; he may also combat his shame through defiant shamelessness. If he compensates for a sense of powerlessness by overmanipulating himself and the environment, "such hollow victory is the infantile model for compulsion neurosis."[29] His sense of doubt about the products of the bowels "finds its adult expression in paranoiac fears concerning hidden persecutors and secret persecutions threatening from behind (and from within the behind)."[30] Again, in Mailer's fiction we see a frequent struggle for autonomy. The feelings of shame and doubt, the sense of powerlessness, and fears of persecution are common among his characters. The critic Philip Bufithis goes so far as to say, "The fiction of Norman Mailer up to and including *The Deer Park* concerns man trying to achieve a self-fulfilling autonomy. . . ."[31] It is more likely that *all* of Mailer's fiction concerns the struggle for autonomy. In his idiosyncratic fashion, Mailer is a bit like Emerson and Thoreau, those earlier American apostles of "self-reliance."

If psychoanalytic terminology seems to reduce Mailer's fiction to the expression of anally-oriented fantasies, it is worth recalling that all of us are subject, to one degree or another, to such fantasies. Yet few of us have the power to create believable art out of our emotional lives. The power of the artist is in managing and convincingly dramatizing feelings. Thus Mailer is able to parcel out different parts of himself to the various characters in *The Naked and the Dead* and let their conflict express his own ambiguous feelings, or he observes his own behavior in *The Armies of the Night* from a distance, as one observes a fictional creation. By making his feelings serve the purpose of his art, Mailer can, if only temporarily, transcend them. As Alfred Kazin says, "Mailer is able to make more of a world out of his obsessions than other writers are able to make out of the given material of own common social world."[32]

Notes

1. Norman Mailer, *The Presidential Papers* (New York: Putnam's, 1963), p. 38.

2. Norman Mailer, *Of a Fire on the Moon* (Boston: Little, Brown, 1970), p. 38.

3. Ibid., p. 152.

4. Ibid., p. 159.

5. Ibid., p. 161.

6. See Jean Radford, *Norman Mailer: A Critical Study* (New York: Harper, 1975), p. 27.

7. Norman Mailer, "A Transit to Narcissus," *The New York Review of Books* 20, no. 8 (May 17, 1973): 3.

8. Philip Bufithis, *Norman Mailer* (New York: Ungar, 1978), p. 2.

9. Howard Gardner, *The Arts and Human Development* (New York: John Wiley, 1973), p. 340.

10. D. H. Lawrence, *Studies in Classic American Literature* (New York: Viking, 1966), p. 2.

11. Richard Poirier, *Norman Mailer* (New York: Viking, 1972), p. 2.

12. Sigmund Freud, "On the Transformation of Instincts with Special Reference to Anal Erotism (1917)," in *Character and Culture*, ed. Philip Rieff (New York: Collier, 1963), p. 206.

13. Sigmund Freud, "The Predisposition to Obsessional Neurosis (1913)," in *Sexuality and the Psychology of Love*, ed. Philip Reiff (New York: Collier, 1963), p. 92.

14. Sigmund Freud, *Three Essays on the Theory of Sexuality*, trans. and ed. James Strachey (New York: Avon, 1962), p. 97.

15. Freud, "On the Transformation of Instincts," *Character and Culture*, pp. 206–7.

16. Freud, "The Predisposition to Obsessional Neurosis," *Sexuality and Psychology of Love*, p. 90.

17. Sigmund Freud, *A General Introduction to Psychoanalysis* (New York: Washington Square, 1965), pp. 352–53.

18. Freud, "Predisposition to Obsessional Neurosis," *Sexuality and Psychology of Love*, p. 95.

19. Freud, *General Introduction*, p. 411.

20. Ibid., p. 308.

21. Paul Kline, *Fact and Fantasy in Freudian Theory* (London: Methuen, 1972), p. 3.

22. Ibid., p. 349.

23. Ibid., pp. 116, 29.

24. Karl Abraham, "Contributions to the Theory of Anal Character," in *An Outline of Psychoanalysis*, ed. Clara Thompson, Milton Mazer and Earl Wittenberg (New York: Random, 1955), pp. 298–319.

25. Otto Fenichel, *The Psychoanalytic Theory of Neurosis* (New York: Norton, 1945), pp. 300–04.

26. Robert Solotaroff, *Down Mailer's Way* (Urbana, Ill.: University of Illinois Press, 1974), p. 118.

27. Melanie Klein, *Contributions to Psychoanalysis* (London: Hogarth Press, 1948).

28. Erik M. Erikson, *Childhood and Society*, 2d. ed. (New York: Norton, 1963), p. 82.

29. Ibid., p. 252.

30. Ibid., p. 254.

31. Bufithis, *Norman Mailer*, p. 131.

32. Alfred Kazin, "The Alone Generation," in *Recent American Fiction: Some Critical Views*, ed. Joseph J. Waldmeir (Boston: Houghton Mifflin, 1963), p. 23.

An American Dreamer

1 Mailer, Freud, and Reich: The Novelist as Psychoanalyst

" 'Isn't it a little obvious to be hostile to psychoanalysis?' " says Denise to Sergius in Norman Mailer's short story "The Time of Her Time" (*ADV*, p. 493). Mailer's own relationship as a novelist to psychoanalysis over the years has been much like his relationship to his audience: a combative affair, mixed with equal parts of love and hate. Mailer has used psychoanalysis in a very conscious and sophisticated way in his fiction, and at the same time he has carried on a crusade, both in his essays and in his fiction, against the power of psychoanalysis in popular culture.

Mailer is not alone among contemporary novelists in his distrust of analysis and therapists. Vladimir Nabokov was another psychoanalytic sophisticate even more openly contemptuous than is Mailer of the fruits of Sigmund Freud.

This study aims to examine Mailer's fictional creations, using Freudian psychology as a critical tool. Before we can begin to do this, however, we must understand the reasons for Mailer's ambivalence toward Freudianism.

The incorporation of Freud into popular culture created a dilemma for the artist, and, in particular, for the novelist, who had to come to terms with this radically new way of evaluating and delineating human character. The novelist could respond to psychoanalysis in three basic ways: accept the analyst as a colleague working in a parallel field and absorb his insights as a valuable supplement to traditional ways of depicting character in fiction; proceed as if he were still writing in the nineteenth century; or consider the analyst as a rival or dangerous enemy to the art of the novelist. In any case, the discoveries of Freud represented to the novelist a loaded weapon with a potentially heavy recoil. However the novelist chose to respond, that is, whether he accommodated himself to psychoanalysis, ignored it, or declared war against it, the novelist was still dealing with the raw material of fantasy, and, as such, his creations were invariably grist for the analyst's mill and could be interpreted as high-class sublimations of his neurotic needs. Freud himself may have admired the artist and stood in awe of the mysteries of his craft, but this did not ease the anxiety in the mind of the novelist. A magician has reason to feel

31

threatened by someone who he believes can see through the tricks.

Mailer's literary career, although undeniably unique, is representative of the range of responses of a modern novelist attempting to cope with psychoanalysis. Mailer moves in psychological loyalty from Freudian to Reichian to "existential psychology," Mailer's own brand of guerrilla therapy. Throughout, Mailer demonstrates the role confusion and identity crisis of the modern novelist, precipitated in part by the rise of the psychoanalyst, who seems to the novelist to have usurped part of the novelist's previous role—to have, in a sense, rendered him obsolete.

Mailer began as an ardent Freudian, trying to assimilate into his fiction what was then the fashionable psychology. *The Naked and the Dead* exhibits a good awareness of Freudian ideas about behavior. The "Time Machine" sections in this novel give rapid, capsule histories of the various characters through a series of flashback scenes. This literary device derives from naturalistic novelists such as Dos Passos, but Mailer adds to the sociological determinism of Dos Passos a form of psychological determinism.[1] The character traits of Mailer's soldiers are largely predetermined by the social strata and geographical location into which they are born and by the personalities of their parents. Mailer makes use of certain Freudian commonplaces to explain the behavior patterns of the men in the action of the story. For example, the mother of young Edward Cummings encourages him to sew, but his father beats him when he finds him using a needle and thread. This "Time Machine" episode is presumed to explain the suppressed homosexuality and will to power that Cummings later manifests.

Mailer's use of Freud here is rather makeshift, but it serves his purposes in this massive novel, where he is dealing with an epic cast of characters and has to account for the motivation of each individual as rapidly and efficiently as possible. What is absorbing in *The Naked and the Dead* is not the Freudian overlay but rather the dynamic interplay between the characters, and inexplicable, mystical yearnings of a man such as Croft in the assault on Mount Anaka—elements that cannot be entirely accounted for by psychological commonplaces. Finally, it is Mailer's intuitive grasp of psychology and not his mechanical incorporation of Freud that lifts this novel into the realm of interesting art.

In his second novel, *Barbary Shore,* Mailer is dealing with a much smaller cast of characters, but they are all so alienated, living in the savage wilds of "the enormous present" (*ADV.*, p. 93), their past histories either erased or obscured, that the techniques of "The Time Machine" no longer apply. The behavior of the

Sam has felt the nervous glee of an adolescent locking himself in the bathroom. Anal fixation, Sam thinks automatically" (p. 166).

One critic has suggested that the counteractive to Dr. Sergius and the true therapist of the tale is the anonymous narrator.[2] In Mailer's later short story "The Time of Her Time," the anonymous narrator is replaced by an active narrator, the hipster Sergius O'Shaugnessy, who serves as the self-appointed sexual liberator and therapist for a frigid woman. This "Dr. Sergius" is at the opposite pole from Sam's Dr. Sergius.

Dr. Sergius in "Yoga" is the original for a stock character in Mailer's fiction: the therapist as comic villain. The type includes Dr. Joyce in "The Time of Her Time" and Dr. Rothenberg in *Why Are We in Vietnam?* Dr. Leonard Levin Fichte Rothenberg is affectionately called by his patient Hallie Lee Jethroe, in a deliberate Freudian slip, "Dr. Rottenbug" and "Dr. Fink Lenin Rodzianko." The "Lenin" tag unmistakably implies Mailer's message: the totalitarian character of the psychotherapist.

Despite his hostility toward analysts, Mailer never completely abandoned his earlier faith in Freud. In reply to an interviewer's question, "Are you a Freudian?" Mailer was careful to distinguish between his respect for the mind of Freud and his distaste for Freud's social conservatism. "I believe Freud was a genius, an incredible mighty discoverer of secrets, mysteries, and new questions. But the answers he gave were doctrinaire, deathlike, and philosophically most dreary. . . . He had so little optimism . . ." (p. 273). As Diana Trilling notes, Mailer makes Freudianism "the target of some of his sharpest attacks on the modern dispensation." However, Mailer "directs his criticism not so much at Freud himself as to his disciples today," followers of Freud who "live too cosily with the traditional attitudes of our society."[3] Mailer objects not to the discoveries of Freud but to the abuses to which Mailer believed this new science had been subjected, in particular the use of psychotherapy as another instrument for social control. According to Jean Radford, "The reasons behind his wholesale rejection of psychoanalysis lie in his reactionary notion that instinct is more 'authentic' than socially acquired behavior, and the treatment of sex and violence in his work can only be understood in this light."[4]

In *Advertisements*, Mailer admits to a certain kinship between the task of the novelist and the analyst. "The novelist, like the analyst, spends his life absorbed with the nuances of human nature . . ." (p. 302). After the failure of *Barbary Shore*, Mailer even felt for a while that "maybe I was not really a writer. I thought often of becoming a psychoanalyst" (p. 108), as though an analyst were

characters in *Barbary Shore* is so bizarre and path(
secondhand Freud is useless to explain their motiv;
inexplicable frenzy is a given, presumably accepted b'
as one of the inevitable consequences of living in the
scape of the postwar, nuclear era, in which there is
worth believing in. Although *Barbary Shore* cannot reall
stood except as a psychological romance, Mailer had
he wrote it no psychology that was adequate to explain
creations, because he was at a period of his life when he
ability to explain himself. Mailer admits as much la
vertisements for Myself:

> *Barbary Shore* was really a book to emerge from the l
> cellars of my unconscious, an agonized eye of a n(
> tried to find some amalgam of my new experience and
> horror of that world which might be preparing to des
> I was obviously trying for something which was at the \
> my reach, and then beyond it, and toward the end of
> collapsed. . . . Yet, it could be that if my work is alive on
> years from now, *Barbary Shore* will be considered t
> of my first three novels for it has in its high fevers a kin(
> insight into the psychic mysteries. . . . (p. 94)

Out of his postwar disillusionment and his personal psy(
crisis, Mailer had to discard nearly all of his previous b(
build anew. One of these discards was psychoanalysis. "
Who Studied Yoga," his short story of 1952, crystallizes the
toward traditional psychotherapy that characterize Mail(
from then on.

The therapist is now the villain, the representative (
society, and the enemy of the liberating guerrilla force o(
force that in his famous essay of 1957, "The White Negro,'
was to label "Hip." Sam Slovoda, the protagonist of "Yo
middle-class square, a failed radical, and a failed artist in s
to a deadening psychoanalytic jargon and to the powe
analyst, Dr. Sergius. The domineering Dr. Sergius, with his
accent, represents the forces of creeping totalitarianism
which Mailer wages war. The Doctor is a caricature, persor
his "bald skull and horn-rimmed glasses" (p. 162), th
developed head and the probing eye. He is the archenem'
infantile residues in the personality and the spontaneous i
of the body. Sam finds himself hemmed in by psychoanaly
and categories, which, like the superego, have become a reg
voice incorporated in his own head. "Ever since Marvin μ

only a kind of novelist *manqué*. Nevertheless, he came to the conclusion that the novelist and the analyst "approach their vocation diametrically opposed. . . . I wonder if their ends are not essentially different, the artist a rebel concerned with Becoming, the analyst a regulator concerned with Being?" (p. 302).

Mailer wrote *Advertisements for Myself* in part to define for himself his new conception of his relationship as an artist to society. At the opening of the book, Mailer announces, "The sour truth is that I am imprisoned with a perception which will settle for nothing less than making a revolution in the consciousness of our time" (p. 17). He has come to believe that the artist could have a direct effect on society by exerting an influence upon its consciousness. Mailer is positing an extremely hypothetical revolution: not an uprising by force of arms, but a rebellion that takes place inside the individual psyche. Having given up on conventional politics, he wants to believe in internally liberating forces by which the individual can free himself. Mailer admits that he is searching for a dialectic "which can infuse material notions of energy into that philosophical country of the ideal (read: the individual unconscious) which psychoanalysis now occupies with a middle-class mechanistic *weltanschauung*" (p. 365). As such a potentially revolutionary artist, Mailer is attempting to muscle in on the territory that has been staked out by the psychoanalyst; he is setting himself up as nothing less than a countertherapist for the collective unconscious of society.

Mailer puns on the slang notion of the analyst as "shrink," contemptuously calling him an "educated ball-shrinker" (p. 371). The analyst, suggests Mailer, does not treat neurosis: he reduces the patient, shrinks him to fit into place in the well-regulated society, and, in effect, castrates him. "The result for all too many patients is a diminution, a 'tranquilizing' of their most interesting qualities and vices. . . . He is thus able to conform to that contradictory and unbearable society which first created his neurosis" (p. 346).

There is an element of fanciful distortion in Mailer's typecasting of the artist and the analyst, and in the vision of the therapist as an omnipotent social regulator. Nevertheless, Mailer's picture of the psychoanalyst, although exaggerated and not applicable to all analysts, does have a basis in fact. There does exist a therapeutic orthodoxy that can have an inhibiting effect on self-expression. In an argument with Dr. Sergius, Sam Slovoda expresses the pathetic situation of the artist, his impotent rage as he is defeated in argument and frustrated by the all-powerful force of psychoanalysis, the science that has an answer for everything: "'How can I discuss these things . . . if you insist that my opinions are the expression of neurotic needs, and your opinions are merely dispassionate medical advice?'" (p. 164).

One senses the same rage and frustration in Mailer as he grapples for some way to battle with this lofty and evasive opponent. In one of his columns for the *Village Voice*, Miler issues a challenge to any analyst to debate him in print. It smacks of the old barroom brawler's dare, "I can lick any man in the house," but it is Mailer's way of smoking out the enemy, a faceless opponent who prefers to remain above the combat. Mailer tries to provoke psychoanalysts into a fight by taunting them. "I doubt, frankly, if any analyst will come forward . . . there is a certain tendency among all too many of them to avoid psychoanalytic discussion with laymen on the theory that the mysteries of the new religion might suffer . . . " (p. 302). Later Mailer confesses, "The sad reality, I'm afraid, is that an artist must step up in class these days to challenge an analyst, for the greater part of the public listens far more carefully to a third-rate practitioner than a first-rate novelist" (p. 306). There is a touch of professional jealousy in this attitude; for Mailer the high priests of this new religion, who presume to have all the answers and all the cures, have usurped the position that was once held by the novelist.

Mailer is harking back to a hypothetical "Golden Age" of the novel. Whether the novelist was ever held in such high esteem by most of the public, or in the sort of esteem now held by the analyst, is dubious. Is the storyteller really expected to perform the same functions as the medicine man?

When Mailer finally receives a reply from an analyst, the encounter is inconclusive. The doctor sends him a letter, and Mailer breaks down the substance of the letter sentence by sentence, interjecting his responses to give it the semblance of a real dialogue. Mailer, of course, holds all the aces in such a contrived exchange. The doctor sounds cool, clinical, and condescending, whereas Mailer is malicious and mocking. He concludes the pseudo-debate by turning the analyst's own weapons against him, indulging in a mock analysis packed with the jargon of the trade and intended to dispose of the doctor once and for all through ridicule.

Doctor Y. impresses me as being only mildly neurotic, and in ways which most people consider socially constructive. He suffers from small compulsions and expulsions of guilt, undoubtedly anal-retentive in their seat, but so relatively harmless, given his successful sublimation of sadism, that his conditioned conservatism allocates powerful super-ego energies to control the mildly paranoid element revealed today by his literary style and his obvious (to any clinician) projections upon me of all his conflicts. One may add that Dr. Y. is ambitious beyond his means, but is covertly aware that his powerdrives are unrealistic. This expresses itself beneath his general depression by ambivalence and general timidity. . . . He would be suitable for treating weak unfortunate patients. . . . (pp. 308–9)

Ironically, this vindictive analysis could apply just as well to Mailer himself. Mailer satirizes far more skillfully in *Why Are We in Vietnam?*, where Dr. Rottenbug, in D.J.'s comic fantasy, indulges in bastardized, high-flown and garbled rhetoric about "a choir task force of libidinal cross-hybrided vectors" (*WV*. p. 14).

Mailer confesses with pride in *Advertisements* that "I have never been analyzed, but . . . I have spent the last year in analyzing myself" (*ADV*, pp. 301–2). Mailer prides himself on being independent, on bucking the trend in an age when it has become fashionable to take one's miseries to the analyst's couch. He is aware that others could use against him the argument that Denise uses against Sergius: "'Isn't it a little obvious to be hostile to psychoanalysis?'" Nevertheless, although Mailer psychoanalyzes himself at great length in print, he bridles at allowing someone else to use the same techniques on him. For Mailer, therapy other than self-therapy constitutes an invasion of privacy and an infringement on individual liberty. He prefers that the individual be totally self-reliant.

But Mailer is not equally hostile to all forms of therapy. He adds, "As a hint, I will add that if I were ever to look for an analyst, I would get me to a Reichian" (p. 301). *Advertisements* records Mailer's gradual shift in allegiance from the more conservative Freud to the more radical, one-time disciple of Freud, Wilhelm Reich.

It is impossible to state precisely when Mailer first came under the influence of Reich. We do know that Reich's *Character Analysis* and *The Sexual Revolution* were first published in translation in the United States in 1945, followed by *The Mass Psychology of Fascism* in 1946 and *The Emotional Plague* in 1953. The critic Robert Lawler says, "At some point in his career—perhaps as early as *The Naked and the Dead*—Mailer had appropriated some of the ideas of Wilhelm Reich and his belief that the achievement of sexual orgasm would in itself initiate the cure for any so-called 'mental' disease."[5] It is difficult to make a case for Reich as a major influence in Mailer's first two novels. There is one brief mention of McLeod's "rigid muscle armor" in *Barbary Shore* (*BS*, p. 235), but that is all. However, the portrait of Sam Slovoda in "Yoga" in 1952—an uptight, impotent square who is not helped by conventional therapy—

suggests that Mailer had either started to take Reich's psychology seriously as the potential answer for modern man or was ready to move in that direction.

Mailer's first reference in print to Reich comes in a 1954 essay entitled "The Homosexual Villain," written for a homosexual magazine.

> I had been a libertarian socialist for some years. . . . Very basic to everything I had thought was that sexual relations, above everything else, demand their liberty. . . . For, in the reverse, history has certainly offered enough examples of the link between sexual repression and political repression. (A fascinating thesis on this subject is *The Sexual Revolution* by Wilhelm Reich.) (*ADV*, p. 225)

Since this essay was written after *The Deer Park*, the conclusion of that novel, in which Sergius, on a mystical flight of fancy, imagines God telling him that "Sex is time, and Time is the connection of new circuits," may be a subliminal reference to Reich's electrical theory of the nature of sexuality. This same concept recurs, somewhat altered, in D.J.'s mystical vision of the aurora borealis at the conclusion of *Vietnam*, although in the latter it is much easier to trace the direct connection between the ideas of the novel and the ideas of Reich.

It is not surprising that Mailer should have affiliated himself with Reich during the mid-1950s; it was fashionable, and many other discontented artists, intellectuals, and socialists turned in that direction at that time. As Diana Trilling wrote in 1962, "Jung, Fromm, Reich: it is among these analytic dissidents that protest now regularly seeks the psychology (and perhaps the parental support) with which to replace . . . Freudian psychology."[6]

Leslie Fiedler asserted that, among the Jewish novelists, "a flirtation with Zen, and especially a commitment to Reichianism . . . often indicates a discontent with simple or conventional plot resolutions and hence a deeper awareness of the contradictions in the situation of the Jewish-American writer."[7] Reich appealed to both the young and the middle-aged in revolt against Freudian orthodoxy:

> Freud has come to seem too timid, too puritanical, and above all too *rational* for the second half of the twentieth century. His notion of the reclamation of the unconscious ("where *id* was, *ego* shall be!") strikes the present age as beside the point; and his celebration of sublimation as the basis of civilization seems to that age a cowardly concession. It is Reich who moves the young, with his antinomianism, his taste for magic, and his emphasis on

full genitality as the final goal of man. The cult of the orgasm developed in his name has won converts in recent years, even from members of the generation of the Forties and the Fifties, approaching middle-age and disillusioned with orthodox Marxism and Freudianism. Isaac Rosenfeld, Saul Bellow, Paul Goodman, and especially Norman Mailer, trying to live a second, meno-pausal youth, have chosen to live it . . . under Reichian auspices, and Mailer . . . has seemed to the young a model and leader in this respect.[8]

It is also natural for Mailer to have been attracted to Reich; Mailer was trying to achieve as a novelist the same synthesis of Marx and Freud that Reich had attempted. According to one critic, Reich had formulated "a theory of sex economy that contains within itself both a theory of psychopathology and a critique of capitalist society."[9] Reich said that "psychic disturbances are the results of the sexual chaos brought about by the nature of our society."[10] Mailer had been moving for some time toward the same conclusion. Leo Braudy writes that

> *Barbary Shore* is Mailer's first attempt to bring together his interests in politics and psychology. In *Advertisements for Myself* he will describe this imaginative synthesis as an effort to build a bridge between Marx and Freud. . . . A Marxist analysis of society could stand in the wings behind the naturalistic novel, but Mailer wanted also to include Freud, to emphasize the imaginative and psychological effects of ideology.[11]

This statement should be qualified to the extent that Mailer had been working toward a union of Marx and Freud as early as *The Naked and the Dead*. The synthesis there is makeshift and pessi-mistic—what class and sexuality have in common is that they are oppressive, deterministic forces that interact to circumscribe and fix the individual permanently—but, nevertheless, the attempt is made.

Mailer's imaginative synthesis of Marx and Freud reaches a peak in "The White Negro." Mailer's friend the French Marxist Jean Malaquais goes so far as to assert that the philosophy of Hip merely transfers the romantic myth of the proletariat onto the psychopath (pp. 359–62). "The White Negro" is a seminal work, forming source material that Mailer is to mine is his essays and fiction for years to come. For the psychological content of the essay, Mailer acknowl-edges a debt to two main sources: Robert Lindner and Wilhelm Reich.

Lindner was another friend of Mailer's, a psychoanalyst and psychological theorist who is best known as the author of *Rebel without a Cause—The Hypnoanalysis of a Criminal Psychopath*. Mailer devoted several columns in the *Village Voice* to a discussion of Lindner's work, and he quotes from Lindner at length in "The White Negro":

". . . the psychopath is a rebel without a cause, an agitator without a slogan, a revolutionary without a program. . . . The psychopath, like the child, cannot delay the pleasures of gratification. . . . He must rape. He cannot wait upon the development of prestige in society: his egoistic ambitions lead him to leap into the headlines by daring performances." (p. 344)

"Yet even Lindner," says Mailer,

who was the most imaginative and most sympathetic of the psychoanalysts who have studied the psychopathic personality was not ready to project himself into the essential sympathy—which is that the psychopath may indeed be the perverted and dangerous front-runner of a new kind of personality which could become the central expression of human nature before the twentieth century is over. (p. 345)

However, where Lindner's theories were based on case studies, Mailer's theory of the importance of the psychopath is more fiction than fact.

What "The White Negro" owes to Wilhelm Reich is primarily the cult of the good orgasm as the cure-all for mental and physical ailments. As Mailer writes, "In the Western sexual literature with which I am familiar, classical, technical, and pornographic, I can remember—with the harsh radical exception of Wilhelm Reich—almost no incisive discussion of male orgasm" (p. 369). Again, Mailer writes that "the intellectual antecedents of this generation can be traced to such separate influences as D. H. Lawrence, Henry Miller, and Wilhelm Reich" (p. 340).[12] What these three figures have in common is their radical candor about sex and their exaltation of the orgasm.

The second concept that Mailer derives from Reich in "The White Negro," which is connected to the cult of the orgasm, is the importance of the instinctual life. According to Charles Rycroft, Reich was convinced that "if man could live by his instincts and not in submission to his character armor not only would life be freer and richer than it is but also many moral problems and indeed many physical illnesses including cancer would never occur."[13]

In "The White Negro," Mailer is crossing Lindner with Reich, taking the psychopath as Lindner delineated him and interpreting him in terms of Reichian categories. Reich tended to glorify the id and the instinctual and to mistrust the ego and the superego; by Reichian standards, the psychopath might indeed be considered the liberated man.

Thus, Mailer's attempt to create a bridge between Marx and Freud, to find "a calculus capable of translating the economic relations of man into his psychological relations and then back again" (p. 358), of necessity forced him to adopt the role not only of philosopher of economics but of amateur psychoanalytic theorist. Out of a desperation with the bland and security-minded culture of America in the 1950s, with a therapy that offered only tranquilizers and soothing platitudes, with an impotent Left, and with his own lack of impact on the culture, Mailer decided to do some consciousness raising of his own. Mailer chose to ennoble a perverse fringe group who were primarily a product of his own invention: the hipsters. He wanted to shake the bourgeoisie out of their indifference and their smug complacency. Like Reich, he wanted to move away from Freudian pessimism back to a romantic affirmation of the essential goodness of man. However, Mailer goes even further than Reich; like the true anarchist, Mailer wants to remove *all* social restraints. Reich also never talked very much about violence, except as another instance of the perverse behavior into which a sex-denying civilization drove individuals: "The vital energies, under natural conditions, regulate themselves spontaneously, without compulsive duty or compulsive morality. . . . Antisocial behavior springs from *secondary drives which owe their existence to the suppression of natural sexuality.*" [14] One can compare this statement by Reich to the following from "The White Negro" to see how Mailer's attitude toward antisocial behavior differs from Reich's:

> . . . the nihilism of Hip proposes as its final tendency that every social restraint and category be removed, and the affirmation implicit in the proposal is that man would then prove to be more creative than murderous and so would not destroy himself. . . . Hip, which would return us to ourselves, at no matter what price in individual violence, is the affirmation of the barbarian, for it requires a primitive passion about human nature to believe that individual acts of violence are always to be preferred to the collective violence of the State; it takes literal faith in the creative possibilities of the human being to envisage acts of violence as the catharsis which prepares growth. (pp. 354–55)

Paradoxically, Mailer had moved from the fear expressed in *Barbary*

Shore that mankind was drifting toward barbarism to the affirmation in "The White Negro" that only in individual barbarism is
there hope for salvation.

Moreover, Reich's therapy required the aid of a trained psychoanalyst, whereas the therapy of the psychopath is self-administered.
Mailer seems to have great faith in the "instinctive wisdom" of the
psychopath. Whether the extreme form of cure he depicts works or
not is entirely theoretical.

> What characterizes almost every psychopath is that they are
> trying to create a new nervous system for themselves. . . . The
> fundamental decision of his nature is to try to live the infantile
> fantasy, and in this decision (given the dreary alternative of psy-
> choanalysis) there may be a certain instinctive wisdom. . . . The
> psychopath exploring backward along the road of the homosexual,
> the orgiast, the drug-addict, the rapist, the robber and the mur-
> derer seeks to find those violent parallels to the violent and often
> hopeless contradictions he knew as a child. . . . In thus giving
> expression to the buried infant in himself, he can lessen the tension
> and so free himself to remake a bit of his nervous system. Like
> the neurotic he is looking for the opportunity to grow up a second
> time, but the psychopath knows instinctively that to express
> a forbidden impulse actively is far more beneficial than merely
> to confess the desire in the safety of a doctor's room. . . . So his
> associational journey into the past is lived out in the theatre of the
> present . . . he can be aware actively (as the analysand is aware
> passively) of what his habits are, and how he can change them.
> The strength of the psychopath is that he knows (where most of us
> can only guess) what is good for him and what is bad for him. . . .
> (pp. 346–47)

As an archetype for the age, the "White Negro" is an interesting
figure, a sort of modern version of Rousseau's "noble savage," who
lives at the opposite end of the spectrum from that other archetype
of the 1950s, "the man in the gray flannel suit." The trouble with
the essay is that one is never certain whether Mailer is merely
explaining Hip or *advocating* it. The complete avoidance of the first
person and the intricate and frequently ambiguous language used
in this essay complicate the problem. It does appear, however, that
Mailer is not so much describing a phenomenon as he is promoting
it, creating a mythical character who is the avant garde of a hypothetical movement and endowing that character with heroic and
noble qualities. [15]

Mailer also seems to have fabricated the psychology of the hipster
out of whole cloth, apparently depending upon the imaginative lee-

way one is supposed to allow a novelist. Mailer really has no evidence of the "instinctive wisdom" of the hipster, and the psychology that he posits for him may be just so much wish fulfillment. In an interview, Mailer proposes this argument himself only to dismiss it, thereby anticipating his critics. He speculates that perhaps "everything I have said is merely an intricate and ingenious rationalization to defend my neurotic . . . perversities, anh? Of course, I don't believe this is true" (p. 383). Like Reich, Mailer believes that what we call civilization is the perverted product of a "psychic plague." For Mailer, it is not the hipster who is the psychological aberration, but modern civilization itself.

According to Mailer, the violent situation into which modern man has been thrust demands a violent cure. The individual must assert his will against the collective violence of the state by an expression of individual violence (which is presumably more creative and more authentic), acting out and expelling his rage. Unlike revolutionary violence, however, the selfish behavior of the White Negro sounds as creative and authentic as a temper tantrum, and Mailer seems heedless of the effects of such sadistic rage on the innocent victims. The form of radical self-therapy he posits as an amateur psychoanalyst has its obvious dangers. In a piece of comic fiction, *American Mischief*, the novelist Alan Lelchuk envisions a gruesome kind of poetic justice for Mailer. Lelchuk's hero, a radical leader and fledgling psychopath named Pincus, reads "The White Negro" and takes it as a license to kill. As he reads Mailer's description of the murder of a fifty-year-old candy store owner by two young hoodlums, Pincus admires Mailer's use of the term *therapeutic* in reference to the act. "Ah, I loved that 'therapeutic' just there, in that discussion." In an excess of revolutionary zeal, Pincus decides to take Mailer up on his own ideas and assassinates him. "Didn't I at least owe it to him to push the event to a Maileresque extreme? . . . A last act violent and extraordinary enough to satisfy his wild teachings. . . ."[16]

One of Mailer's motives behind "The White Negro" seems to be revenge against the psychoanalyst. Because the psychoanalyst, the new keeper of the unconscious, has usurped some of the functions of the novelist, the novelist must fight to regain his lost territory. The hipster cures himself, and the hipster may be the wave of the future. Mailer evidently hopes that in the future there will be less need for analysts and more room for novelists.

Sergius in "The Time of Her Time," Rojack in *An American Dream*, and D.J. in *Why Are We in Vietnam?* are all variations on the White Negro or hipster. Each attempts to purge himself of frustration and impotent rage through violence; none is entirely successful. Mailer issued this clarion call in *Advertisements*: "So, yes, it may be time to say that the Republic is in real peril, and we are the cowards who must defend courage, sex, consciousness, the beauty of the body, the search for love, and the capture of what may be, after all, an heroic destiny" (p. 24). One suspects that Mailer's heroes do not quite succeed because they are still "cowards" at heart, forever in the process of becoming hipsters. By the early 1960s, the term *Hip* had become an embarrassment to him, and Mailer speaks instead of "existential politics" and "existential psychology" in *The Presidential Papers* (among his many incarnations, Rojack is "a professor of existential psychology"), but he admits that it is essentially the same thing.[17]

Sergius O'Shaugnessy in "Time" is endowed with many of the attributes of the hipster. He is one with "the saint and the bull-fighter and the lover" (p. 342), as Richard Poirier has noted.[18] To quote from "The White Negro":

> At bottom, the drama of the psychopath is that he seeks love. Not love as the search for a mate, but love as the search for an orgasm more apocalyptic than the one which preceded it. Orgasm is his therapy—he knows at the seed of his being that good orgasm opens his possibilities and bad orgasm imprisons him. (p. 347)

The drama of Sergius O'Shaugnessy's life in "The Time of Her Time" is the search for the apocalyptic orgasm, and his instrument in the search is Denise Gondelman, a bourgeois square (her father is a hardware wholesaler in Brooklyn) who aspires to become a bohemian. Worse yet,

> she was being psychoanalyzed, what a predictable pisser! and she was in the stage where the jargon had the totalitarian force of all vocabularies of mechanism. . . . She was enthusiastic about her analyst . . . he was really an integrated guy, Stanford Joyce. . . . (pp. 488–89)

Denise personifies everything that Sergius as hipster despises. According to Mailer, the actions of true hipsters are guided by their instinctive wisdom, "the navigator at the seat of their being" (p. 386). When Sergius hears Denise parroting the opinions of Dr. Joyce, he says contemptuously, "'You make him sound like your navigator'" (p. 493). In other words, the hipster regulates himself but the square is dependent upon outside control. As Reich writes, "the therapeutic task consists in changing the neurotic character into a genital character, and in replacing moral regulation by self-regulation."[19]

Thus, Sergius has his work cut out for him: to transform Denise from a neurotic and frigid girl into a genital character, a woman who will be self-regulating. He must break through her "Amazon's armor" (p. 498). Just as Mailer sets himself up as a countertherapist, so Sergius sets out to outdo Dr. Joyce by applying his own potent brand of Reichian orgasm therapy to Denise.[20] There is, of course, a large element of vanity in the attempt. No matter the cost, Sergius must be "the first to carry her stone of no-orgasm up the cliff, all the way, over and into the sea" (p. 496).[21]

There is an unmistakable element of Freudian therapist versus Reichian therapist in their confrontation. "'Vaginally, I'm anesthetized,'" Denise informs Sergius with grave clinical detachment, "'a good phallic narcissist like you doesn't do enough for me'" (p. 493). But Sergius responds in kind:

> "Aren't you mixing your language a little?" I began. "The phallic narcissist is one of Wilhelm Reich's categories."
> "Therefore?"
> "Aren't you a Freudian?"
> "It would be presumptuous of me to say," she said like a seminar student working for his pee-aitch-dee. "But Sandy is an eclectic. He accepts a lot of Reich—you see, he's very ambitious, he wants to arrive at his own synthesis." (pp. 493–94)[22]

Ironically, if Sergius is Mailer as hipster, then Sandy Joyce is Mailer as square. Like Dr. Joyce, Mailer is eclectic: he accepts a lot of Reich but is very ambitious and wants to arrive at his own synthesis.

But again, in "The Time of Her Time" as in *The Naked and the Dead*, the psychological ideas are applied mechanically, even diagrammatically. Insofar as it illustrates Mailer's newly formulated psychoanalytic theories, "Time" offers a predictable dichotomy of Hip versus Square. But the confrontation between Sergius and Denise is a power struggle between two individuals as well as a clash of opposing ideas. It is in the unpredictable, very human elements that the story becomes interesting, particularly in the rich multiple ironies and ambiguities of its ending. The reader is uncertain who triumphs in the end. Is it Denise, who puts down Sergius by accusing him of being a homosexual and then walking out of his life, slamming the door behind her? Is it Sergius, who has achieved his goal but cannot reap the fruits of his reward? Or are they both losers, phonies so hung up in their role playing that they cannot relate to each other as human beings? Through its inconclusive ending, the story transcends its dialectical framework and becomes something other than straight propaganda for neo-Reichian orgasm therapy and the Hip way of life.

An American Dream has rarely been discussed in terms of its use of Reich, and yet many elements of this often puzzling novel become more comprehensible when viewed in this light. "There were clefts and rents which cut like geological faults right through all the lead and concrete and kapok and leather of my ego, that mutilated piece of insulation," says Stephen Rojack (*AD*, p. 12). The elaborate metaphor seems to be based on Reich's notion of "character armor."[23] The stress in the novel on the precise quality of the orgasm as an index to one's mental and spiritual condition, which carries the theme of "Time" one step further, is certainly inspired by Reich. The concern with cancer as a psychically induced disease also probably derives from Reich, who believed that there was a direct connection between sexual and emotional repression and cancer. "Cancer in women is predominantly localized in the sexual organs. The connection with frigidity is obvious and known to many gynecologists. Furthermore, chronic constipation is, as a rule, in the background of cancer of the intestinal tract," writes Reich.[24]

Most significantly, Rojack's progress in *An American Dream* can be charted in terms of Reich's three-tiered conception of character structure. According to Reich's theory, there are three layers of character in civilized man; in descending order they are the social mask, the Freudian "unconscious," and the deepest level of all, the biological core.

The surface layer is "an artificial mask of self-control, of compulsive, insincere politeness and of artificial sociality."[25] Rojack manifests this first layer in one of the novel's early scenes, where he is chatting with an old friend at a cocktail party. Although Rojack is consumed with jealousy over his wife Deborah since their separation, and wonders if his sincere-sounding buddy has been one of the men who cuckolded him, the conversation carefully avoids any mention of Deborah. Rojack speaks "in a tone I had come to abhor, a sort of boozed Connecticut gentry" (p. 11). Wracked with a sudden and overwhelming spasm of nausea, "I stood up in the middle of my conversation with old friend rogue and simply heaved my cakes" (p. 11). His vomiting represents the eruption of his real feeling through the surface mask of sociality. In Reichian terms, it is an orgasmic breakthrough, an expulsion of repressed and bottled-up energy.[26]

The surface layer "covers up the second one, the Freudian 'unconscious,' in which sadism, greediness, lasciviousness, envy, perversions of all kinds, etc., are kept in check, without, however, having in the least lost any of their power."[27] Beneath this layer of sickness lies the third and deepest layer, what Reich believed to be the naturally good, biological character of man. Unfortunately, there is a catch involved in trying to approach level three. "One cannot penetrate to this deep, promising layer without first eliminating the sham-social surface. What makes its appearance when this cultivated mask falls away, however, is not natural sociality, but the perverse antisocial nature of the character."[28] Thus, when Rojack penetrates below level one, he first murders his wife and then indulges in bizarre sexual gymnastics with her German maid, Ruta, a scene of "sadism, greediness, lasciviousness and perversion" if there ever was one. Rojack has broken through the social mask, but he must now work through all the horrors of the Freudian unconscious, Reich's level two, before he can reach the biological core. Viewed in a Reichian sense, Rojack's perverse and antisocial actions would not seem to be an indulgent wallowing in unhealthy fantasies, as so many critics complain, but a *purgation* of the negative instincts which is a necessary part of the therapeutic process. (However, it remains to be seen what a Freudian interpretation could make of these fantasies.)

Reich's third and final layer of character consists of *"natural sociality, spontaneous enjoyment of work, capacity for love. This third and deepest layer* [represents] *the biological nucleus of the human structure. . . ."*[29] As Rojack goes to see Cherry, a brief respite between his encounter with the police and his upcoming bout with Barney Kelly, he pleads, " 'God,' I wanted to pray, 'let me love that girl, and become a father, and try to be a good man, and do some decent work' " (p. 162). Nevertheless, Rojack realizes that he is not through yet; "like a soldier on a six-hour leave to a canteen, I knew I would have to return" (p. 162). He must still do battle with Shago and Kelly, go back to the struggle against the murder and the potential for suicide that live within him, and fulfill his contact with the forces of death and the Devil. But Rojack's goal, which he never quite reaches, perhaps because he is not good enough to make it, is to dissolve the habits of a lifetime, to work through the horrors within him and become Reich's biological man. Rojack's yearning toward that goal is intended to show that, despite his perverse tendencies, his fundamental instincts are in the right place. "Knowledge, work and natural love are the sources of life," writes Reich. "They should also be the forces that govern our life."[30]

Aside from the possible influence of Reich on *An American*

Dream, the novel is also in tune with the ideas of the psychiatrist R.D. Laing, which gained wide popularity in the sixties, about schizophrenia as a personal voyage of discovery outside of the normal mode of experience, a breakthrough rather than a break-down. In *The Politics of Experience*, Laing claims that "the experience and behavior that gets labeled schizophrenic is a special strategy that a person invents in order to live in an unlivable situation"[31]; this behavior appears bizarre only because society perceives it as such. According to Laing, "normal" people are crazy because they have adjusted themselves to a mad contemporary civilization: "What we call 'normal' is a product of repression, denial, splitting, projection, introjection, and other forms of destructive action on experience. . . . It is radically estranged from the structure of being."[32] Rojack's experience of madness could serve to illustrate this theory. Whether or not Mailer was aware of R.D. Laing's ideas at the time of writing *Dream*, Mailer's alignment with Reich anticipated the movement in the sixties in America toward the radical left in psychoanalytic thinking, the tendency to see society as insane, and the individual as either a victim of that society, a collaborator, or a lone hero struggling against it. Mailer had always viewed the individual and society in this light; Reich merely gave him a system with which to analyze and categorize behavior and experience.

Mailer's adherence to Reich's theory of human character points to certain attitudes that he shares with Reich: romanticism, faith in the individual and distrust of the society, and a belief in the instinctual life. "Beneath these neurotic mechanisms," writes Reich, "behind all these dangerous, grotesque, irrational phantasies and impulses, I found a bit of simple, matter-of-fact, decent nature."[33] That sentence could almost be used to refer to the plot of *An American Dream*.

Mailer's style of thought from *Advertisements* on comes to resemble more closely that of Reich; like Reich, Mailer mixes the systematic and the dogmatic with equal parts of the mystical and the messianic. Mailer also approaches Reich in his Manicheism and in his creation of a private cosmology which one is unsure whether to take as a poetic construct or sheer superstition. In his later work, Reich seemed to become increasingly paranoid and his proposed solutions for psychological problems sounded grandiose and even simple-minded (put everyone in an orgone box). In *An American Dream* and *Vietnam*, the two novels written after he became a serious devotee of Reich, Mailer makes an aesthetic leap into a more extreme, cosmic, and sweeping treatment of his characters' conflicts. One should not, however, make too much of the similarities between the psychology of Mailer and Reich, for the differences are even more marked. Mailer possesses a capacity for complexity, irony, and detachment from himself, and a sense of humor that Reich always lacked.

Mailer becomes both more ironic, playful, and self-detached and more mystical and messianic in his next novel, *Why Are We in Vietnam?* It is here that he draws directly from the later Reich, the Reich who went further and further out until he was believed to be insane. The creation in this novel of a mysterious field of electrical energy, manifested in the aurora borealis, a force which energizes the entire globe and into which the minds of all creatures are plugged, is similar to Reich's belief in the existence of "orgone energy," a form of tangible, measurable libido that activates all living things. "The orgone energy can be demonstrated visually, thermically and electroscopically in the soil, the atmosphere and in plant and animal organisms . . . the blue-gray *Northern lights* . . . are manifestations of the orgone energy."[34]

Reich believed that one could actually tap into this life force with an accumulator called an orgone box; Mailer's novel posits certain nodes, such as the Brooks Range, which act as natural antennae, radio receivers for his brand of cosmic emanation. As a scientific theory, "orgone energy" is as absurd as phlogiston, but when it is borrowed as the core idea for a piece of fiction, it takes on a kind of metaphoric believability. Mailer's narrator, D.J., shows some of the characteristics of paranoid schizophrenia. He is obsessed with notions of Godlike or Satanic forces in control of man, forces as tangible as electricity. Electricity runs D.J.'s universe; he even conceives of himself as a disc jockey broadcasting over the airwaves. D.J. is the messiah as pitchman, "here to sell America its new handbook on how to live, how to live in this Electrox Edison world, all programmed out" (*WV*, p. 8). "Did you ever know the seat of electricity?" he asks us. "It's the asshole. But what then is the asshole of electricity? Why Creation . . ." (p. 23). His climactic, poetic vision of electricity saturating the universe in a field of force, man and animal and nature connected in a cosmic conspiracy for some unknown purpose, comes as an appropriate fantasy, the transcendently logical conclusion of his metaphysical train of thought.

Roger Ramsey, a critic of Mailer, asserts that the schizophrenia of D.J. is "clearly related to the source of Mailer's ideas about sex, the works of Wilhelm Reich." Ramsey cites one particular case history from Reich's *Character Analysis*, "The Schizophrenic

Split," as a gloss on D.J.'s mental state. In Reich's conception of schizophrenia, the individual is first possessed by the Devil and then tries to battle his influence and align himself with God. Reich considers schizophrenics brave individuals who "had the courage to approach what is commonly evaded" with no help from society and who hoped "to emerge from the inferno into the clear, fresh air where only great minds dwell." According to Ramsey, Reich's schizophrenic is "the same character as the White Negro, the hipster, and doubtlessly D.J." Reich's conception of the Devil and God as, respectively, man's perverted nature and cosmic electricity also seems to Ramsey to be similar to Mailer's conception. Most significant of all, Ramsey cites an instance in the same case history where the woman patient asks, "What is the Aurora Borealis?" and mentally projects herself to "where the 'forces' are."[35]

Since Reich refers elsewhere in his writings to "Northern lights," it is difficult to prove the direct influence of this case on *Vietnam*, but it is safe to say that Mailer has studied Reich carefully and appropriated his psychology as an integral part of his private cosmology. Reich is a valuable asset to Mailer's art as a framework for generating metaphor and as a device for interpreting reality.

It is difficult to say how much Mailer actually believes in Reich and in the metaphysic he has evolved partly from Reich. Mailer's system has its witty and playful aspects as well as its serious side. Frederic Jameson speculates that Mailer does not believe in his own system "scientifically or positivistically, but perhaps aesthetically. For the novelist, indeed, these occult paraphernalia amount to a kind of *stylistic superstition*: they permit the writing of vivid sentences and constitute a new kind of characterological shorthand."

Jameson does admit that, whereas Mailer's ethic is "aggressive and anti–middle class," his metaphysic is a sort of private, occult religion that "holds out the false comfort of all mystifications." In Mailer's system, nothing happens by accident, which can "be a way of fleeing the absurdity and contingency of life itself."[36] According to Mary Ellman, "It will not be admitted, by Mailer, that even the bowels move without personal meaning, the sewers reek with messages."[37] One wonders whether Mailer sometimes gets carried away by his own system and his own metaphors and confuses them with reality.

Another difficulty with Mailer's absorption of Reichian psychology into his fiction is the same as with his incorporation of Freudian psychology in *The Naked and the Dead*: overschematization. Mailer's belief in Reichianism interferes with his art when he makes his characters into walking stereotypes or mouth-pieces for his theories. For example, when all the characters in *An American Dream* begin talking about "God" and "the Devil," they stop sounding like themselves and begin sounding like the author. Rather than allowing the ideas to issue as the logical by-products of their situation, the characters often appear to have been concocted to illustrate Mailer's beliefs, or else we sense the author injecting or forcing the ideas from outside onto characters who cannot bear the ideological weight, such as Cherry. This is one reason why *An American Dream* so much resembles a medieval allegory and why all the characters in *Vietnam* are blown up out of human proportions. Mailer's ideology sometimes tends to over-whelm the believability of his characters.

Thus, we see Mailer's progress as a novelist and an intellectual trying to cope with modern psychoanalytic theories. An emotional and ideological incompatibility led him away from his early al-legiance to Freud and into an alignment with the ideas of the more romantic and anarchistic Reich. At the same time, Mailer's in-creasingly grandiose conception of the role of the artist led him to view the psychoanalyst as the enemy and to arrogate to himself the role of countertherapist, an unorthodox, guerrilla doctor to the sick mind, body, and spirit of his society.

From *Advertisements* on, Mailer shows a cavalier attitude toward psychoanalytic theory, a sublime confusion that sometimes leads him into excess. Disregarding the basis of psychiatry in science and medicine, Mailer treats the psychoanalyst as a generally in-ferior type of artist and the artist as a potentially superior type of analyst. For example, in *Of a Fire on the Moon*, Mailer views Freud's theory of dreams as an interesting fiction, and proposes his own theory to replace it. As Richard Poirier writes, "While he can't supply it, he must therefore call for a theory of dreams beyond Freud, thus showing, if only for a moment, his alignment with the kind of intellectual who thinks that questions not answered by Freud and Marx have not even been asked."[38]

Mailer's role confusion illustrates the redefinition of self that the modern artist is still undergoing in the wake of Freud. The novelist had always been an intuitive, amateur psychoanalyst; how could the novelist hope to compete with these professionals who had codified human behavior and made its study into a science? Mailer seems to feel that the territory is not big enough for both of them; it is up to the novelist to outpsych the shrink.

While it is proper for Mailer as a writer to enjoy unlimited freedom of imaginative speculation, it is also necessary to remember that the art of fiction and the science of psychology belong to different universes of discourse. Although the artist and the psychologist offer different kinds of knowledge, there is no reason why the two ways of knowing should be incompatible. According to the critic Bernard J. Paris, "The psychologist enables us to grasp . . . experience analytically, categorically. . . . Fiction lets us know what it is like to be a certain kind of person. . . . Psychology helps us to talk about what the novelist knows, fiction helps us to know what the psychologist is talking about."[39] Whereas Mailer as intuitive psychologist in his fiction is frequently worthwhile, Mailer as pop psychological theorist in his nonfiction is more often pretentious, offering myth rather than verifiable hypothesis.

It is not my intention here to defend the profession of psychoanalyst. Mailer has a justifiable grudge. As a novelist, he resents the debasement of the language and the confining of the imagination through psychoanalytic jargon. As a social libertarian, Mailer resents the use of therapy as an instrument for social control, as one more way for the establishment to normalize and tame the individual. The problem is that Mailer carries his grudge too far; he feels forced to invent his own system to rival the therapeutic orthodoxy. When he applies this set of ideas to his art, Mailer sometimes becomes the prisoner of his own system. Often it appears that he has merely replaced one kind of jargon with his own brand.

Notes

1. See John M. Muste, "Norman Mailer and John Dos Passos: The Question of Influence," *Modern Fiction Studies* 17 (1971): 361–74, for an interesting discussion of *The Naked and the Dead* in relation to *USA* and *Three Soldiers*.

2. Theodore Gross, *The Heroic Ideal in American Literature* (New York: Free Press, 1971), p. 278.

3. Diana Trilling, "The Moral Radicalism of Norman Mailer," in *Norman Mailer: The Man and His Work*, ed. Robert F. Lucid (Boston and Toronto: Little, Brown, 1971), p. 130.

4. Jean Radford, *Norman Mailer: A Critical Study* (New York: Harper, 1975), p. 61.

5. Robert W. Lawler, "Norman Mailer: The Connection of New Circuits" (Ph.D. diss., Claremont, 1969), p. 98.

6. Trilling, "Moral Radicalism," p. 53.

7. Leslie Fiedler, *Waiting for the End* (New York: Dell, 1965), p. 93.

8. Ibid., p. 160.

9. Charles Rycroft, *Wilhelm Reich* (New York: Viking, 1971), p. 33.

10. Wilhelm Reich, *The Function of the Orgasm*, trans. Theodore P. Wolfe (New York: Bantam, 1967), p. xxiv.

11. Leo Braudy, "Norman Mailer: The Pride of Vulnerability," in *Norman Mailer: A*

Collection of Critical Essays, ed. Leo Braudy (Englewood Cliffs, N.J.: Prentice-Hall, 1972), p. 4.

12. It is interesting that Mailer should link D. H. Lawrence with Henry Miller here. Mailer returns to these two figures in an eloquent defense of their art in *The Prisoner of Sex* and in *Genius and Lust*. For Mailer, they represent examples, like Hemingway, of the artist as hero.

13. Rycroft, *Wilhelm Reich*, p. 33.

14. Reich, *Function of the Orgasm*, p. xxiv.

15. The critical consensus is that "The White Negro" is a myth or fiction. See, for example, Robert Solotaroff, *Down Mailer's Way* (Urbana: University of Illinois, 1974), p. 92; Laura Adams, *Existential Battles: The Growth of Norman Mailer* (Athens, Ohio: Ohio University, 1976), p. 59; and Radford, *Norman Mailer*, p. 92.

16. Alan Lelchuk, *American Mischief* (New York: Farrar, Strauss, 1973), pp. 281, 292.

17. Norman Mailer, *Existential Errands* (Boston and Toronto: Little, Brown, 1972), p. 210. "I came to use the words existential and existentialism rather than Hip. Hip, I knew, would end in a box on Madison Avenue."

18. Richard Poirier, *Norman Mailer* (New York: Viking, 1972), p. 73.

19. Reich, *Function of the Orgasm*, p. 121.

20. Poirier, *Norman Mailer*, p. 73. "An allusion is intended here to the Reichian idea of body armor, thereby lending some support to Sergius's claim that his 'avenger' is an instrument of therapy rather than revenge," says Poirier.

21. The quest for the apocalyptic orgasm is imbued with existential overtones by Mailer's metaphor here, which suggests Camus and the myth of Sisyphus.

22. For a discussion of the phallic narcissist, see Reich, *Function of the Orgasm*, pp. 106–7. "A fourth group is formed by the men who show excessive erective potency, for fear of the woman and in defense against unconscious homosexual phantasies. The sexual act serves the purpose of proving their 'potency,' the penis serves as a piercing instrument with sadistic phantasies."

23. See also Norman Mailer, *St. George and the Godfather* (New York: New American Library, 1972), p. 198. ". . . so Nixon promenading toward them exhibits again that characteristic gait which is his alone and might have provided thought for analysis in even so profound a student of body movements as Wilhelm Reich, for Nixon has character-armor, hordes of it!"

24. Reich, *Function of the Orgasm*, p. 250. See also n. 12.

25. Ibid., p. 157.

26. See Wilhelm Reich, *Character Analysis*, trans. Theodore P. Wolfe (New York: Farrar, Strauss, 1949), p. 388. Reich believed that "the total movement of the body in vomiting is . . . the same as in the orgasm reflex." This notion explains some of the significance of the two graphic descriptions of vomiting in *An American Dream*, on the balcony and in the rest room of Cherry's nightclub. In Reich's psychology, vomiting is simulated orgasm. The nightclub incident means that, even as Rojack is breaking down Cherry's muscular armor with his psychic bullets, he is also breaking through some of his own character-armor and is on the way to good orgasm with her.

27. Reich, *Function of the Orgasm*, p. 157.

28. Wilhelm Reich, *The Mass Psychology of Fascism* (New York: Orgone Institute Press, 1946), p. viii.

29. Reich, *Function of the Orgasm*, p. 157.

30. Ibid., p. xxix.

31. R.D. Laing, *The Politics of Experience* (New York: Ballantine, 1968), pp. 114–15.

32. Ibid., p. 23.

33. Reich, *Function of the Orgasm*, p. 114.

34. Ibid., pp. 263–64. Emphasis added.

35. Roger Ramsey, "Current and Recurrent: The Vietnam Novel," *Modern Fiction Studies* 17 (1971): 427–29.

36. Frederic Jameson, "The Great American Hunter; or, Ideological Content in the Novel," *College English* 34 (November 1972): 189.

37. Mary Ellman, *Thinking about Women* (New York: Harcourt, Brace, 1968), p. 101.

38. Richard Poirier, "The Ups and Downs of Mailer," in *Norman Mailer*, ed. Leo Braudy, p. 173.

39. Bernard J. Paris, *A Psychological Approach to Fiction: Studies in Thackeray, Stendhal, George Eliot, Dostoyevsky, and Conrad* (Bloomington: Indiana University, 1974), p. 27.

2 *The Naked and the Dead:*
The Triumph of
Impotence _____

> Say I'm anally oriented? OK. Say I'm anally oriented. I'll say I'm
> Cassius Clay. Fuck you.
>> Norman Mailer in an interview with Paul Carroll of *Playboy*

In an astute critical examination of Mailer's novel *Why Are We
in Vietnam?*, John W. Aldridge cites the two forms of obscenity in
the novel, "scatological and fornicatory," and notes that "over the
years, Mailer has evolved a sort of eschatology of scatology, a highly
idiosyncratic metaphysics of feces. . . . The route of salvation is thus
from the anus to the phallus. . . ."[1] This valuable insight could be
carried much further, for the anal-phallic mode is more than an
"idiosyncratic" theory of Mailer's; it stems instead from deep
psychic conflicts that have powered every element of his fiction
from the beginning. The evolution toward the eschatology of
scatology has been a completely natural development for Mailer,
for what has always most deeply concerned Mailer is what he terms
"the worst lust, the excretory lust."[2]

One of Mailer's earliest works is a four-page tale entitled "Maybe
Next Year," written when he was an eighteen-year-old junior at
Harvard, and published in 1958 in his critical self-scrutiny, *Advertisements for Myself*. This story contains, in microcosm, Mailer's
obsession with dirt, along with the connected cluster of themes
that are to dominate his unconscious, and in part determine the
development of his future writings.

The narrator of "Maybe Next Year," a young boy, trapped in
a circle of misery, plagued and mistreated by a domineering, nagging
mother, and a henpecked, cruel father, keeps running away from
home to the nearby railway tracks, an abode of filthy, unpleasant
hoboes. "I'd . . . slide down the steep part of the grass where it was
slippery like dogs had been dirty there . . ." (*ADV*, p. 85). The tramps
are

> dirty old men, they just sat around, and smoked pipes and washed
> their dirty old shirts in the yellow water spot where I used to go
> swimming before Mom started yell yell yell about the dirty
> old men. . . . *They're filthy old things, you'll get sick and die,
> they're diseased, they're diseased, why did the town let them*

*camp and flop in a meadow . . . why should they be flopping
so near our house?* (p. 86)

The anal imagery here is abundant: in the dog droppings, the
dirt, the yellow water, and the double meaning of "flop."

The story revolves around the child's ambivalence toward the
tramps, who are associated, on the one hand, with the power of the
railway, escape from the family situation, and the chance to dirty
himself in freedom which every small child desires, and, on the other
hand, with the repulsive aspects of dirt. The tramps torment the
boy, threatening to soil him against his will: "one of them said
he was going to take my shirt and use it as a snotrag, and they all
laughed again, the big man in the middle of them making believe
he was going to throw dirt at me . . ." (p. 86). At the same time,
the child's mother's nagging whine, which appears in his stream
of consciousness as an italicized superego, connects the tramps'
dirtiness with disease and homosexuality, as she belittles the masculinity of every man around.

*God knows what those bums are doing to him, they're all vile,
they don't live like men, they're not men I heard, they're no more
men than you are, both of you are, why don't you take care of
him, he'll turn out weak in everything like you, those bums will
get him into trouble.* (p. 86)

The mother has deprived the boy of any male figure with whom
he can strongly identify, and when his loyalties are tested, he breaks
down and projects all his hate onto an old bum. The bum, badly
wounded by a vigilante committee inspired by the mother and
led by the father, pleads for aid from the child, who is disgusted,
and responds by stoning the tramp and then fleeing home. The
wounded tramp is described as "yowling" like a dog, and crawling
like a snake; the snake image is obviously phallic, whereas the
dog suggests anality. (Throughout the story, dogs are mentioned
in terms of their leavings, and the parents mistreat and whip both
their dogs and the boy in the same manner.) Whereas one would
expect the child to empathize with the plight of the tramp, he is
instead horrified by him:

. . . he started crawling to me, I could see it was his foot that
was hurt 'cause it was all bloody like, and bleeding near the knee.
Help me kid, help me kid, he kept yelling.
Go ahead, hit the child, hit it, hit it, it deserves it, playing with

dirty old men, hit it, it's a terrible child, it never listens to us,
there's something wrong with it.
The old man . . . looked like a snake, only bleeding. (p. 87)

Just at the moment when there is a possibility of the boy's identifying with the old man, the voice of the mother intervenes, warning
of punishment.

In repudiating the tramp, the boy may be said to be taking
vicarious revenge on his father, and also repudiating his own emasculation. The boy identifies instead with his mother, the aggressor,
because the imagined consequences of disobeying her are too
frightening. The rejection of the father is strengthened by the
ironic reversal at the conclusion, in which the father identifies
with the bum—"I might be one of them myself, maybe next year"—
and weeps like a child for what he has done, while the boy feels like
an adult. ". . . I'd seen two men cry that day and maybe that meant
I was getting bigger too, and that was an awful good feeling" (p. 88).
In the boy's mind, sadism comes to equal manhood. Mailer makes
us aware that this sense of power is illusory, for the real victor
is the mother, who has managed to control or defeat all the males.

The family triangle of son, father, and mother depicted in "Maybe
Next Year" is repeated in all of Mailer's fiction. First is the innocent,
tormented, basically blameless hero, who must prove his masculinity in a sordid world. He is reincarnated as Lieutenant Hearn
in *The Naked and the Dead*, Mike Lovett in *Barbary Shore*, Sergius
in *The Deer Park* and "The Time of Her Time," Rojack in *An
American Dream*, D.J. in *Why Are We in Vietnam?*, and as "Norman
Mailer" in *The Armies of the Night*.

There is often a split in the novels between heroes who are weak,
liberal, and masochistic (such as Hearn and Lovett) and their
"bad brothers," who are strong, reactionary, and sadistic (such as
Croft and Hollingsworth). We might call this doubling of heroes
a reflection of the division between the "anal-erotic" weakling
and the "anal-sadistic" strongman.

In his later fiction, Mailer achieves a synthesis, the "good-bad"
hero, who incorporates both extremes: he is weak yet strong, left-
conservative, and sado-masochistic. The good-bad hero is characterized by an ambivalence between impulses of love and hate;
he seems to embody many of the contradictions and warring impulses of the author. These ambivalent heroes include Sergius in
"The Time of Her Time," Rojack, D.J., and the "Mailer" of *Armies*.

The father figures, however, remain split into the two diametrically opposed types: the good (weak, liberal, and masochistic)

and the bad (strong, reactionary, and sadistic). The hero always
tries to best these older men. The "good fathers" are McLeod in
Barbary Shore and Eitel in *The Deer Park*; the bad ones are General
Cummings in *The Naked and the Dead*. Herman Teppis (H. T.) in
The Deer Park, Barney Kelly in *An American Dream*, and Rusty
Jethroe in *Why Are We in Vietnam?* The good fathers are always
pitied, and the bad ones are viewed with a mixture of revulsion,
fascination, and awe. In either guise, however, the father figure
is impotent or compensating for his sexual inadequacy through
violence.

It would not be overly speculative to say that every male in
Mailer's fiction, hero or villain, suffers from psychic impotence or
has grave doubts about his manhood. Mailer's heroes are drastically
incomplete: Hearn is "nothing but a goddamn shell" (*ND*, p. 347);
Lovett has amnesia; Sergius looks impressive but feels like "an
unemployed actor who tries to interest a casting director by dressing
for the role" (*DP*, p. 5); and Rojack is another actor who compares
himself to "movie stars who are not only profiles for a great lover,
but homosexual and private in their life" (*AD*, p. 7).

To the family portrait of son and father, we can add the mother
figure, around whom the action usually pivots. The same division
that exists among the male characters also occurs among the females. On the one hand are the slightly soiled yet innocent heroines,
vulnerable, suffering women (weak, liberal, and masochistic like
their male counterparts): Lannie Madison in *Barbary Shore*, Elena
Esposito in *The Deer Park*, and Cherry Melanie in *An American
Dream*. Their names suggest their characters: the mad, the exposed,
and the virginal. On the other hand are the bitch goddesses, shameless, powerful, domineering, and emasculating, not so much soiled
as foully corrupt: Guinevere in *Barbary Shore*, Lulu Meyers and
Dorothea O'Faye in *The Deer Park*, Denise in "The Time of Her
Time," Deborah Rojack in *An American Dream*, and Alice Jethroe
in *Why Are We in Vietnam?* Although *The Naked and the Dead* is
an all-male novel, the absence of women plays a prominent part
in the action.

The critic Howard Silverstein notes the repeated triangular
relationships in Mailer's fiction, in which a group of people becomes
sexually and romantically involved. Silverstein sees this repeated
pattern as a family romance:

> What distinguishes all of these inter-relationships is that love
> and romance in Mailer's world is essentially a "family affair."
> Because they have not broken the circle of their connections with
> childhood, many of Mailer's characters seek involvements with

women who are representative of the mother figure. Basically, Mailer's characters have not solved their oedipal conflicts; their recurring need to form a closed circuit of relationships is a way of representing incestuous drives.[3]

Given this family triangle, we can now view "Maybe Next Year" in terms of psychological development. The boy, acutely conscious of his inferior status, longs for power, which involves usurping the father's role and winning the undivided affection of the mother. In this instance, however, the mother is viewed as fearful. His father is so henpecked that the son fears that his mother will do to him what she seems to have done to his father, that is, emasculate him. Empathy with the paternal plight is about to lead the boy into the arms of his father, but he flees instead, afraid of the homosexual implications of such an act. The boy then regresses to an earlier, narcissistic stage of development, in which fulfillment revolved around his own feces. The fixation intensifies the dilemma, since his anally compulsive mother has instilled a fear of all sexuality as "dirty." The boy's inhibition against anality then is as powerful as that against genital sexuality.

The anality and sexuality become united in the boy's unconscious as destructive, befouling, and potentially uncontrollable forces against which he must defend himself. As D.J. announces in the first paragraph of *Why Are We in Vietnam?*, "there's blood on my dick" and "out out damn fart." In other words, the evil of the phallus and the anus is inescapable. Mailer's novels are filled with impotent murderer heroes who feel that they deserve to be castrated. Ultimately, this is a shaky manner of dealing with an emasculating, anally constricted image of the mother and a father who is perceived as impotent yet cruel. Every one of Mailer's stories represents an unconscious working out of this dilemma, a shifting of the variables in an endless search for a viable solution. As Rojack puts it, "I had my fill of walking about with a chest full of hatred and a brain jammed to burst, but there is something manly about containing your rage. It is so difficult. . . The exhilaration comes I suppose from possessing such strength. Besides, murder offers the promise of vast relief. It is never unsexual" (*AD*, p. 8). The phallic imagery here is right on the surface, though the linked anal imagery is slightly hidden: "containing your rage" suggests constipation. When the dammed up force is released, it destroys, just as the little boy restrains himself until he heaves the rock. No wonder Mailer should conceive of America as having two currents, the surface one dull and factual, and the barely restrained "subterranean river" just beneath the surface, the repository of untapped "ecstasy and violence."[4] This is a portrait of Mailer himself: Mailer the meticulous observer and reporter versus Mailer the self-proclaimed "Beast" of *The Armies of the Night*; Mailer restrained or Mailer letting go. The tension is immense and the psychic balance is always precarious, like Rojack walking the parapet. When Mailer pulls it off, the result is masterful. This vacillation between the modes of containment and expulsion also helps to account for the peculiar dichotomy that Diana Trilling notes in her critical survey of Mailer, of "so much moral affirmation coupled with so much moral anarchism . . . so much defensive caution but such headlong recklessness. . . ."[5] Mailer labels himself "a Left conservative," a paradoxical position which attempts to bridge the gap between the two modes.

Mailer has been at war even before he was drafted into the army in 1942—at war inside himself. Unintentionally emulating Stephen Crane, Mailer wrote a bitter, vivid war story called "A Calculus at Heaven" before he left Harvard. The hero, Bowen Hilliard, abandons his artistic ambitions, knuckles under to his father and father-in-law, marries the castrating bitch, but then leaves all this to go and fight in the Pacific and court suicide. At the end of the tale, Hilliard is waiting for dawn and the inevitable death by a Japanese machine gun it will bring. In both technique and subject matter, "A Calculus" anticipates the story of Lieutenant Hearn in *The Naked and the Dead*.

The Naked and the Dead, Norman Mailer's first novel, published in 1948, is a sweaty, pessimistic, mercilessly realistic view of men at war, littered with decaying corpses and filled with the smell of jungle rot. Mailer's fragmented narrative, which owes much to the social realism of American fiction of the 1930s, develops a group consciousness by shifting between the inner thoughts of more than a dozen soldiers. The specter of death is omnipresent, and the violent struggle to preserve their lives and their manhood consumes them. Their unsatisfactory confrontation with the civilian forces that have determined their characters seems only a prelude to the inevitable carnage of the battlefield.

Diana Trilling raises the central critical problem of the novel when she notes the curious fascination which is evident toward the ostensible villains, the brutal and reactionary General Cummings and his less sophisticated counterpart, Sergeant Croft, when one would expect the author to focus instead on the disaffected humanists, Lieutenant Hearn and Private Red Valsen, who oppose the totalitarian Cummings and Croft.[6] However, there is more than a question of political or moral sympathy at stake here. John W. Aldridge is justifiably disturbed because *neither* side is favored, and the novel comes to no positive conclusion: "the good are humiliated or suffer a fatal deception; the evil are made ridiculous, and the mediocre ride to victory on an accident . . . the novel descends through a series of reductions to an absolute zero."[7] Though Aldridge's statement contains more truth than that of Diana Trilling's, we are still left without an explanation of the disturbing impact of the novel and its mood of tension deteriorating into ultimate inconclusiveness. An inkling of the solution is provided by Ihab Hassan:

> The explicit statement of the novel asserts defeat. Croft does not climb his mountain, and the general wins the campaign despite himself. Omnipotence, as private motive or historical destiny, gives way to impotence.[8]

One could add that this impotence holds, even in a very physical sense. Martinez, the Mexican, is insecure and feels incomplete as a man until he can succeed with "white Protestant girls, firm and aloof" (*ND*, p. 66). Stanley discovers he is "inept, incapable of controlling himself. His love spasms had been quick and nervous; he had wept . . . in his wife's arms at his failure" (*ND*, p. 294). Wilson, once an invincible stud, is now rotting away from venereal disease and jungle diarrhea and fears the Japanese will "cut mah nuts off" (p. 516). As Hearn says blithely, " 'If I'm afraid of having my dick cut off or something like that, I don't care to know it' " (p. 348). In fact, every male in this novel, without exception, is unsure of his potency and terrified of being less than a man.

Finally, even violence becomes impotent in the novel. For all their narcissism and drive for power, both Cummings and Croft prove incapable of even controlling themselves; in the end, the battle is determined by mere chance. The pattern is established in the first chapter, where Croft bets heavily in poker because "he had a deep unspoken belief that whatever made things happen was on his side, and now, after a long night of indifferent cards, he had a potentially powerful hand" (p. 9). Naturally, Croft's premonition proves false; chance is not on his side, and he is left to rage. Croft drives his platoon members pitilessly, but they exhaust themselves in a meaningless struggle without ever achieving their goal, defeated by circumstances outside of their control. *Power* and *control* are the two most frequently employed words in the novel, but the terms next highest in frequency are *impotent rage* and *failure*. The truth of the novel is revealed in its title: those who are stripped *naked* and are yet sexually *dead*.

The psychological makeup of the protagonists is precisely the same as that of the boy in "Maybe Next Year": fear of impotence and emasculation coupled with anal regression and latent homosexuality. Like the long-suffering child, the men in the novel put a clamp on their emotions, for the expulsion of emotion itself is excremental. "There was something nasty, unclean about the emotion Roth was showing. Red always curdled before emotion" (p. 576). Feelings must therefore be smothered until they can no longer be controlled. "It was the old pattern," Hearn thinks, "when he could take something no longer, he flared up . . ." (p. 75). There is no cessation of struggle for any of them. The cycle is suggested in the first incident in the book, when a soldier retreats to the latrine, looking for relief, and finds none.

In a primitive physical sense, relieving one's bowels is connected with destruction, for the men who die lose control of the sphincter first. Hennessy, Wilson, and Roth all break the cardinal rule of the soldiers, which is "Keep a tight asshole." Diarrhea presages disaster, impotence, and death. When the wounded Wilson finds himself about to defecate on his stretcher, he feels it as an intense pain, and fights it "with a childish fear of punishment, and then relapsed into the heat and pleasure of voiding. . . ." Sexual images fill his head, and impart "a lazy sensuality to his loins," but an attempt to urinate is prevented by his painful syphilis, so that "it shattered the images, left him aware and troubled and perplexed, conscious for the first time of the way he had soiled himself. He had a picture of his loins putrefacted and a deep misery passed through him" (p. 628).

The protagonists attempt to cope with their doubts about their masculinity through a drive toward omnipotence. General Cummings indulges in a battle plan that is pure homosexual fantasy: "his mind kept picturing the pincers of a frontal assault and an invasion from the rear" (p. 398), that is, overpowering the enemy through simultaneous emasculation and buggery. Cummings believes that " 'Man's deepest urge is omnipotence' " and " 'when we discover that the universe is not us, it's the deepest trauma of our existence' " (p. 323). The Oedipal implications of such a statement are self-evident. In a similar fashion, Croft says, "I hate everything which is not in myself" (p. 164). Lieutenant Hearn is horrified with himself when he discovers his own attraction toward the ruthless power of the effeminate Cummings. "Divorced of all the environmental trappings . . . he was basically like Cummings" (p. 392). As he comes later to realize, leadership is

as filthy as everything else. And he enjoyed it now. After the
unique excitement, call it the unique ecstasy, of leading the
men. . . . Beyond Cummings, deeper now, was his own desire
to lead the platoon. It had grown, ignited suddenly, become one
of the most satisfying things he had ever done . . . when he searched
himself he was just another Croft.

> That was it. All his life he had flirted with situations, jobs,
> where he could move men, and always . . . he had dropped things
> when they were about to develop, cast off women because deep
> within him he needed control and not mating. (p. 580)

Even in this self-confrontation, we can see the constant shift between anal and phallic metaphors: from "filthy" to the overtly
sexual "unique excitement," "unique ecstasy," "desire," "grown,"
"ignited suddenly," "satisfying" and "flirted," back to anal in
"dropped things," concluding with the highly charged word "control" and a sudden switch into the sexual realm with "mating."
The two layers of castration anxiety and anal anxiety seem to coexist, even in the structure of the prose, and are subsumed under
a desire for control, for omnipotence.

The necessity for omnipotence is foiled in the confrontation
with authority, since the men suffer from an admitted "father
dependence" (p. 74). Hearn's hatred for Cummings is tempered
by his awe and need for approval, and his ambivalence is matched
by the resentment the soldiers feel toward Croft: " 'He's probably
the best platoon sergeant in the army and the meanest. . . . There
ain't a worse man you could be under or a better one, depending
on how you look at it' " (p. 17). Valsen keeps edging away from
a confrontation with the hated Croft; when it actually takes place,
Croft wins by whipping out his gun. In Croft's own case, the unnecessary and futile attempt to climb Mount Anaka is triggered
by his irrational need for omnipotence. The awesome peak seems
to symbolize for him, along with various vague metaphysical goals,
the power of the father. "Far in the distance they could see Mount
Anaka rising above the island, . . . it looked like an immense old
gray elephant erecting himself. . . . The mountain seemed wise
and powerful, and terrifying in its size. . . . The mountain attracted
him, taunted and inflamed him with its size" (p. 447). The relationship with the mountain is not without its homosexual overtones: "behind him Mount Anaka bored into his back as if it were
a human thing" (p. 543).

Hearn also is upset by "the disturbing, fascinating intimacy"
(p. 301) of his unnatural relationship with the effeminate general.
He chooses to combat the degrading pressure of the overly hy-
gienic Cummings through an anal assault, a cigarette butt mashed

into his immaculate floor "in a tangled ugly excrement of black ash, soiled paper, and brown tobacco" (p. 317). Faced with such open defiance of his power, the general temporarily loses control: he suffers from diarrhea and then "a furious uncontrolled anger." Underneath the rage there is "a curious troubled excitement, a momentary submission as if he had been a young girl undressing before the eyes of a roomful of strange men." Cummings overcomes his fear of homosexual submission by an explosive rage which is symbolically both anal and phallic: "his rage choked this off, expanded inside him until it clotted all the conduits of his emotion, and left him trembling with unendurable wrath" (p. 318). In retaliation, he humiliates Hearn by forcing him to pick up the cigarette butt, thus manipulating the junior officer into a kind of homosexual submission. "For almost an hour he [Hearn] lay face down on his cot, burning with shame and self-disgust and an impossible impotent anger" (p. 326). In a sense, Hearn has been buggered by the general, so that his shameful face-down position is appropriate.

This homoerotic struggle for dominance between father and son surfaces again when a few of the soldiers are breaking down under the tropical heat and physical exhaustion, trekking through the jungle with their burden, the dying Wilson, on a stretcher. Sergeant Brown, who outranks the others, feels himself losing command and urges himself on, remembering at the same time a fearful scene in combat when he had nearly succumbed to drowning: "he could not control himself from gulping . . . he had learned then that he was helpless in the shattering gyre of war . . ." (p. 630). The men's fatigue is momentarily relieved by a rainstorm, but the relief is illusory, for it converts their solid footing to mud, and they begin to lose "all puissance" as they sink into the muck. The cycle is from loss of control into helplessness, then regression to anality, only to be trapped through anality into a recognition of powerlessness once more. At this point, young Corporal Stanley, who had won advancement by flattering Brown, now turns on Brown, as the sergeant simultaneously attacks him. It is the son tackling the father, but as in "Maybe Next Year," both battle from a position of enraged and feeble impotence. Brown, an admitted cuckold, hurts the younger man by claiming that Stanley's wife is also unfaithful. In other words, it is the fickle woman who has bested both father and son, and troubles them at the deepest level. Their quarrel is only a cover for the fear of facing the fearful woman, so the battle comes to nothing. Immediately afterward, Brown and Stanley both quit as litter bearers, overcome by a "spongy powerless sensation." Brown feels that he should turn in his stripes, but he knows he is too much of a coward to resign his authority. Just as Hearn saw his likeness to Croft, Brown now recognizes the similarity between himself and Stanley. "Aaah, the two of us are just alike. He'll be having my troubles soon" (p. 634). In truth, it is like father, like son. What is this except the bitter realization of masculine powerlessness at the conclusion of "Maybe Next Year" all over again? "I'm not going to do anything about it, what with the boy between us, and the job ruined, and everything God-damn else, I might be one of them [the tramps] myself, maybe next year."

As in the short story, the secret conqueror of *The Naked and the Dead* is the woman that no one can face, the mother, and this repressed truth helps to explain the basic inconclusiveness of the work. Such a supposition is reinforced by the all-male environment of the book. Even though Mailer in this novel deals with the civilian lives and amatory concerns of his soldiers, the women are a series of ciphers, with no more substance than the life-size photograph of a movie star over which the ineffectual Dalleson drools in the closing scene. The novel stubbornly maintains tension for over seven hundred pages, but instead of reaching a climax, it is defensively reticent, like a man gingerly maneuvering through a mine field which, we later discover, was planted with duds all the time. It is a war story without major battles; all the energy is expended in skirmishes and squabbling, and its heroes keep approaching and receding from conflict. The scenes in which the bickering and bitching, the perpetually suppressed anxiety, momentarily rise to explosive tension are given no more emphasis than the surrounding mass of incident. The psychic content of the novel is mirrored in its form, which one can liken to a state of coitus interruptus. Tony Tanner, reviewing another work by Mailer, refers to its "fragmentary spasmodic structure," "kept simmering at a high degree of excitability just short of hysteria."[9] These descriptive terms apply as well to the structure of *The Naked and the Dead*.

The physically defensive nature of the novel manifests itself in abundant images of castration and buggery, the latter being itself a projection of emasculation fears. As Leslie Fiedler has noted about Mailer's fiction, anal intercourse is an expression of sadistic impulses: "buggery is the essential aspect of a sexual connection whose aim is annihilation, not fulfillment. . . ."[10] This attitude is clear in the hateful feelings of Cummings toward Hearn. "Women would have wanted to excite some love from him, but for himself—to see Hearn afraid, filled with shame if only for an instant" (p. 322). Diana Trilling notes that when Cummings cannot quite *seduce* Hearn, he must therefore *kill* him.[11] The underlying conception is one of sex as a violent struggle for dominance, and it colors all of Mailer's fiction. As Private Minetta says in *The Naked and the Dead*, " 'If you're not on top you just get the shitty end of the stick' " (p. 315): that is, if you are not aggressively potent, you will be entered from behind.

The controlling metaphor of anal intercourse makes the novel sometimes appear like a progress through a series of slimy tunnels. For Mailer, it is truly as Yeats puts it in "Crazy Jane Talks with the Bishop": "Love has pitched his mansion in/The place of excrement." When the soldiers are forced to carry a field piece through a deeply rutted jungle trail, the struggle with the gun becomes a form of forbidden sexual encounter, like sodomy: "they felt as though they were groping their way through an endless tunnel. Their feet sank into the deep mud . . ." (p. 130). The metaphorical sodomy in turn conjures up images of emasculation: "the file at last broke into separate wriggling columns like a worm cut into many parts" (p. 131), and the final impotence occurs when the men lose their grip and the gun slides downhill.

Cummings himself "gropes with distaste" through the "slimy" walls of a muddy tent (p. 110), and Hearn repeats his action later on in the novel with a similar response. Hearn opens the hatch door of a ship and starts down a ladder. "The heat smote him with an unexpected shock; he had forgotten how unbearable a ship's hold could become. And of course it stank. He felt like an insect crawling through the entrails of a horse. 'Damn,' he muttered in disgust" (pp. 306–7).

The symbolic equation between the anus and the lethal vagina becomes evident in a later episode. The platoon is on patrol, significantly headed toward "the Japanese rear" (p. 455). Suddenly, the men encounter a jungle, "a tunnel whose walls were composed of foliage and whose roadbed was covered with slime." They are "absorbed" in the stench, which released "a stifled horror, close to nausea. . . . 'Smells like a nigger woman,' Wilson announced" (pp. 456–57). They progress upriver "with the motions of salmon laboring upstream for the spawning season" (p. 467). It is a struggle upstream all the way in *The Naked and the Dead*, and the journey into the dark tunnel is a particularly chancy trip, filled with "stimulations and terrors" (p. 458), because one might not return intact.

Corpses symbolize the various forms of sexual death in the novel. As they are searching for plunder among the Japanese dead that litter the battlefield, the drunken soldiers uncover one hideous specimen: "he was stretched out on his back with his legs separated and his knees raised" (p. 211). One notes the feminine sexual posture of the body.

> The singed cloth of his uniform had rotted away and it exposed his scorched genitals. . . . Martinez prodded with his shoe the genitals of the charred corpse. The genitals collapsed with a small crispy sound as if he had stuck his finger into a coil of cigar ash. (p. 211)

As though this image of emasculation were inadequate, there are also in the same chapter withered trees, a headless corpse, and a dangerous snake that the soldiers reduce to pulp with a gunshot.

Mailer's hyperdeveloped sense of smell comes into play here. Scattered amidst the debris of the battlefield are thousands of rotting corpses, which give off an odor of decay " a good deal like ordure leavened with garbage and the foul odor of a swamp" (p. 210). The men enter yet another slimy cavern, in which Martinez steals the gold teeth from a decaying Japanese soldier. This scene displays the full gamut of anal-phallic associations; feces are connected with money, corpses, and emasculation.

The equation recurs in a later scene when, shortly after the death of his wife, Gallagher encounters a dead giant sea kelp washed ashore on the beach, "dark brown and very long, perhaps fifty feet, and its dark rubbery skin glistened like snakes, and gave him a jolt of horror. He was remembering the bodies in the cave" (p. 284). The symbol of the sea kelp appears elsewhere (pp. 287 and 338), where it is identified as a "withered brown frond" used as fertilizer. Like the corpses, the kelp is simultaneously phallic and fecal; like castration and defecation, it represents a *loss of power*.

In the same manner, when Cummings finds himself "temporarily powerless" to control his troops, it is described in terms that could apply almost equally to detumescence or diarrhea:

> For five weeks the troops had functioned like an extension of his own body. And now . . . he had lost his sensitive control. No matter how he molded them now the men always collapsed into a sodden resistant mess like dishrags, too soft, too wet to hold any shape which might be given them. At night he would lie sleepless on his cot, suffering an almost unbearable frustration; there were times when he was burning with the impotence of his rage. (pp. 300–301)

This wording is echoed later in the description of Hearn's humiliation: "he lay face down on his cot, burning with shame and self-disgust and an impossible impotent anger" (p. 326).

The Naked and the Dead is, in fact, peopled with curiously similar anally oriented personalities. Hearn is always searching for the dirty motive behind everything, Cummings and Croft both hate waste and hate to be touched, and Valsen is perpetually stifling his emotions. All of them have an overwhelming need to "Keep a tight asshole"; all of them fear being reduced to a lower, more vile order of being—a homosexual or a woman.

It should be evident by now that the reason for the final cancellation of all conflict in the novel is that the central action is a mere dodge, a regressive way of avoiding, at all costs, the fearsome mother. " 'Ah, you're just a bunch of women,' " Croft keeps contemptuously saying to his platoon. " 'Course Sam got mother's milk if ever a one did,' " says Mr. Croft about his son (p. 156). Croft tries to burn out the mother in himself through violence. At one point, Roth is mothering a tiny crippled bird, and Croft takes it in his fist and deliberately crushes it to death. " 'It's like killing a baby,' " says Goldstein in horror (p. 531).

The Mailer hero usually suffers from "a fatal taint": he has "the softness of a man early accustomed to mother love" (*AN*, p. 134). In *The Naked and the Dead*, Martinez' earliest memories are of "big fat momma with the smell" (*ND*, p. 63). The Mailer hero wants to eliminate this image, to extirpate the soft, tainted woman he hates in himself.

In the same way, the war in *The Naked and the Dead* is not against any external enemy: it is a war against the introjected image of the mother, an image that has become confused with the feces. The external conflict, the plot machinations, are a mask for an internal conflict that remains fairly static. There is no woman here for the men to fight against, so they fight against their own fears, against their own sense of inadequacy, and against each other. It is not surprising then that the action results in a draw; the internal conflict is stalemated.

Twenty years after *The Naked and the Dead*, Mailer wrote a war novel in miniature: *Why Are We in Vietnam?* Again, the enemy D.J. cannot defeat is the mother. "D.J. is full of mother-love received in full crazy bitch perfume aromas from Hallie" (*WV*, p. 160), Hallie being his mother, who perfumes herself all over, even on the behind. D.J. identifies his anus with his mother's vagina, "his dangerous hard-ass soft mother's cherry" (p. 203). Once again, the critics have noted that the conflict of the novel is unresolved.[12] As though to underline the similarity between these two war novels, Mailer ends *Vietnam* with an echo of the end of *The Naked and the Dead*. Major Dalleson in *The Naked and the Dead* says " 'Hot dog!' " and D.J. turns off with "Vietnam, hot damn."

Given the static conflict of *The Naked and the Dead*, we can offer a tentative solution for another critical problem that has been debated for years: who is the hero of the novel? Is it Croft or Cummings, Valsen or Hearn, or is this a novel with no real hero?[13] We have noted a fundamental similarity in psychological makeup between the characters in the novel. Hearn resembles Cummings and Croft, and Valsen is like Croft and Hearn. Each one undergoes the same emotional crises and burns with endless frustration, self-disgust, and impotent rage. They all persevere heroically in spite of the fact that they are trapped on a hopeless treadmill of despair. All of them, aggressors and underdogs alike, have impossibly grand ambitions but are dogged by failure. "Like Valsen and Hearn," writes Norman Podhoretz, "the platoon sergeant and the general have so much in common that they seem to be the same person in two different incarnations."[14]

Each character is only a different version of a single character, a composite personality who suffers from an unresolved Oedipal crisis, anal ambivalence and consequent homosexual ambivalence, psychic impotence, and an inability to cope with authority or deal with women. Once we recognize the repetitiousness of the central conflict and the essential similarity of all the characters, there is really nothing to choose among them. The author seems to have parceled himself out among the various characters to create this composite personality.

The narrow emotional range of the characters makes *The Naked and the Dead* an excessively gloomy, pessimistic work.[15] We see characters reduced by starved emotions to the level of beasts. The soldiers are, almost to a man, pitifully deficient in feeling, manipulative, and self-absorbed.[16] Their human interaction is limited primarily to mutual animosity. Hearn does not like people, Croft hates everything not in himself, and Cummings is not close to anyone. Roth is smothered in self-pity and Gallagher boils over with rage. The Croft-Martinez friendship is distorted by racism, and the Cummings-Hearn relationship by power plays and sado-masochism. The only comradeship is that of temporary fellow sufferers, as in the scene of the aftermath of the storm, but even that feeling quickly evaporates.

One could see this alienation and emotional starvation as part of the tradition of literary naturalism in which Mailer is writing; naturalism always tends toward a bleak determinism. Alternately, one could say that this is Mailer's pessimistic view of the products of the American social and military machine. Nevertheless, the portrait is exaggerated: it seems to correspond not so much to the reality of masculine relationships as to the author's own psychological reality.

There is also a lovelessness in the characters' relationships with women.[17] With few exceptions, sex is used as a substitute for power or a form of aggression, or is reduced to a purely animal, sensual level, as with Wilson.

Whereas Mailer is obviously highly critical of the inadequacies of the men's emotional and sexual relationships, the similarity of their conflicts and of their responses suggests an underlying pattern of psychological ambivalence. None of the characters is successfully able to balance rage and compassion, hate and love, aggressive and passive impulses. Hearn and Valsen are capable of both hate and love, but choose to stifle their compassion. Cummings and Croft are disgusted by their tenderer emotions; both are consumed by rage. Compassion is considered soft and effeminate—it leaves one open and vulnerable—and is associated with the Jews, Roth and Goldstein. The two most sympathetic characters at the novel's end, Ridges and Goldstein, possess abundant compassion but almost no capacity for anger. Their virtue is the passive one of endurance.[18]

Nevertheless, despite the lack of emotional range and emotional balance in the characters, *The Naked and the Dead* would be a much weaker and thinner work if it did not acknowledge the conflict. The novel reflects the tension of emotional ambivalence: the force of repression is great, but that tenderness is still there, struggling to surface.

In sum, then, the central psychological conflict in *The Naked and the Dead* is the struggle for power and control over the self and over outside objects, an effort that is doomed again and again to humiliating failure. It is an oedipal struggle with anal overtones. The desire for omnipotence is countered by impotence, the struggle for autonomy defeated by shame and doubt.

The only one truly in control in the novel is that mastermind, the omniscient narrator, who organizes his campaign, marshals his forces, and deploys his troops with the skill of a great military strategist. *The Naked and the Dead* is the triumph of General Mailer.[19] For the novel does build an impressive force in several ways: first, through raw physical realism which stays close to the body—this is a novel that you feel in your guts; second, through the massive accumulation of detail[20]; and third, through the repetition of the central conflict in various characters—the struggle for power constantly foiled, leaving a sensation of bitter frustration and helplessness. The pressure builds until that final, exhausting long patrol wears down the reader as well as the soldiers. The novel recreates in the reader the sense of impotent rage and helplessness of the child struggling for autonomy and failing.

These are the virtues of the novel, and if we look at them carefully, we see that they are also virtues commonly associated with the anal character: an intimate concern with bodily processes, stubbornness, repetition, and a scrupulous attention to detail. Finally, both the weaknesses and the strengths of *The Naked and the Dead* derive from the same psychological source.

Notes

1. John W. Aldridge, "From Vietnam to Obscenity," in *Norman Mailer: The Man and His Work*, ed. Robert F. Lucid (Boston and Toronto: Little, Brown, 1971), pp. 188–89.

2. Norman Mailer, "Homage to El Loco," in *Existential Errands*, p. 59.

3. Howard Silverstein, "Norman Mailer: The Family Romance and the Oedipal Fantasy," *American Imago* 34, No. 3 (Fall 1977), 277.

4. Norman Mailer, *The Presidential Papers* (New York: Putnam's, 1963), p. 38.

5. Diana Trilling, "The Moral Radicalism of Norman Mailer," in *Norman Mailer*, ed. Lucid, p. 110.

6. Ibid., p. 118. For other criticism along these lines, see also Norman Podhoretz, "Norman Mailer: The Embattled Vision," in *Norman Mailer*, ed. Lucid, pp. 62–68; and Chester E. Eisinger, *Fiction of the Forties* (Chicago: Phoenix, 1965), pp. 33–38.

7. John W. Aldridge, *After the Lost Generation* (New York: McGraw-Hill, 1951), p. 139.

8. Ihab Hassan, *Radical Innocence* (Princeton: Princeton University, 1961), p. 144.

9. Tony Tanner, "In the Lion's Den," *Partisan Review* 34 (Summer 1967): 467.

10. Leslie Fiedler, "Master of Dreams," *Partisan Review* 34 (Summer 1967): 354.

11. Trilling, "Moral Radicalism," p. 117.

12. See, for example, Frederic Jameson, "The Great American Hunter; or Ideological Content in the Novel," *College English* 34 (November 1972): 190. Jameson says *Vietnam* is "structurally unresolvable."

13. See David F. Burg, "The Hero of *The Naked and the Dead*," *Modern Fiction Studies* 18 (1971): 387–401, for a summary of the arguments. Burg himself opts for Valsen as the hero.

14. Podhoretz, "Norman Mailer: The Embattled Vision," p. 66.

15. See, for example, Robert Solotaroff, *Down Mailer's Way* (Urbana: University of Illinois, 1974), p. 5: "*The Naked and the Dead* seems, in moral terms, to be a wasteland vision of a dying world."

16. See Philip Bufithis, *Norman Mailer* (New York: Ungar, 1978), p. 26: "Self-absorption . . . is the indelible attribute of every man in the platoon."

17. The best analysis of Mailer's view of male-female relationships in *The Naked and the Dead* (and in Mailer's other works) is Jean Radford, *Norman Mailer: A Critical Study* (New York: Harper, 1975), pp. 124–30.

18. Ibid., p. 16. Also see Stanley T. Gutman, *Mankind in Barbary: The Individual and Society in the Novels of Norman Mailer* (Hanover, N.H.: University Press of New England, 1975), p. 27.

19. See Bufithis, *Norman Mailer*, p. 21: "General Cummings represents, then, Mailer's self-projection as the Romantic artist convinced that he is posessed of the ability to recreate the world."

20. See Robert Alter, "Norman Mailer," in *The Politics of Twentieth-Century Novelists*, ed. George A. Panichas (New York: Crowell, 1974), p. 322. Alter says that *The Naked and the Dead* has a "painstaking accumulation of acute observation. . . . a massive solidity unlike anything he would write afterward." Alter is not quite correct. *Of a Fire on the Moon* shows the same painstaking accumulation of detail, although it ultimately bogs down under its own weight.

3 *Barbary Shore:* Growing Up in Brooklyn

Barbary Shore is an intriguing failure of a novel, an overly-ambitious and finally unsuccessful attempt to mix political allegory with existential closet drama, myth, and family romance. The ghosts of George Orwell and Franz Kafka meet in a room in one of Nathaniel Hawthorne's haunted mansions.

It is, at best, a transitional work for Mailer.[1] The naturalism of *The Naked and the Dead*, with its political and sociological stereotyping and exaggerated despair, gives way to an unreal, self-contained nightmare world filled with grotesque characters— and exaggerated despair. According to Robert Langbaum, "Mailer's vision of general disease and madness becomes ever more comprehensive and strident with each novel."[2] Mailer's view of society as perverse and corrupt forced him away from literary realism and into the feverish distortions of the dream vision. Nevertheless, the political allegory and polemic in *Barbary Shore* clash with the nightmarish surrealism.[3] Later, Mailer will write a more realistic, plausible version of the same plot in *The Deer Park*, and improve on the nightmarish sexual intensity in *An American Dream* and *Why Are We in Vietnam?*.

What happens in *Barbary Shore* is that the overt, political concerns are swamped by the unconscious, psychosexual concerns. Leslie Fiedler claims that Mailer was trying to rewrite the old "novel of political disillusionment," but "only the hectic sexuality which threatens, despite his conscious attempt, to replace politics completely, seems his own."[4] Robert Solotaroff believes that, in *Barbary Shore*, "Mailer's interest in sexual disturbance ranges beyond its availability as a symbol and symptom of total social dislocation. It intrigues him in its own right."[5] The uniformly bizarre, perverted sexual relationships in the novel are best understood as the eruption of unconscious concerns. "On one level," writes Howard Silverstein, "*Barbary Shore* is a novel about the compulsive incestuous drives of the characters. All the emotional attachments take place between characters living under one roof. In this sense, the novel is a 'family romance,' a dramatization of the character's earliest sexual desires focused on the members of the family circle."[6]

Barbary Shore is an autobiographical novel in disguise. In his comments about the writing of the novel, Mailer says, "my life seemed to have been mined and melted into the long reaches of [*The Naked and the Dead*]. And so I was prominent and empty, and I had to begin life again. . . . Success had been a lobotomy to my past, there seemed no power from the past which could help me in the present, and I had no choice but to force myself to step into the war of the enormous present . . ." (*ADV*, pp. 92–93). Given these circumstances, Mailer ponders the possibilties for a second novel: "If my past had become empty as a theme, was I to write about Brooklyn streets, or my mother and father, or another war novel (*The Naked and the Dead* go to Japan), was I to do the book of the returning veteran when I had lived like a mole writing and rewriting . . ? No, those were not real choices. I was drawn instead to write about an imaginary future . . ." (*ADV*, p. 93–94).[7] Thus the hero, Mike Lovett, is a reflection of Mailer's situation: Mailer has been lobotomized from his past, and Lovett has amnesia, probably as the consequence of war injuries. Lovett essentially has no identity of his own: his wounds have resulted in a surgically rebuilt face, and his amnesia has robbed him of all but a few phantom memories. He is reborn and forced to live in "the enormous present."

In "The White Negro," Mailer claims that the psychopath is seeking "the opportunity to grow up a second time" (*ADV*, p. 346). In creating Lovett, Mailer is seeking the same opportunity for himself. *Barbary Shore* is as much concerned with reenacting the past as it is with speculating about the future. Ironically, all the possibilities that Mailer discards for his novel become the subject of *Barbary Shore*: the novel takes place in Brooklyn, concerns a war (not the Second World War but the Cold War), and has as narrator a returned veteran who lives like a mole in a rented room, trying to write a novel. Moreover, *Barbary Shore* is about a mother and father (McLeod and Guinevere) and a young hero (Lovett) trying to grow up again who attaches himself to this substitute family. Despite himself, Mailer wrote the novel about growing up in Brooklyn he had tried so hard to avoid writing.

In *The Myth of the Birth of the Hero*, Otto Rank describes the typical pattern of the family romance: the orphan hero has been deprived of true knowledge of his identity and discovers that his parents are royalty.[8] This is the pattern of *Barbary Shore*. Lovett is symbolically an orphan, stripped of his identity. Determined to write a novel, he saves some money and rents a cheap room for the summer on the top floor of a Brooklyn Heights rooming house. There he becomes involved in the lives of the various residents: Guinevere, the buxom but blowsy landlady, attracts him sexually; McLeod, a shrewd, severe older man, befriends him; Hollingsworth, an aggressive young man who claims to be a clerk in a Wall Street brokerage, puzzles and offends him; and Lannie, a deranged young woman, arouses both his pity and his desire.

As the summer goes on, Lovett is in for a series of shocks and surprises as he discovers that none of them is exactly what he or she appears to be. McLeod is not a mere department store worker, but an ex-Commissar for Stalin. Once known as "the hangman of the Left opposition," he had participated in the Stalinist purges until, disillusioned with the course of the Revolution, he defected to the West. He then worked in a government office until, as disgusted with capitalism as with communism, he stole some vital, unnamed "little object" and went into hiding under an assumed name. McLeod also turns out to be the mysterious missing husband of Guinevere. Hollingsworth, in turn, is a government agent sent to spy on McLeod and retrieve the little object, and Lannie is an ex-Trotskyite who joins forces with Hollingsworth because she blames McLeod for the death of Trotsky. Lovett becomes involved in the web of suspicion and conspiracy, with each spying on the others, and all of them involved in a daisy chain of sadomasochistic love affairs: Lovett is tempted but frustrated by Guinevere, and has a brief, abortive affair with Lannie; Lannie in turn romances both Hollingsworth and Guinevere; and Hollingsworth in the end kills McLeod and runs off with Guinevere. At the novel's end, Lovett is bequeathed the little object (which seems to symbolize the hope for revolutionary socialism) by his newfound spiritual and political father, McLeod.

Critics have noted the political allegory and Arthurian myth that underlies this implausible plot. Lovett is the aliented young postwar radical who has lost his socialist culture; McLeod is the disillusioned Stalinist; Lannie, the betrayed Trotskyite; Hollingsworth, the oppressive American right wing; and Guinevere, the mindless, apolitical masses.[9] Everyone romances Guinevere, who is up for grabs but really can only love herself; Hollingsworth wins her because he is the most ruthless and sadistic. On another level, the failed Russian Revolution is symbolically equivalent to King Arthur's Round Table. McLeod then is Arthur, Guinevere his "burlesque queen," and Hollingsworth is Lancelot, who betrays Arthur and steals his queen.[10] All this is supported by the mystery, rumor, and awe which surround McLeod. Moreover, Hollingsworth has some of the attributes of a mythic hero: he claims to be of "humble birth" (*BS*, p. 11), but Guinevere suspects "he's the son

of a prince. . . living here in disguise" (p. 90). His first name,
Leroy, means "the king," and he has a black shield emblazoned
on his silver cigarette lighter (p. 108). These Arthurian and mythic
attributes tend to reinforce the element of family romance in the
tale, with McLeod and Guinevere as symbolic King and Queen,
father and mother to the other characters.

There is also a religious allegory connected to the political and
Arthurian allegory. Guinevere speaks of herself fancifully as a
Jehovah's Witness. She says, " 'there's going to be wars and plagues
and famines, and the Witnesses'll be the only ones saved because
they bear true witness to the ways of the Lord, and they don't have
false idols' " (p. 31). At the end of the novel, Lovett has inherited
from McLeod the role of keeper of the faith and possessor of the
Holy Grail, the "little object." He will be a Witness to the inevitable
apocalypse of the Third World War, which he awaits in hiding,
a Witness who hopes to be saved because he no longer believes
in the false idols of Capitalism or Commmunism. However, as a
Witness, he is not equipped to live in this world. His bleak existence
is merely a preparation for the imagined revolutionary future
that will presumably follow the apocalypse.

On a parallel level of mythic meaning, McLeod is a sorcerer
out of a fairy tale, and Lovett calls himself "the sorcerer's apprentice" (p. 7). When Lovett first meets him, McLeod resembles "a
witch" and is holding a broom (p. 20). In bequeathing Lovett "the
remnants of my socialist culture" (p. 312) and the mysterious and
much sought-after "little object," he is passing on the mysteries
of the faith to the new apprentice. Having passed his initiation
rites, Lovett graduates into adulthood upon the death of McLeod.

According to Otto Rank, every myth is a paranoid structure
revealing the wish to get rid of the parents, particularly the father.
Nevertheless, through reaction formation, the hero often appears
"not as the persecutor of his father . . . but as the avenger of the
persecuted father."[11] In *Barbary Shore*, everyone is conspiring
to get McLeod, spying on him, pressuring, and persecuting him
to relinquish the little object. Only Lovett remains true to him.

For that matter, most of Mailer's plots depend upon conspiracies.
In *The Naked and the Dead*, Cummings and then Croft conspire
against Hearn. In *The Deer Park*, movie studio executives and the
government conspire against Eitel. And in *An American Dream*,
almost everyone is out to get Rojack.

Along with the paranoid conspiracy in *Barbary Shore* goes an
atmosphere of mutual suspicion, shame and doubt. Everyone is
keeping secrets and living in hiding or under assumed names and

fake identities. They all spy on one another, and their deepest fear is of being found out. Even Lovett, that apparently innocent witness, is as guilty as the rest of them: he spies on Guinevere, and bursts in on the bedroom of McLeod and Guinevere. Each time, he is forced to do it, as if against his will: Guinevere makes him hide when Hollingsworth arrives, and it is Hollingsworth who drags him into the apartment to catch Guinevere with her secret husband, McLeod. Besides being a spy, Lovett is as fake as any of them, since he does not know his real name or age, or even what his face looked like before it was remodeled. He conceals the fact of his amnesia from everyone except McLeod.

Like the mythic hero Oedipus, Lovett is set apart from other men because of his lack of knowledge of his true identity and because of his wounds: "There is the mark of a wound behind my ear, an oblong of unfertile flesh where no hair grows. It is covered over now. . . . but no barber can hide the scar on my back" (p. 3). That "unfertile flesh" suggests that, like the typical Mailer hero, he is not a complete man. Because he has lost his memory, Lovett compares himself at the opening and the close of the novel to others who have lost their faculties: the blind and the deaf. Guinevere accuses him of being "a cripple" (p. 7), and McLeod calls him "a castrate" (p. 224). Emotionally, Lovett is indeed crippled or stunted. He is one of many Mailer heroes unmanned by war wounds who must forge a new identity and a new manhood for himself; Sergius in *The Deer Park* and Rojack in *An American Dream* fit the same pattern. Mailer may be deliberately borrowing the idea of the emasculating war wound from Hemingway, but it seems to fit his myth of himself and his need as an author to recreate his identity and seek renewed proof of his manhood in each new work.

Unfortunately, Lovett is the weak link in the story. He is the narrator and ostensible protagonist, but he is the least realized character. Moreover, he is a most unsatisfactory hero, since he is reduced primarily to the role of a passive witness to events.

Lovett's passivity is compensated for by the aggressive energy of Hollingsworth, that other mythic hero, who is symbolically Lovett's "bad brother." Just as we saw a split in *The Naked and the Dead* between the masochistic, self-defeating heroes (Hearn and Valsen), and the sadistic, self-aggrandizing ones (Cummings and Croft), so we see the same doubling of male characters in *Barbary Shore*. This doubling also occurs in *The Deer Park*, where the active and sadistic Marion Faye becomes a much more compelling character than the ostensible hero, Sergius.

Lovett is given to fantasizing and Hollingsworth to acting out. For example, when Guinevere fails to keep an appointment to meet Lovett in his room, he is at first angry and frustrated, but shortly feels "relief that Guinevere had not kept her word" (p. 57).[12] He imagines the two of them together in bed:

> The door is locked, and I lie with my head at her breast. . . . We are happy, we are content, and we are safe. Suddenly there is a knock. We start up, looking desperately at one another, search for an escape. There is none. . . . We make no sound and draw the bedclothes to our necks. . . .Then a key is inserted in the lock, turns back and forth. We wait, petrified, and the door opens, and on the threshold stands a stranger. His arm lifts in a menacing gesture, and I close my eyes and turn my head to the pillow. (p. 58)

The fantasy is obviously infantile: he lies like a blissful infant at the breast, and the protective gestures he makes are childlike, such as pulling the bedclothes up and turning his head to the pillow. It is a fantasy of being caught in the act and punished by that terrible stranger, the father; thus Lovett's relief that he does not succeed with Guinevere.

Lovett also fantasizes about Guinevere's mysterious absent husband. Willie Dinsmore, Lovett's writer friend, was the previous occupant of the room, and was also attracted to Guinevere, whom he called "a nymphomaniac." He tells Lovett, " 'I might have entertained ideas, but there's her husband involved, and although I never met the guy I think it's kind of sneaky seeing a dame when her husband sleeps in the same building' " (p. 12). Ironically, Lovett finds himself confessing his passion for Guinevere to McLeod and speculating about what her husband might be like: " 'He must be a retiring man, overshadowed by her. . . . He could be just as easily seven feet tall and with a big red face and whip her every night' " (p. 75). These are a child's conception of the father figure as either harmless mouse or giant ogre.

One night, as Lovett passes Guinevere's door, he thinks, "Her husband must be home now, and between them was passing the daily exchange of their marriage. . . . On an impulse I thought of ringing her bell" (p. 107). Instead, he leaves, and meets Hollingsworth, who reveals that he has spied on Guinevere and discovered the identity of the mysterious husband. He dares Lovett to accompany him to their apartment. Once there, the drunken Hollingsworth begins to slap Guinevere, and she pummels him in return: "It might have been a scene in a bawdyhouse . . ."(p. 115). Lovett is led against his will into the bedroom by Monina, Guinevere's three-year-old daughter. There, to his shock, he discovers that the man in Guinevere's bed is McLeod, who says, " 'Well, Lovett, the lassie's uncovered me. . . . Once you've found a father, you'd do better not to track him to a brothel' " (pp. 116–17). In other words, Lovett's fantasy of uncovering the father is fulfilled through the agency of Hollingsworth, his alter ego or demon brother.

It might be useful to consider Lovett as Mailer's conception of himself as artist: good, Socialist, and passive. The later Mailer might call him an example of a man soft with "mother love." Richard Poirier suggests that, for Mailer, writing is imagined as an essentially feminine activity.[13] Hollingsworth, on the other hand, is Mailer's conception of himself as a masterful man of action and power, a descendant of Croft: evil, fascistic, and aggressive. Hollingsworth is the other type of Mailer hero, the man hard with "daddy love." This same dark figure recurs in all of Mailer's novels, revealing the hero's hidden evil desires: Croft, Marion Faye, Shago Martin, and Tex Hyde (Mr. Hyde to D.J.'s Dr. Jekyll in *Why Are We in Vietnam?*).

Hollingsworth expresses most of the sexually perverse desires in the novel, the oedipal hostilities and the anal and oral sadism. As the hero's psychic proxy, he acts out Lovett's fantasies and wards off any blame that might accrue to Lovett.

As he does with all the characters in the novel, Mailer deliberately exaggerates Hollingsworth's psychological quirks, as if he could better control these perverse drives by rendering them unmistakable. The ambivalent love/hate, persecutor/victim relationship between McLeod and Hollingsworth is an almost textbook case, an acting out of paranoid delusions of persecution. loaded with unmistakable homoerotic overtones.

McLeod and Hollingsworth are an odd couple with complementary hangups; they are made for each other. When we first encounter McLeod, he is, rather obviously, down on his knees scrubbing a bathroom floor. "'I've got a mania about neatness,'" he tells Lovett (p. 20). "In everything he did there were elements of such order, demanding, monastic. . . . And his room, clean as any cell could have been in our aged mansion, described an unending campaign against the ceiling which sweated water and the floor which collected dust" (p. 34).[14] Later this passion for cleanliness seems an expression of guilt over his crimes in the service of Stalin.

Hollingsworth, in contrast, looks like a clean-cut, blond, All-American boy, yet McLeod says he has "a mind like a garbage pail" (p. 36). Hollingsworth is a mass of contradictions; he is clean and freshly-shaved, yet "his room was unbelievably messed," dirty clothes and trash strewn everywhere. "Yet the floor had no dust, the woodwork was wiped, and the windows had been washed . . ." (p. 37). He likes his job because he says "'It's clean work, and I always prefer clean work, don't you?'" (p. 38). Orderly yet disorderly, neat yet dirty, kind yet cruel at the same time: Hollingsworth shows many of the characteristics of a compulsive neurotic.

In his monastic passion for order and cleanliness, McLeod resembles General Cummings in *The Naked and the Dead*. In turn, in his disorderliness, Hollingsworth resembles the rebellious son, Lieutenant Hearn. In a scene parallel to Hearn's childish insubordination in mashing a cigarette butt into the General's immaculate floor, Hollingsworth deliberately provokes McLeod by dumping some pencil shavings onto his clean floor. The repetition of such episodes suggests a similar psychological conflict at the root of both novels: the son's impulse to defy the father through anal rebellion.

The barely disguised homosexual love play between the persecutor and victim, father and son is repeated frequently in Mailer's fiction. Besides the power games between Cummings and Hearn, and McLeod and Hollingsworth, there is also the loving persecution of Charles Eitel by Collie Munshin in *The Deer Park* and of Rojack by Kelly in *An American Dream*. In all of these relationships except *The Naked and Dead*, persecutor and victim share the same woman.

Hollingsworth is a government agent sent to do a job; he is under strict supervision by the Home Office. There is no reason for him to become personally involved in the case, alternately to persecute and to woo McLeod, and no rational reason for him to murder McLeod and run off with his wife. It is clear that Hollingsworth wants to seduce McLeod, and if he cannot do that, he will eliminate him. Even his wooing of Guinevere is a substitute for making love to McLeod. "'You're his wife,'" Hollingsworth says as he embraces Guinevere. "'Why don't you tell me what it was like with him?'" (p. 204). Although he persecutes McLeod, he expresses awe and admiration for the man. For Mailer, "homosexuality as a direct struggle for virility between men themselves is always a murderous symbol, a sign of impending Evil," according to one critic.[15] Thus, the temptation that Hollingsworth offers McLeod just before he kills him is transparently homosexual:

> "You know, I think I first had the idea for my offer when it occurred to me that I could also save you." And he said this with passion so suppressed that the effort made him lean almost against the the body of McLeod. "You're such a stern sort of fellow," he murmured. "I've always liked your type. And deep down, now don't answer cause I know better than you, I feel that you could get to like me." He caught himself short. (p. 303)

The murder that follows is described in ambiguous terms that could suggest homosexual rape: "I could almost see the weapon uncovered and the slow rapt movement of each man about the other. There was some sound of attack, a thick cry which followed . . ." (p. 307).

Is Hollingsworth's desire to possess or kill the father figure supposed to be a symptom or a cause of political repression? The link between the sex and the political allegory is never made clear. In any case, the same sadomasochistic relationship between males is repeated so often in Mailer's fiction that it seems as if he has subsumed his own struggle for manhood into artistic generalizations about the uncertain sexual identity of all modern American men. Hollingsworth is another of Mailer's fictional psychopaths, a type that begins with Croft and Cummings, and is repeated in Marion Faye, Sergius in "The Time of Her Time," the "White Negro," Rojack, and D.J. All of these characters are sexually confused and tormented; their sadistic sexual urges are always hinted to be a denial of latent homosexuality. As Denise accuses Sergius, "'your whole life is a lie, and you do nothing but run away from the homosexual that is you'" (*ADV*, p. 503).

Along with anal sadism, Hollingsworth is also extremely orally aggressive. He is always smiling and showing his teeth and biting down hard on his pipe. Lovett watches Hollingsworth flirt with a waitress: "His head lowered, he was plunged into a conversation directed at her throat" (*BS*, p. 132). Later, Lovett gets vicarious gratification by spying on Hollingsworth and Guinevere. He overhears Hollingsworth making a savage, cannibalistic declaration of love, one of the most striking passages in the novel:

> As though language were a catapult he proceeded to tell her how much he loved her, his speech containing more obscenity than I had ever heard in so short a space, and in rapid succession with a gusto . . . he named various parts of her body and described what he would do to them, how he would tear this and squeeze that, eat here and spit there, butcher rough and slice fine, slash, macerate, pillage, all in an unrecognizable voice which must have issued between clenched teeth, until his appetite satisfied, I could see him squatting beside the carcass, his mouth wiped carefully with the back of his hand. With that, he sighed, as much to say, "A good piece of ass, by God." (p. 203)

The tone here seems a mixture of satiric exaggeration, horror, and delight at Hollingsworth's barbaric energy. If, as the novel claims, mankind is drifting toward "barbary shore," Mailer still puts his greatest imaginative energies into the descriptions of barbarism.

Hollingsworth's cannibalistic desires resemble those of many other scenes in Mailer's fiction. For example, Cummings tells his wife as they make love, "'I'll take you apart, I''ll eat you, oh, I'll make you mine, I'll make you mine, you bitch'" (*ND.* p. 416). And in *American Dream*, Rojack fantasizes that Kelly is inviting him to "pitch and tear and squat and lick, swill and grovel . . . fuck until our eyes were out" (*AD*, p. 254). For that matter, the hunt in *Why Are We in Vietnam?* is almost entirely a matter of acting out anally and orally sadistic desires. This tendency toward cannibalism, toward oral or anal savagery, seems to be always present in Mailer's characters, ready to surface and prompt them into violence or guilt or revulsion. They fight the impulse even though they wish to fulfill it.

McLeod also confuses sex with cannibalism. He "rooted in all the sweating and lurching of unfulfillment until the flesh of his wife had become just that, and as flesh was the denominator of meat and all the corpses he had ever seen and some created" (*BS*, p. 204). Similarly, Sergius in *The Deer Park* becomes impotent because of guilt over his wartime experiences. When he makes love, he can think only of "bursting flesh, rotting flesh, flesh hung on spikes in butcher stalls" (*DP*, p. 229).

In one memorable scene in *Barbary Shore*, little Monina acts out the oral aggression which obsesses so many of the novel's characters: "like a missile whose fuse was her mouth, she buried her teeth into Hollingsworth's hand, emitting in advance one single shriek which graduated her at a bound from a child to an avenging banshee" (*BS*, p. 147).

Mailer attempts to rationalize the impulses toward cannibalism in *Barbary Shore* as instances of political degeneracy. Lannie says that "'the world devours'" (p. 212), and McLeod claims that "'the first stage of cannibalism has been reached'" in modern totalitarianism, and that the state begins to devour its own (p. 280). The secret police are put to the task of "'the swallowing of all opposition'" (p. 223). Hollingsworth, says McLeod, is "'the perfection of the policeman for it is never enough to bring the man in, you've got to swallow him first'" (p. 245). Thus, "'the voracious appetite of Mr. Hollingsworth'" is supposed to be symptomatic of encroaching barbarism (p. 246). Years later, Mailer entitles one of his volumes *Cannibals and Christians* (1966); that title also seems to describe the characters in *Barbary Shore*. All of them are consumed with cannibalistic desires. In Hollingsworth, these desires are expressed sadistically; in McLeod, they are transformed by the masochism of guilt feelings into impotence.

Finally, beneath the conscious political and intellectual structures of *Barbary Shore* is enacted a family romance filled with impulses of anal and oral sadism. These fantasies interest the author so much in their own right that they take over the novel and subvert its surface meaning as a political allegory.

In the context of the family romance, Lovett, Hollingsworth, and Lannie do not stand for differing political ideologies but for children. Lovett feels like "an adolescent first entering the adult world" (p. 10). His age, like that of all the other characters, is uncertain. He could be anywhere from twenty to thirty, but he looks so young everyone calls him "kid" or "boy." The rooming house makes him feel at one point "as unashamedly miserable as a child in the immensity of an empty house" (p. 289). McLeod calls Hollingsworth "a child" (p. 244), and Hollingsworth complains, "'Everybody wants to hurt me,' he said like a boy of twelve" (p. 302). McLeod also gives Lannie paternal reassurance: "'Go to sleep,' he said almost tenderly, 'and when you wake everything will be better.' A mist from childhood came near to whisking her away" (p. 294).

McLeod is the father as guilty murderer, a projection of the son's own murderous oedipal desires. McLeod served Stalin, symbolically the "bad father," and helped assassinate Trotsky, who stands here for the betrayed "good father." Lastly, McLeod killed a young political associate who had been like a son to him. Now McLeod repents and offers himself masochistically as a sacrifice to Hollingsworth, the avenging son. Hollingsworth wants both to love and destroy the parents—like Mailer's later invention, the hipster or "White Negro," to rape and murder them. Hollingsworth is the rival of Lovett for the affections of McLeod and Guinevere. Lovett, the good son, stands passively by the sidelines, getting a vicarious, voyeuristic pleasure out of the conflict. He first pursues Guinevere, but later transfers his loyalties to McLeod. As Howard Silverstein writes, "Ultimately, Lovett's need for the father's approval is much greater than his attraction to Guinevere, and he chooses to serve McLeod's cause rather than to go along with his mentor's scheming wife." [16] At the end of the novel, Lovett takes the place of the dead McLeod, living like him a monastic existence, in hiding, devoted only to the "little object" which stands for the hopes of a coming revolution. Symbolically, Lovett keeps the father figure alive by becoming him; he is also doing penance for the destruction of the father.

Guinevere, whom Diana Trilling describes so well as "a sharp, slobby lady who is always bartering or withholding her fly-blown sexuality in some strange, awful enterprise of personal advantage," [17] is the debased mother, the mother as prostitute up for sale to the highest bidder. Guinevere is a memorable comic creation, a kind of vulgar, seductive earth mother with huge hips and breasts. Every character, male or female, tries to make love to her. According to Otto Rank, mythic plots are often "impelled by the pleasurable emotion of placing the mother, or the subject of greatest sexual curiosity, in the situation of secret unfaithfulness and clandestine love affairs. . . . Frequently they do not hesitate in crediting the mother with as many love affairs as there are rivals."[18]

Guinevere is narcissistic, emotionally unstable, and unremittingly greedy. She has even turned her little daughter Monina into a miniature sex pot and has been grooming her for Hollywood. Like the typical Mailer "bitch goddess," such as Lulu or Dorothea in *The Deer Park*, Denise in "The Time of Her Time," or Deborah in *An American Dream*, Guinevere is capricious, bestowing or withholding her favors arbitrarily. We realize finally that she is incapable of any affection apart from self-love and self-aggrandizement.

Barbary Shore is partially redeemed by the flair for satire shown in the creation of Guinevere and Hollingsworth, a talent for comedy Mailer will develop in his later work. One also has to give Mailer high marks for trying to write a political novel during a period of repression; one critic calls *Barbary Shore* "the most serious novel to emerge from the McCarthy period."[19] Nevertheless, *Barbary Shore* is an incoherent work: the sex competes with the politics, and the comedy competes with the tragedy. For example, Jean Radford notes that the poetic despair of the maddened Lannie, who has been in and out of mental institutions, "is not integrated with the comic, neo-surrealist elements which centre around Guinevere and Monina."[20] We are left finally with what Diana Trilling calls "a web of finespun fantasies, as obscure as they are frightening."[21]

Incoherence in a work of art may indicate ambivalent or unresolved feelings in the artist. Mailer admits that, at the time he wrote *Barbary Shore*

> My conscious intelligence . . . became obsessed with the Russian Revolution. But my unconscious was much more interested in other matters: murder, suicide, orgy, psychosis, all the themes I discuss in *Advertisements*. Since the gulf between these conscious and unconscious themes was vast and quite resistant to any quick literary coupling, the tension to get a bridge across resulted in the peculiar feverish hothouse atmosphere of the book.[22]

The rigid polemical structure of the novel can be seen as a kind of unsuccessful defense against the dangerous unconscious meaning of the tale, which surfaces in the violent passions of the characters.

These passions have little basis in rational motivations. It seems as if Mailer is uncertain how he feels about the violent sexual fantasies he is unearthing: are they perverse and horrifying instances of modern political and cultural degeneracy, or are they stimulating and funny? Because Mailer does not know how to handle the fantasies, neither does the reader.

What we see in *Barbary Shore* is a clash between two coexisting but imperfectly connected levels of meaning, one polemical and intensely rational, and the other unconscious and wholly irrational. The schism prefigures the split in Mailer's later works, in which the dogmatic and the systematic coexist with the fanciful and the fantastic. The ideology in *Barbary Shore* serves a function that is similar to that of the cosmology and the Reichianism in *American Dream* and *Vietnam*, but instead of being integral to the plot, the ideology in *Barbary Shore* seems only loosely connected to it, and instead of generating metaphor, it inhibits the style. In *Barbary Shore*, Mailer has as yet no way to mediate successfully between the opposing pulls of his personality—the intellectual ideologue and the irrational primitive—and make them work for him. Consequently, the novel is overdefensive and *overwrought* (in both senses of that term).

The Naked and the Dead was so long and fairly mechanical in form, impersonal in its narration, and filled with characters that its psychological conflict was diffused. *Barbary Shore* is a more aesthetically ambitious, intensely personal, even claustrophobic novel. It reflects the novelist's agony at having to begin all over again, having to grow up in Brooklyn a second time. Thus it seems less like a second novel, and more like the sort of flawed, semi-autobiographical first novel many young writers produce.

Barbary Shore was worthwhile for Mailer, for it showed him the direction in which he had to go. In it, he began to explore directly the tensions in his own psyche as a clue to the anxieties of modern man:

> Working on *Barbary Shore* I always felt as if I were not writing the book myself but rather as if I were serving as a subject for some intelligence which had decided to use me to write this book . . . if I hadn't heard of the unconscious I would have had to postulate one to explain this phenomenon. For the first time I became powerfully aware of the fact that I had an unconscious which seemed to have little to do with me.[23]

Unfortunately for the reader, Mailer was not yet able to handle conflicts that were so close to home except by attempting to overwhelm them with polemics.

Notes

1. See Theodore L. Gross, *The Heroic Ideal in American Literature* (New York: Free Press, 1971), p. 277. Gross calls *Barbary Shore* "a transitional work, in which form and theme have not cohered, in which Mailer is breaking with old techniques and old ideologies and searching for a distinctive style and point of view."

2. Robert Langbaum, *The Modern Spirit: Essays on the Continuity of Nineteenth and Twentieth-Century Literature* (New York: Oxford, 1970), p. 149.

3. See John Stark, "*Barbary Shore*: The Basis of Mailer's Best Work," *Modern Fiction Studies* 17 (1971): 405.

4. Leslie Fiedler, "The Breakthrough: The American Jewish Novelist and the Fictional Image of the Jew," *Midstream* 4 (Winter 1958): 26.

5. Robert Solotaroff, *Down Mailer's Way* (Urbana, Ill.: University of Illinois, 1974), p. 50.

6. Howard Silverstein, "Norman Mailer: The Family Romance and the Oedipal Fantasy," *American Imago* 34, No. 3 (Fall 1977): 279.

7. Mailer's mention of "an imaginary future" shows the possible influence on *Barbary Shore* (1951) of George Orwell's *1984* (1949): both novels are speculative fiction set in a possible near future. Both are political novels intended as prophetic warnings to the postwar world about coming totalitarianism. Both Orwell and Mailer reject the encroachments on individual freedom of the modern bureaucratic state, whether that state be politically Left or Right.

8. Otto Rank, *The Myth of the Birth of the Hero and Other Writings*, ed. Philip Freund (New York: Vintage, 1959), p. 65.

9. For a discussion of *Barbary Shore* as political allegory, see Stark, "Mailer's Best Work," 405–6.

10. For a discussion of *Barbary Shore* as Arthurian myth, see L. Moffitt Cecil, "The Passing of Arthur in Norman Mailer's *Barbary Shore*," *Research Studies* (Washington State University) 39, No. 1 (March 1971): 54–58.

11. Rank, *Birth of the Hero*, p. 65.

12. Silverstein, "The Family Romance," 278 also cites this scene as an example of Lovett churning up "repressed oedipal fantasies."

13. Richard Poirier, *Norman Mailer* (New York: Viking, 1972), p. 107.

14. Jean Radford, *Norman Mailer: A Critical Study* (New York: Harper, 1975), p. 18, mentions that "each room is used to symbolize the character of its occupant."

15. Frederic Jameson, "The Great American Hunter; or, Ideological Content in the Novel," *College English* 34 (November 1972): 189.

16. Silverstein, "The Family Romance," 279.

17. Diana Trilling, "The Moral Radicalism of Norman Mailer," *Norman Mailer: The Man and His Work*, ed. Robert F. Lucid (Boston: Little, Brown & Company, 1971), p. 120.

18. Rank, *Birth of the Hero*, p. 70.

19. Ruth Prigozy, "The Liberal Novelist in the McCarthy Era," *Twentieth Century Literature* 25, No. 3 (October 1975): 260.

20. Radford, *Norman Mailer*, p. 83.

21. Trilling, Moral Radicalism," p. 120.

22. "An Interview with Norman Mailer," by Steven Marcus, in *Norman Mailer: A Collection of Critical Essays*, ed. Leo Braudy (Englewood Cliffs, N.J.: Prentice Hall, 1972), p. 29.

23. Ibid., p. 25.

4 "The Man Who Studied Yoga": The Womb of Middle-Class Life

"The Man Who Studied Yoga," Mailer's short story written in 1952 following *Barbary Shore*, seems to anticipate all the major concerns of his next three novels, *The Deer Park, An American Dream*, and *Why Are We in Vietnam?*: self-betrayal into the deadening trap of American life, middle-class security and freedom from dread purchased at the price of one's soul. In Sam Slavoda, protagonist of "Yoga," we see a failed radical and failed artist subsiding into a middle-class coma. At the opposite pole of Mailer's scheme of values is Sergius O'Shaugnessy in "The Time of Her Time," the existential hipster battling the square world. These two short stories might even be considered as thesis and antithesis, complementary segments of Mailer's ongoing quixotic quest, in both fiction and reality, for a hero fit for our times. The hero must be able to cope with the chaos by moving with the flux, and he must be tough and resourceful enough to battle the bitch to a draw. The bitch can be the establishment itself, one's own cowardice, a tough woman, or even, as in *Vietnam*, a bear. The opponents are equivalent and interchangeable and the battleground shifts from internal to external, but the rules of the game and the essence of the struggle remain the same; it is, at heart, all one continuous stream of psychological warfare.

The major theme of "Yoga," as in most of Mailer's work, is the craving for omnipotence and the fear of its inevitable corollary, total impotence. Sam's story is "the day of a small frustrated man, a minor artist manqué" (*ADV*, p. 154). It is a kind of domestic tragicomedy with an underlying feeling of anguish and entrapment. Richard Poirier calls the story "the most Bellovian Mailer has written, similar in mood but not equal in distinction to *Seize the Day*."[1] Nevertheless, Mailer intended "Yoga" only as a warm-up exercise, a prologue to an admittedly "Napoleonic" (p. 155) scheme, an eight-novel cycle. This short story about failure and impotence was to be a prelude to a novelistic try for omnipotence.

The novelist, thinks Sam, perspiring beneath blankets, must live in paranoia and seek to be one with the world; he must be terrified of experience and hungry for it; he must think himself

nothing and believe he is superior to all. The feminine in his
nature cries out for proof he is a man; he loves himself and therefore despises all that he is. (p. 184)

This congregation of paradoxes is more than a prescription for a novelist; it is a formula that could describe Mailer, who, says the critic
Theodore L. Gross, "is a romantic who reasserts his self-reliance,
his self-importance against the authoritarianism of America. . . .
At times he is more than half in love with that authority . . . like
Sam Slavoda, 'he dreams of power and is without capacity to gain
it.' . . ."[2]

In the character of Sam Slavoda, Mailer has created a poignant
middle-class archetype for the overwhelming impotence of modern
man. Sam is mass man alienated and powerless in mass society.
The poignancy of the portrayal springs partly from the fact that
Sam incarnates some of his creator's deepest fears of failure, fears
of becoming only "a small frustrated man," a man of potentially
vast achievement who has allowed himself to be trapped in mediocrity by submission to the powers that be. "In tone, feeling, even
in phrasing, Sam is a portrait of what Mailer, in 1952, might have
feared in himself," writes Poirier.[3] The critic Frederick Busch
concurs: "It seems entirely possible that Mailer the writer is also
psychoanalyzing himself, or at least studying himself, as he creates
a voice which might speak for him about Sam. . . ."[4]

In Mailer's writing, being mediocre has always been the worst
curse, worse than being evil, for mediocrity is equivalent to being
ground down to the lowest common denominator, to excrement.
In a work published in 1972, Mailer contemptuously calls the
formless political center of the American populace "the Wad . . .
this inert lump which resided in the bend of the duodenum of the
great American political river. . . ."[5]

Mailer could be said to have introduced Sam Slovoda in the
prologue intended for an epic novel as a sacrificial offering designed
magically to ward off failure in the task at hand. If Sam is several
steps above "the Wad," there is still the suggestion of "the Slob"
in his name. Sam also aspires to write the Great American Novel,
but he has deteriorated to the point of merely going through the
motions, "giving a day once or twice a month to a bit of thought
and a little writing" on the vast and ambitious project he hopes
to begin someday (p. 163).

Toward the end of the story, Sam bitterly excoriates himself
for his failure:

He has wasted the day, he tells himself, he has wasted the day

as he has wasted so many days of his life . . . while that huge
work with which he has cheated himself, that enormous novel
which would lift him at a bound from the impasse in which he
stifles, whose dozens of characters would develop a vision of life
in bountiful complexity, lies foundered, rotting on a beach of
purposeless effort. Notes here, pages there, it sprawls through
a formless wreck of incidental ideas and half-episodes; utterly
without shape. He is not even a hero for it. (p. 183)

As we can see from this passage, a markedly anal form of self-
disgust is linked with Sam's fears of failure and artistic impotence.
His life is "wasted" and the deadlocked constipation of his situation,
"the impasse in which he stifles," can produce only a shapeless,
formless, "rotting" wreck instead of a work of bounty. Sam, like
Rojack, or like almost any Mailer hero, is a man stung by the fear of
failure. This failure is always conceptualized in anal terms: Carter,
the hero of Mailer's short story "The Language of Men," feels "mired
in the rut of his own failure" (*ADV*, p. 128); Rojack says, "Every
cockroach has the memory of a revolting failure" (*AD*, p. 257);
and Mailer describes the young Henry Miller as suffering from
"failure backed up in all the pipes."[6] As D.J. puts it bluntly, "Excrement is defeat" (*WV*, p. 151).

And in Mailer, the only alternative for excrement is to exit with
violence that turns against others, or to bottle up that violence,
which turns into a kind of constipated, powerless rage that only
destroys the self.

Sam even perceives the environment as a shapeless mass that
threatens him. "I know what Sam feels," the narrator sympathizes,
"the Sunday papers are strewn around him . . . mummery of a
real world which no one can grasp" (*ADV*, p. 164). The scattered
papers on the floor represent the terrifying chaos of the world,
a shapeless fecal horror. Sam cannot grasp it and he cannot organize
it; things are too formless to deal with. Symptomatically, he cannot
write his novel because he cannot find a form. "However could
he organize his novel? What form to give it? It is so complex. Too
loose, thinks Sam, too scattered" (p. 185).

Sam's situation may be likened to that of Hennessy, the first
soldier to die in *The Naked and the Dead*. Hennessy, a raw young
recruit, is left isolated in a foxhole during the assault on the beach
at Anopopei. It is his first time under fire. Scared and helpless
as an infant abandoned by its parents, he curls into the fetal position
in his foxhole. The pounding enemy bombardment causes him to
lose control through terror. To his shame, disgust, and horror, he
discovers that he has unwillingly voided his bowels. The hole now

seems foul and menacing, so he races in panic down the beach, attempting to purify himself, caught in a hysterical dilemma between the threat from outside (the exploding Japanese mortars) and the threat from inside (his own perfidious bowels). The result is his death, a virtual suicide.

Sam avoids Hennessy's fate only by crawling into his hole and staying there. He burrows permanently into "the womb of middle class life" (p. 177). As the story opens, Sam is unhappily returning to consciousness, and as it ends, he is once again drifting into sleep. "Like most humans, he prefers sleeping to not sleeping" (p. 157).

Sam is like an infant in the womb, and it is suggested that the womb is his wife Eleanor's. Yet even as he clings to her in bed, Sam feels "a sweaty, irritable resentment of the woman's body which hinders his limbs" (p. 183). The theme of regression to the womb recurs in Mailer's fiction. In the original version of American Dream, serialized in Esquire, Rojack says to Cherry, "I was a breech birth. . . . They had to go in with forceps and pull me out. It must be that my preference then was to die in the womb rather than enter life. I must have been more attached to where I had been before than to where I was going now."[7]

The deadly womb is also equated unconsciously with the bowels. "Yoga" is filled with images of blocked and thwarted power, of pleasure turning into pain, feelings of irritability and helpless rage, creative and emotional constipation, and an overwhelming sense of being stifled, suffocated, and strangled. What Sam feels is akin to the self-disgust, shame, and powerless rage of a child who is overcontrolled and deprived of true autonomy, and thus finds himself perpetually fixated at the anal stage of development. He is trapped in a dilemma between the threat from authority and the threat from within himself, from his own bodily functions.[8]

When we are first introduced to Sam, we find him in a characteristically helpless position, semiconscious in bed, "twisted, strangled and trussed in pajamas which are too large for him" (p. 147). Significantly, he is suffocating because Eleanor has shut the bedroom windows and left the radiator turned on. As Sam rises to open the window, he sees outside "an irritable little boy who plays by himself among the empty benches, swaddled in galoshes, muffler, and overcoat" (p. 159). The isolated, overprotected, and overdressed little boy is like Sam in his oversize pajamas. Both are smothered in mother-love, strangled by their swaddling clothes. The images of strangulation in this story recur in An American Dream, where Rojack retaliates against a domineering wife by choking her to death.

The two central figures in Sam's life, his wife Eleanor and his analyst Dr. Sergius, constitute a set of substitute parents, evil step-mother and stepfather. " 'Oh, you know Sam, he not only thinks I'm his mother, he blames me for being born,' " says Eleanor jok-ingly, but it is no joke (p. 159). Eleanor is deliberately depicted as androgynous, vivacious and appealing but with strong teeth, a sharp tongue, and hair "cropped in a mannish cut" (p. 160). She reappears later, complete with her middle-class bohemian pre-tensions, as the man-eating Jewish witch Denise in "The Time of Her Time." Dr. Sergius is Mailer's portrait of the analyst as men-acing father figure, a social regulator and "educated ball-shrinker" (p. 371).

Sam must ask Eleanor and Dr. Sergius for permission for his every action—like a child in a classroom who must raise his hand to ask to go to the bathroom. The two of them rule his life; they are in collusion to deprive Sam of his creativity, his freedom, and his masculinity. Sam submits and betrays himself. While Eleanor wields the shears, Dr. Sergius accommodates him to his gradual gelding. For Mailer, this is a fate worse than quick, violent death: to lose one's soul day by day while still being alive.

The world in which Sam exists is debased and compromised, in effect, castrated. Intellectual concepts are reduced to jargon and platitudes, cocktail party chatter. Art is debased into the cheap fantasies of comic strips (which Sam creates for a living) and por-nography, and romance dwindles into comfortable, deadening middle-class marriages. The main action of the story is the viewing by several couples of the simulated passion of a dirty movie. Sam fantasizes that perhaps the film will stimulate his friends into the honest passion of a spontaneous orgy, but it only strengthens their hypocrisy and reinforces what Marcuse would later call "repressive desublimation." After the others have left, Sam and Eleanor make love in front of the movie: "It is dirty, downright porno dirty, it is a lewd slop-brush slapped through the middle of domestic exasperations and breakfast eggs. It is so dirty that only half of Sam . . . can be exercised at all" (p. 181). As Frederick Busch sees it, this scene symbolizes the defeats of Sam's life: "false artist imitating false art in a story about artistic failure."[9]

In part, Mailer's portrait of Sam's world is the anguished re-sponse of an artist to the oppressive historical realities of the 1950s in America. It is also, in part, the heightening of art, but this ex-aggerated, one-sided picture is partially a response to the author's own anxiety about failure and loss of manhood.

In this regard, we could compare "The Man Who Studied Yoga"

to an early Mailer story, "The Greatest Thing in the World," which was written in 1941. We can see the advance in terms of narrative control and complexity in "Yoga," but the two stories share the same exaggerated, one-sided view of their respective historical eras, a tough, naturalistic, antiromantic heightening of reality, which yet throws the lurid light of romanticism on all the events it depicts. The world of Al Groot in "The Greatest Thing in the World" is the typical Mailer jungle, filled with constant terror and the brute struggle to survive. The dread is the same for Sam Slovoda, except that he has retreated into the false security of the womb.

No heroes exist in Sam's world of "dreary compromise" (p. 185). Every potential heroic figure is cut down, even as he is invoked, by impotence. First there is Jerry O'Shaugnessy, a former man of action and labor organizer who has become a bum, another victim of "a stinking time" (p. 178). At the center of the tale is the title character, Cassius O'Shaugnessy, the man who studied yoga. Cassius is the twentieth-century man, the man who has been everywhere, seen everything, and known everyone, participated in all the major political and artistic movements of his age, and finally retreated into spiritualism. He studies Indian mysticism, meditates deeply, and one day, in the midst of his concentration, comes to believe that he can actually unscrew his navel. At the cost of enormous effort, he does so. His reward is that his "ass" falls off.

Why does Mailer add such elaborate trappings to such a hoary old joke and then feature the long-winded tale at the center of his story? The life history of Cassius is rich and varied and seems to promise much but winds up being merely "irritating and inconsequential" (p. 173). It offers a symbolic parallel to the life of Sam. Like Cassius, Sam is a modern everyman with heroic potential who tries too many things, never with a whole heart, and turns into a failure and something of a fool.

The joke also works on an emotional level. A shaggy-dog story moves from the sublime to the ridiculous: after a long buildup, it offers a deliberately ludicrous and pathetically inadequate punch line. It capitalizes on tension and suspense and then frustrates the audience. The typical response to a shaggy-dog story is a groan of suppressed rage. The lame joke about Cassius recreates in the reader the same state of emotional blockage that Sam experiences continually as his grandiose dream life is frustrated by a demeaning reality.

In psychological terms, the Cassius joke fits the story because it is a perfect parable of anal-phallic impotence. Cassius retreats from the world into solitary meditation; Sam retreats into the womb. Cassius and Sam try to relinquish power in the world for power over themselves and wind up losing both. Cassius falls into a fantasy of omnipotence, of total control over his body, that is rudely interrupted by a complete loss of control of even the crudest body functions. " 'Damn,' said Cassius, 'if my ass didn't fall off' " (p. 173). In other versions of this well-known joke it is not his ass that the hero loses but his testicles.

So at the center of the story is an anal-phallic terror of complete loss of control (we joke about those things we most fear), of loss of physical power over the body and shaping power over the environment. This anxiety gives way to a regressive solution, a yearning to retreat into the deathlike security of the womb. These problems are not solved within the plot, which concludes with Sam as helpless, trapped, and frustrated as he was at the beginning.

If the problems are countered in any way, it is through the medium of the secret hero of the story, who is its narrator. According to Theodore L. Gross, the power of the tale resides in

> the straightforward, almost Tolstoyan analysis of Sam Slovoda's marriage by an anonymous narrator who defines the meaning of Sam's life and who stands in opposition to Sam's psychoanalyst, Dr. Sergius. Although Sam Slovoda refers his every action to Sergius . . . he clearly doesn't need Sergius. . . . The true analyst is the narrator, for he hasn't compromised himself to society and to a host of sociological and psychoanalytic clichés. . . .[10]

The anonymous narrator acts as curative, as therapist for both the tale and its hero. He shows us what Sam could not possibly admit to himself, that his unhappiness springs from his voluntary servitude to the power of society in the form of his wife and his psychiatrist.

This narrator also seems to prefigure the technique that fully blossoms in *The Armies of the Night*, that unique combination of objectivity and subjectivity achieved by an almost schizophrenic splitting of the self into heatedly active participant and coolly detached commentator. Mailer has always been writing his autobiography, has always been talking about himself, or rather one part of himself carries on a dialogue with another and the reader is allowed to eavesdrop. The triumph of Mailer's career has been discovering a way to get away with this without seeming egotistical: he considers himself as an aesthetic object, as a character in one of his own novels.

The disembodied narrator of "Yoga," who speaks in the first

person but remains deliberately anonymous and immune from our judgment, who floats above the action and comments upon it, and who even has certain omniscient, telepathic powers, is a stand-in for the artist with his magical ability to manipulate reality. Whereas Sam is trapped by everyday detail and his fixed identity, the narrator is above such contingencies.

Out of a terror of failure, Sam clings to things he does not really need, to his possessions, his jargon, his analyst, his wife, and to the false security of the womb. Sam is an object lesson in fixity, but the anonymous narrator has let go of everything, including his name. Finally, we can see Sam and the narrator as two opposite poles of an anal ambivalence, an inability to deal with the self and with love objects: Sam represents the pole of *holding on*; the narrator, the pole of *letting go*. Mailer's success in this story lies in the power to maintain both possibilities in his mind simultaneously and in finding an experimental narrative technique that is complex enough to express them both.

Notes

1. Richard Poirier, *Norman Mailer* (New York: The Viking Press, 1972), p. 44.

2. Theodore Gross, *The Heroic Ideal in American Literature* (New York: Free Press, 1971), p. 279.

3. Poirier, *Norman Mailer*, p. 43.

4. Frederick Busch, "The Whale as Shaggy Dog: Melville and 'The Man Who Studied Yoga,' " *Modern Fiction Studies* 19, no. 2 (Summer 1973): 195.

5. Norman Mailer, *St. George and the Godfather* (New York: New American Library, 1972), p. 138.

6. Norman Mailer, *Genius and Lust: A Journey Through the Major Writings of Henry Miller* (New York: Grove Press, 1976), p. 8.

7. See *Esquire* (April 1964), p. 148.

8. See Erik H. Erikson, *Childhood and Society*, 2d. ed. rev. (New York: Norton, 1963), pp. 251–54.

9. Busch, "Whale as Shaggy Dog," 201.

10. Gross, *Heroic Ideal*, p. 278.

5 *The Deer Park*: The Ambivalence to Power

"And with the pride of the artist, you must blow against the walls of every power that exists, the small trumpet of your defiance."

Charles Eitel, *The Deer Park*

I

The critic Bruce Cook has suggested that "what Norman Mailer is most interested in is power."[1] "I want to know how power works," Mailer once said to his friend, novelist James Baldwin, "how it really works, in detail."[2] Unfortunately, if Mailer ever found out how power really works, he would have very little left to write about. Most of his work romanticizes power, both the possession and the loss of it.

In both his work and his life, Mailer is fascinated and yet repelled by power. Repeatedly, he is drawn to the arenas of power, the boxing ring and the bull ring, the machinations of political conventions, and the steps of the Pentagon. He tries to expand art into a force that can compete with politics, or failing that, he writes open letters to presidents, or even runs for mayor of New York City himself. If the impulse is vain and romantic, Mailer admits it, but still considers it one of his assets.

Yet how is one to cope effectively with authority over others? The ambivalence toward power provides a central conflict in each one of Mailer's novels, for behind the temptation to power he always sees the lustful drive for total omnipotence. His novels demonstrate again and again the ways in which power inevitably corrupts the man who holds it and leads to excessive and unnecessary violence. In *The Naked and the Dead*, both Cummings and Croft become power-mad and have a malign influence as leaders. Hearn is ambivalent toward power: he enjoys it, and yet he feels that his satisfaction is perverse and "dirty," that he is just as bad as Cummings and Croft. Nevertheless, Mailer's admiration focuses more on the ruthless manipulators of power than it does on the squeamish Hearn.

How can a man maintain power without ultimately feeling disgusted with himself? In *Barbary Shore*, McLeod finds himself growing progessively more cruel and evil as he abuses his power.

He renounces his position of authority and goes underground. Finally, he chooses to exercise only the power of defiance and denial against the state. He steals and stubbornly withholds the "little object," but is punished by death.

The roots of Mailer's ambivalence toward power can be clearly seen in a work such as *Of a Fire on the Moon*. As Mailer waits for the launching of the moon rocket, he self-consciously decides to avoid the "greed, guilt, wickedness, and hoarded psychic gold" of the VIPs and instead aligns himself with "his own sweaty grubs, the Press and photographers."[3] This is *nostalgia de la boue*; by this point in his career, Mailer really has much more in common with the celebrities than he does with the ordinary working press.

Later in *Fire*, Mailer reverses himself. Paradoxically, he finds himself admiring Nixon and the Squares and denouncing his own kind. The Squares may be anally repressed, but after all they do hold the power, that "hoarded psychic gold." The writers, the artists, the New Left, and the hippies are at the bottom of the totem pole because they are too anally loose: "an army of outrageously spoiled children who cooked with piss and vomit while the Wasps were quietly moving from command of the world to command of the moon."[4]

One of Mailer's assets as a writer is the range of his identifications; he has the ability to identify with both the aggressor and the underdog, the man at the top of the ladder and the outcast at the bottom. *The Naked and the Dead* was structured by this polarity. Mailer's ability to make these contradictory identifications may account partly for his popularity and for his designation as a peculiarly "American" writer. An author who can identify with both Richard Nixon and the hippies has succeeded in spanning an enormous gap, encompassing within himself the impossible contradictions of the country.

Ironically, this capacity springs from his very ambivalence, his uncertain identity. On the one hand, there is Mailer the left-anarchist, who wants to liberate all the instincts and romantically ennobles the proletariat. "If someone had been part of an experience foreign to his own (being Black, a convict, a prizefighter), Mailer found in him occult powers," writes his friend Joe Flaherty. "This enchantment had to do with . . . his romantic notion of the streets. That the gutter was a spawning ground which produced dullness far more often than genius was never considered."[5] On the other hand, there is Mailer the conservative, in awe of success and raw power, who devotes himself to power in the world through puritanical discipline, self-control, and achievement. In "Yoga," Sam at one moment envies "the life of the executive with the power and sense of command it may offer, but virtually from the same impulses Sam will wish himself a bohemian living in an unheated loft, his life a catch-as-catch-can from day to day" (*ADV*, p. 165).

Like Sam, Mailer romanticizes the upper and the lower classes. He has little affinity for the bourgeoisie. Instead, he is drawn toward the extremes of society, because they symbolize for him the two contradictory impulses of his own personality: the urge to hold on versus the urge to let go. Which shall he choose: the magic at the top or the occult powers at the bottom? Mailer despises the uptight greed of the Square but admires his power; he admires the freedom and lack of materialism of the Hip but would not choose that powerless condition for himself.

George A. Schrader talks about the "despair of defiance" in Mailer's works.[6] It is evident that Mailer's posture of perpetual defiance is a despairing solution to the dilemma of psychological ambivalence. Obstinate defiance of authority for the sake of defiance represents a negative exercise of power; symbolically, it stands for the child's refusal to give up the feces to the parents.

Increasingly, this becomes Mailer's answer to the problem of ambivalence toward power. The hero craves power, but it is dangerous for him to possess it; power is "dirty." The only safe route is to relinquish the ordinary forms of power and hold onto the negative power of defiance against authority.

II

The Deer Park could almost be a rewrite of *Barbary Shore* in a more realistic vein There is the same corrupt, politically repressive climate of the fifties. There are also the same characters: a young first-person narrator (Sergius O'Shaugnessy), a wounded war veteran who wants to be a novelist; an older man (Charles Eitel), a defiant leftist who serves as mentor to the narrator; and a psychopathic young man (Marion Faye), a kind of "bad brother" to the narrator and his rival for the affections of the older man. There is the same mythic pattern concerning the quest of the orphan hero for his identity. Finally, there is the same family romance plot, a complex web of incestuous relationships.[7] As in *Barbary Shore*, everyone except the narrator spies on and conspires against Eitel, the father-figure; and by the novel's end, everyone has been in bed with almost everyone else. The only major difference between the two works is that *Barbary Shore* was primarily about the power of politics, whereas *The Deer Park* is more concerned with the power of art.[8]

In *The Deer Park*, we are presented with two artists, Charles Eitel and Sergius O'Shaugnessy. Each possesses something of great value to the authorities, and each is offered the temptation of power if he gives it over. Sergius passes the test, but Eitel capitulates.

The inability to deal with power is reflected in *The Deer Park* in Eitel, who feels himself divided as an artist "between his desire for power in the world and his desire for power over his work" (*DP*, p. 124). When he operates as a true artist, Eitel can be dignified and heroic, but when he functions as a man of the world, he is frail and easily corrupted.

Considering this uneasy relationship to power, it is not surprising that Mailer's fiction should be filled with scenes of grand temptations and Faustian bargains. There is the homosexual Cummings tempting young Hearn with the possibilities of unlimited power, the father tempting the son, and there is the homosexual Hollingsworth dangling temptation before the tormented McLeod, the son tempting the father. In *The Deer Park*, Collie Munshin, a high-powered producer and "pirate" (p. 50), is the resident Mephistopheles, pimping for Satan, represented by Herman Teppis, an aging autocrat of the film world whose power reaches everywhere. " 'H.T. wants to act like a father to people . . .' " (p. 192). Munshin lures Eitel, a director who has been blacklisted as a consequence of his refusal to name names to a congressional investigating committee, back into the cinema through promises of renewed power. What Eitel has to do is divulge the information the committee wants, and prostitute his art and his conscience to the control of political witch-hunters and Supreme Studios, both of which he fears and despises. Eitel's submission represents one of Mailer's deepest fears concerning power, since the director sacrifices autonomy and control over his work for the illusory power of acceptance by the authorities. For Mailer, fictional potency, sublimation through art, along with the posture of defiance toward authority, is essential to his well-being. In his fiction, the authorities are always envisioned as diabolic figures conspiring to bugger and emasculate the heroes. Thus Eitel's submission is an ultimate defeat, a loss of power in artistic, political, and sexual terms.

Munshin is not quite as successful in his bargainings with Sergius O'Shaugnessy, an ex-Air Force flyer trying to find himself in the world, who comes to Desert D'Or, a southern California resort for the Hollywood film colony, and befriends the ostracized Eitel. The bait is $20,000 for Sergius' life story as an orphan and war hero, which Teppis sees as prime film material, along with the possibility of marrying Lulu Meyers, a blonde sex goddess and showpiece of Teppis' Supreme Studios. " 'Sergius,' " says Munshin with disarming candor, " 'You've been thinking along the lines that you'd be trading your soul for a bag of loot. You're a child . . .' " (p. 221).

The resort is called "Desert D'Or," a city "built out of no other obvious motive than commercial profit" (p. 2), a city of gold but an arid desert nonetheless. Mephistopheles-Munshin offers his bag of loot, but Sergius refuses, managing the temptation to power with more strength of character than poor Eitel.

The temptation posed to Sergius is a dual one: the sexpot and the pot of gold. *The Deer Park* is not only about the power of art but also about how the artist relates to the power of sex and money. And in this novel, sex and money become interchangeable.

The first chapter orients us to the terms of the novel. Hollywood is never named, but referred to obliquely as "the capital," for what Hollywood comes to represent is precisely "Das Kapital." Sergius arrives in Desert D'Or, a "desert of gold," by virtue of $14,000 he had acquired overnight in a poker game. This is a world of fabulous gamblers, of phenomenal good or bad luck, where fortune or love can be won overnight. Desert D'Or was founded by prospectors seeking gold, looking for instant riches, "but there is nothing left of those men" now (p. 2). Evidently they never succeeded; in any case their history has been erased. The streets are filled now with their modern-day counterparts, "small sharp prospectors for pleasure" (p. 4). "Running along the heavy beat of a third-rate promoter trying to raise money, there would come the solo shriek of one hysterical blond or another" (p. 4). Sex and money are entwined in the rhetoric; both "the heavy beat" and "the solo shriek" are suggestive of intercourse. As Sergius admits, he is attracted to Desert D'Or by "the bright green foliage of its love and its money" (p. 5). But both the promise of instant money and the promise of instant love prove to be a mirage in this desert.

At the opening, Sergius is like the city itself: he has a bankroll and a false front. The city is unnatural and sterile, having been established in the middle of a desert, "a place where trees bear no leaves" (p. 3). It is a city of illusion. The architecture is constructed to conceal and to deceive, "its stores look like anything but stores" (p. 2) and "the bars, cocktail lounges, and nightclubs were made to look like a jungle, an underwater grotto, or the lounge of a modern movie theater" (p. 4). No one there has a past history, because, just as in *Barbary Shore*, "everything is in the present tense" (p. 2). Sergius gets by with a convenient fraudulent story of a wealthy family back East and a broken marriage, and everyone takes him for a rich man's son, just as Eitel, whose father was a junk dealer, gives the impression of being a born aristocrat.

Behind the monied luxury and the unnatural phony fronts, everyone is desperately seeking love, or at least sex, Sergius and Eitel included. Desert D'Or is a kind of intricate "maze" (p. 3) or "labyrinth" (p. 96) which leads nowhere. Many get lost in this labyrinth forever.

Sergius uses his temporary fortune, his uniform, and his good looks as bait for sex. Like Lovett or Rojack, he is an actor, a fake whose "personality was built upon a void" (*AD*, p. 7), not a real man at all. Like the typical Mailer hero, Sergius suffers from psychic impotence. "In those days," confesses Sergius, "I was a young man who felt temporarily like an old man" (*DP*, p. 5).

Sergius was a pilot in the air force responsible for napalming Korean villages, until the sight of a burned Oriental boy aroused his guilt and temporarily unmanned him. In a sense, all flesh had become loathsome to him, like the decaying corpses in *The Naked and the Dead*. "We started to make love, and I couldn't think of her or myself or of anything but flesh, and flesh came into my mind, bursting flesh, rotting flesh, flesh hung on spikes in butcher stalls, flesh gone to blood" (p. 229). Images of the wounds he has inflicted on others float before him, connected with the idea of waste: "dead Oriental villages . . . staring their blind eye into the air like the sour black ash of a garbage dump . . ." (p. 230). Sergius is another of Mailer's murderer-heroes, who feels he must be punished for his horrendous sins through psychic emasculation.

This affliction affects more than just Sergius, however, for like the environment of *The Naked and the Dead*, the universe of *The Deer Park* is impotent. "Dead fronds" hang from the trunk of the palms "like an ostrich's muff" (p. 3). All the males suffer from the same problem and face the type of females who are calculated to emasculate. Martin Pelley, an oil man who has nothing to recommend him except his wealth and his sexual incapacity, is picked by Dorothea O'Faye as a mate from her covey of rich, passive escorts. Dorothea, a former singer and gossip columnist, lives like a queen and surrounds herself with a loyal, flattering court. The pathetic Pelley divorces one man-eater only to immediately marry Dorothea, who is another. This kind of hopeless masochistic cycle, a futile lurching from one defeat to the next, which marked Mailer's first two novels, also dominates *The Deer Park*, in which the characters go through meaningless ritual repetitions of love affairs, all equally doomed. At Dorothea's house, everyone plays the games that Dorothea likes, "and we spent evening after evening in doing almost exactly what we had done the night before" (p. 8).

Dorothea O'Faye is the mother as all-devouring beast. Her very name signifies the "enemy" or the "foe" in popular slang. Sergius, the orphan, goes to Desert D'Or, in a sense seeking a family, and is adopted by Dorothea. She is his entrée into the society, the first person to whom Sergius introduces us in the novel, and the last woman he beds down with at the end. Even then, she dominates his existence like a Jewish mother: "she would mop the dirty painted linoleum on my floor and give me lectures on how to handle the janitor" (p. 354). Dorothea is defined by her anal and oral characteristics. Like the landlady Guinevere in *Barbary*, Dorothea cleans up messes. Again, like Guinevere, she is "generous and stingy by turns" (p. 6) in emotional, financial, and sexual affairs, withholding and bestowing with erratic swiftness. As devouring mother, Dorothea uses up "people and time" (p. 9) and "absorbs" (p. 11) men, retaining their used-up hulks as errand boys in her court, like O'Faye, the nominal father of Marion, once a handsome Don Juan and now an alcoholic wreck. Dorothea's romance with Pelley begins "on the sure ground of his incapacity" (p. 11); when he takes her to bed, nothing happens.

Another hero who is unmanned is Eitel, who since testifying before the Committee has felt "'amputated. . . . I haven't had a woman in three months'" (p. 44). Once Eitel had been a famous director, "'a man,'" as Teppis says, "'with a high-powered tool in his hands'" (p. 73). Now he has gone against those who had nourished his power, and, as a consequence, he has lost the famous "Eitel touch," which included his reputation in bed; "he had spent his urge and lost the energy of his talent" (p. 108). The loss of talent seems to be equated with loss of substance and encroaching impotence. As Munshin says, "' His talent is rotting away now . . .'" (p. 223). Eitel's career seems to parallel that of the author; like Mailer he comes from a middle-class Jewish background, fights "against the bonds of his mother's love" (p. 171) and has an early huge success in the arts, followed by a decline and a series of unsuccessful marriages.

Eitel and Sergius, both of whom are temporarily impotent, regain their potency the night of a huge publicity party for Lulu's upcoming picture given by Teppis: Eitel with Elena, the cast-off mistress of Collie Munshin, and Sergius with Lulu. The enjoyment of both men is spiced by the manner in which they defy the power of Teppis, the evil father: Eitel, the social outcast, by flaunting Elena, another social outcast who is the mistress of Teppis' son-in-law Munshin, and Sergius, the outsider, by snatching away Lulu, the guest of honor at the party and Teppis' number one box-office draw.

Eitel enters into an affair with Elena which he hopes "could return his energy, flesh his courage, and make him the man he

had once believed himself to be" (p. 110). Sergius, however, only
succeeds with Lulu after she asserts a usually masculine prerogative:
she picks him up, she drives the car, and finally, after teasing and
tormenting him all night, she seduces him in the rear seat of the
car while he lies flat on his back. The expected sexual roles have
been reversed, and the female becomes the aggressor.

Whereas Teppis is the evil father who demands subservience and
consequently provokes disobedience, Eitel functions for Sergius, and
also for Marion, as the good father. The ambiguity of the love-hate
relationship between Eitel and Sergius is one of the central concerns
of the novel, like the relationship between Cummings and Hearn
and between McLeod and Lovett. "'When I was a kid, I used to
think'—and Faye laughed harshly— 'that Eitel was a god and devil
all in one'" (p. 23). Sergius worships Eitel as an ideal of moral and
artistic integrity, but also derives pleasure from besting him. He
is delighted to find that Lulu considers him the better lover, for
"I wanted to set Eitel at my feet, second to the champion" (p. 138).
In the first draft of the novel, Mailer wrote, "Vizier to the poten-
tate" (ADV, p. 234). What Sergius desires is the potency to cuckold
Eitel. After he first makes love to Lulu, he says:

> It may sound weird, but I was so excited with enthusiasm that
> I had to share it, and I could think of nobody but Eitel. It did
> not even occur to me that he might still be with Elena, or that
> as the ex-husband of little Lulu, he would not necessarily find
> my story a dream. I don't know whether I even remembered that
> Lulu had been married to him. (DP, p. 96)

Sergius' lapse of memory is odd, considering that Lulu and Eitel had
had the following exchange in Sergius' presence at the party only a
few hours before:

> "I'll always be remembered as your second ex-husband,"
> Eitel drawled.
> "It's a fact," she said. "When I think of Charley Eitel, I think
> of number two." (p. 87)

There may even be an element of disguised homosexuality in Sergius' conquest of Lulu, just as Hollingsworth in Barbary Shore wooed
Guinevere as a substitute for making love to McLeod.

Sergius is about to reveal the exciting news about Lulu to Eitel,
when he sees the drunken Teddy Pope being scolded for his homosexual antics by the ubiquitous and ominous Teppis, like a father
chastising a delinquent son. H.T. has uncovered Teddy while making

his rounds as an eternally vigilant "night watchman" in this inferno (p. 98). Teddy, who has just been kicked out by his lover, Marion Faye, screams in a hopeless drunken fury at Teppis after he leaves, "'You bastard Teppis,' he cried out into the empty dawn, 'you know what you can do, you fat bastard, Teppis'" (p. 98). At this grotesque sight, Sergius abandons his plans to see Eitel.

Unconsciously, Sergius' affair with Lulu represents a rebellion against the good father Eitel: a desire to possess his woman, and, in a way, to possess him through her. Teddy Pope, who is homosexual and tyrannized by the evil father Teppis, stands as a psychic proxy for Sergius, suffering the punishment he fears.

Like every male in the novel, Sergius also covets Eitel's mistress Elena, but he never fulfills his ambition. Elena lives with Eitel, then with Marion Faye, and finally marries Eitel. Sergius leaves California, goes to Mexico, befriends a bullfighter and makes love to the bullfighter's girl because she "reminded me a little of Elena" (p. 351). Sergius never seems to be happy with women unless they are secondhand—more precisely, unless they have already had an affair with Eitel.

None of the heroes is man enough to completely satisfy the ladies in *The Deer Park*. At the end of the novel, Lulu has cast off Sergius, married a pretty-boy actor named Tony Tanner, an ex-pimp who gets his kicks by beating up women, and taken back Eitel as one of her lovers. All her men are sexual failures and, even in quantity, they cannot keep her satisfied.

The novel is a sexual round robin; Sergius goes from Lulu, Eitel's ex-wife, to Elena, Eitel's mistress, to Dorothea O'Faye, who also once had a brief fling with Eitel. All three women, like Guinevere, are described as formidable "queens." Elena is "a queen and an empress" (p. 311), Lulu "did the queen, I the slave" (p. 138), and Dorothea has her own "court" which she rules like a tyrannical queen. The same pattern recurs in *An American Dream*, where Rojack's three women, Deborah, Ruta, and Cherry, have all been possessed first by his father-in-law. Like Rojack, Sergius must cuckold the father in triplicate.

Whereas Dorothea represents the evil mother, Lulu and Elena have some of the attributes of the mother, but primarily stand for two sisters, or perhaps one sister split in two, Lulu being the cruel blonde and Elena the kind brunette, to borrow Leslie Fiedler's terminology from *Love and Death in the American Novel*. "[Lulu] gave me a sisterly kiss," says Sergius, "Older sister" (p. 134). Later, when Sergius decides to leave town, he considers inviting Elena to travel with him, and thinks that "we could even make the trip as brother and sister, if she wanted it that way" (p. 327). As sisters, Lulu and Elena are symbolic substitutes for the mother.

While Sergius is briefly wounded in the affair with Lulu, he comes away untouched from his fondness for Elena and Dorothea. As in *Barbary Shore*, Mailer relies on a passive stick figure as a first-person narrator, so that oedipal guilt can be transferred to other male characters, such as the homosexual actor Teddy Pope, who is victimized and ruined by Teppis.

The tortured pimp Marion Faye, the bad son, the equivalent of Hollingsworth in *Barbary Shore*, acts out many of Sergius' desires and is punished for them. "Marion" is a sexually ambiguous name that could apply either to a man or a woman. "Fay" means magical or fairy-like, but it can also mean homosexual (fey) or doomed (fate).

Mailer makes an interesting mistake in one scene: he has Marion remember Teddy Pope leaning drunkenly against a joshua tree (p. 158), when it was actually Sergius who witnessed the scene (p. 98). The novelistic confusion unintentionally reveals what becomes apparent in the course of the novel, that, unconsciously, Marion is an evil double for Sergius, his "bad brother."

Eitel and Marion find themselves trapped in the same bleak fate, a fate that is avoided by Sergius alone. All three men are searching for the same thing: autonomy. One critic calls *The Deer Park* "a fable of self-reliance."[9] Only Sergius maintains the existential freedom to alter his identity at will, a form of power over oneself that Mailer has always cherished, as his career evidences. Marion and Eitel are in limbo; having exchanged power over their lives for power in the world, they are reduced to mere "commercial men" (p. 328). Eitel and Marion hold on, but Sergius learns to let go. The same schism occurs between Sam and the narrator in "Yoga." It is not until *An American Dream*, in the person of Rojack, that Mailer is able to successfully bridge the gap between the two modes and unite these collected personalities into a single psychically integrated character. As in *The Naked and the Dead*, Mailer has fractured his personality and parcelled out the fragments among several characters.

The fragmentation is evident in the way both Sergius and Marion partake of the dimensions of the mythical hero. Mailer originally conceived of Sergius as the "mythical hero" (*ADV*, p. 154) of a never-completed eight novel sequence. Thus Sergius possesses standard mythic attributes: he is an orphan seeking his parents, a warrior, a man who feels destined for greatness and experiences phenomenal alterations of fortune overnight. Sergius also feels touched by magic, "for it was magic to fly an airplane . . ." (*DP*, p. 96). However, Marion Faye crowds out Sergius, for he seems cast for a similar role, having been abandoned by his father, who was supposed to be a European prince, and being a "fay," a man of magic.

Eitel, who had an affair with Dorothea years before the action in the novel takes place, and could even possibly be Marion's father, befriends Marion as a youth and becomes almost a substitute father for him. Eitel is also a member of the mythic royalty; Elena calls him a "king" (p. 103). So we have two young nobles, the black prince and the blond prince, Marion with his royal father and Sergius with his "princely" name (p. 19), two heroes where we would expect one, sharing the same substitute royal father, and two young queens, one light and one dark.

In the play version of *The Deer Park* (1967) Sergius is reduced to a minor character and the main story is that of Marion, Eitel, and Elena. Mailer strips the story down to its essentials: the family romance of these three characters.

In the novel of *The Deer Park*, Sergius desires Elena from a distance for some time, but Marion actually steals her away from Eitel. When Sergius musters enough courage to make Elena an offer, he finds he is too late—Marion has just cracked up his car in order to destroy himself and Elena. Both Marion and Elena are injured, and Marion is in jail for carrying an unlicensed gun in the glove compartment instead of a driver's license. This curious accident, by which Sergius is prevented from sin and saved from guilt, and by which two other sexual transgressors are punished, is similar to the destruction of Shago and Cherry at the end of *An American Dream*, a denouement by virtue of a deus ex machina.

The auto accident suggests an underlying guilt for aggression against the father, and it is Marion rather than Sergius who is punished. In fact, through Sergius' intervention, the estranged Eitel and Elena are reconciled and married after the accident. This conclusion seems a contrived plot device.

Marion's torture is self-induced; his suffering earns him more sympathy and interest from the reader than do the dull problems of the unconvincing Sergius. Like that other psychic proxy, Hollingsworth, Marion Faye is a tormented personality, almost a case study in anal neuroticism blown up into paranoia and compulsion. Marion is the secret hero of the novel,[10] and his personality is the key to the psychic tensions behind the story.

The driving force of Marion's personality is disgust with the world and with himself. For Marion, "'the whole world is bullshit'" (p. 17). "'That's love. Bullshit mountain'" (p. 337). He finds both homosexual and heterosexual love equally repulsive, although he indulges in both. When he lies with Elena, he is "repelled by the odor of her body which Eitel had savored so much . . ." (p. 330). Elena is nothing more or less to Marion than "a trained animal, and he could wipe his fingers in her hair" (p. 334).

Marion's anal neuroticism is also revealed in his fascination for "absolute order" (p. 335) and his secret wish to scorch the earth with atomic explosions in order to "clear the rot and the stench and the stink" (p. 161). At the same time, he is masochistically attracted to all the repellent stench, for he claims that "there is no pleasure greater than that obtained from a conquered repugnance" (p. 146), so that "to be pure one must seek out sin itself, mire the body in offal so that the soul may be elevated" (p. 329). Marion's society operates like a vast whorehouse, and so he has become a procurer. As he bitterly tells his mother, Dorothea, "'I'm just an amateur . . . like you'" (p. 15). The world has failed him, its values and its sexuality are corrupt, and perversely he wallows in the decay.

For Marion, emotion is unclean, as it was for the men in *The Naked and the Dead*. He is plagued with guilt and hopes to eliminate guilt itself by eliminating compassion, "the worst of the vices" (p. 159). Nevertheless, his efforts only intensify his pain, since there is "no pressure in the world like the effort to beat off compassion" (p. 159). Compassion is viewed as excremental: "from some un-willing pocket of his mind there came compassion for her; despite himself it had worked free, a pure lump of painful compassion . . ." (p. 334). Marion spends as much self-defeating and self-destructive energy on hate as some people do on love. In the process of battling all natural emotions, he forces himself to be cruel and inhuman, most of all to himself. Although he lives in constant paranoid anxiety, he never bolts his door, in order to torture himself. These activities could describe the behavior of a "compulsive neurotic who inflicts severe expiatory punishments upon himself and circumscribes his activity because of his unconscious murderous impulses, and there-fore acts as though he were really a murderer."[11]

Fenichel's description of compulsion neurosis fits Marion, whose mind is "like an iron monarch inflicting an alien will . . ." (p. 331). Like a true compulsive, Marion is remarkably lucid and yet strangely irrational. He hears inner voices that command him to do terrible things and he communes with gods and devils, just as Rojack is guided by bizarre and magical psychic ultimatums, devils, gods, and goddesses who plant weird commandments in his brain. Mailer has been concerned since "The Man Who Studied Yoga" with whether there is a God or a Devil, and, if so, which one rules the mind of America. The actions of Marion and Rojack resemble those of the existential man described by Kierkegaard, who must take the leap of faith without having any way of knowing if the orders he follows come from God or the Devil, but their behavior also fits the pattern of the compulsive.

Mailer seems to indicate that the root of Marion's neurotic impulses is in his strange childhood. Like Sergius, Marion is an orphan. Sergius never knows his mother, and is left by his father to be raised in an orphanage. Marion is born out of wedlock and never knows a father. His mother alternately spoils and neglects him. Marion asserts his masculine identity through cruelty, violence, and rebellion, like a prototype of Mailer's "White Negro." Even at this early date, Mailer was obviously thinking about the personality of the "White Negro" as a logical adaptation to the insanity of contemporary civilization. "'You may have a taste for hipsters,'" says Collie to Eitel, "'but they're just psychopaths to me'" (p. 199).

Whereas Sergius finds socially acceptable outlets for his violent instincts (prizefighting, becoming a bomber pilot), Marion's violence moves him toward increasingly antisocial behavior. He is thrown out of several schools, gets arrested for reckless driving, and at eighteen has to ask his mother for money so he can get a girl an abortion. Finally, he becomes a pimp. He seems to find a special delight in degrading women—he is nasty to his mother and keeps thinking of new humiliations for his girls. He imagines himself as "Father Marion" raping his nuns (p. 329). Ironically, Marion is impotent most of the time: "'I got a young face and an old body,'" he admits (p. 336). However, even as he is cruel, it is forced cruelty, and much of it turns in upon himself. His self-hatred and self-disgust are enormous, especially in regard to his homosexual tendencies.

Marion's desire to debase women is symptomatic of the entire novel. As Freud says in his discussion of psychic impotence, "as soon as the sexual object fulfills the conditions of being degraded, sensual feeling can have free play, considerable sexual capacity and a high degree of pleasure can be developed." Only by degrading her can the impotent man "win the mother as an object for sensual desires."[12] Elena, for example, is a girl who has been around, and when she is first introduced to Eitel by Collie, she thinks he is to be a client. Later, she begs Marion to make her into a call girl, but he is reserving the most humiliating of horrors for her: a job in a Mexican whorehouse.

Desert D'Or itself offers "love and money," or rather, love for money. As Mailer explains in the epigraph to the novel, the original Deer Park was a luxurious harem, a "gorge of innocence and virtue," maintained at enormous cost for Louis XV of France. H.T. operates a movie studio as a form of private whorehouse and Collie, his son-in-law, is his procurer. H.T. markets sex sugarcoated with sentiment in his films. Lulu Meyers, his best-selling product, enters his office and is greeted effusively, "'I love a girl like you who brings sunshine into this room'" (p. 271). As she leaves, the enraged Teppis shouts, "'Get out of here. You're a common whore'" (p. 274). When Eitel divorces his second wife, it is as though he is departing from a visit with a prostitute: "he had picked up what he wanted, and paid for it of course" (p. 32).

Every character in the novel—except the noble Sergius, who leaves the resort with his virtue as "intact" (p. 1) as when he arrived—is either a prostitute, a pimp, or a client, some small-time and some big-business. The world of Desert D'Or is a gigantic bordello, with Teppis as the head whoremaster.

H.T. is the evil father, compensating for impotence and lack of control through overmanipulation, an attempt at total, omnipotent control. One of the finest chapters in the novel is set in Teppis' office. This comic set-piece reads like a one-act play. Teppis is shown in action, wheeling and dealing, cajoling and bullying, and our delight increases as Teppis gradually loses control and becomes, like General Cummings, more and more frustrated and enraged at being unable to manipulate events and people to his own liking. After H.T. relieves his sadistic lust for mastery by forcing Bobby, a prostitute, to commit fellatio on him, he is left alone in his office, but his pathetic parting curse rings in our ears:

> Teppis ground out the cigar. "There's a monster in the human heart," he said aloud to the empty room. And to himself he whispered, like a bitter old woman, close to tears, "They deserve it, they deserve every last thing that they get." (p. 285)

Teppis' dowry of hatred is precisely what Marion Faye also wishes on the human race, but whereas Teppis is truly cruel, Marion is a compassionate man who compulsively forces himself to be evil. Earlier in the novel, after taking some money from Bobby, he considers calling her back and forcing her to commit fellatio, "a business she claimed was loathsome" (p. 156). Although Marion congratulates himself on the cruelty of the plan, he is unable to go through with it. When Teppis later debases Bobby precisely as Marion had wished to, we see that the sadism which is checked by guilt in Marion, runs rampant in Teppis. Even in his choice of profession, Marion is a novice at corruption, imitative of big daddy Teppis; they both operate whorehouses, except that Marion is more honest about it.

Coincident with the vision of the world as whorehouse is the vision of the world as doghouse. Everyone in the novel has an enormous fear of being forced down on his hands and knees. Teppis has Bobby get down on all fours. As a junkie named Paco begs Marion for drugs, Marion wonders, "Was that why he had tried to go main-line? So that he could get down on his hands and knees and bark like a dog?" (p. 158). Eitel testifies before the Committee because "'I knew they had me on my knees'" (p. 306). Being doglike represents not only fawning and shameful degradation; it is also linked with anality. As Teppis says, "'Look around before you take a step. There could have been dogs in the grass'" (p. 276).

One of the most canine of the characters in the novel is Lottie Munshin, Teppis' daughter and Munshin's wife, a fanatical dog fancier. "'Do you like dogs?' Lottie Munshin asked me. She gave a short rough laugh for punctuation, and looked at me with her head cocked to one side" (p. 76). She sounds like she is waiting for her master's voice.

Teppis, like his daughter, is a dog breeder, at least in the way he arranges the matings of his kennel of prize stars at Supreme Studios. In another respect, though, H.T. is merely leader of the pack. He clears his throat "with a barking sound" (p. 65). "'Could H.T. be the kind of man who gets down on his hands and knees'" (p. 275), Teppis asks Lulu, but the question is rhetorical.

The producer Munshin, who even has the canine nickname "Collie," is yet another mutt scrambling for power on the dungheap. "'Do you want me to get down on my hands and knees,' Munshin said with a growl" (p. 197). "Collie grinned. He cocked his head to one side with the cunning look of a dog who is being scolded" (p. 54). Like a dog, he ingratiates himself with everyone. "'He's shameless,'" says Eitel. "'You can't stop a man who's never been embarrassed by himself'" (p. 50).

The repeated dog imagery and the terror of being forced down on one's hands and knees may have to do with a fear of being penetrated from the rear in the fashion of a dog. "'I don't care how much slop I've jammed up the hole of more than one cruddy and delirious film product,'" says Collie (p. 196).

"'You love me . . . yes, you certainly do, when you can give your yelps and yowls to any two-bit dog,'" Eitel says bitterly to Elena (p. 294). The remark shows how sex, money, and dirt become interchangeable in the language of the novel. Eitel's eloquent speech to Sergius after he has testified before the Committee could serve to sum up the novel's vision of society as whorehouse or doghouse:

"How do I feel? . . . Oh, nothing so extraordinary, Sergius. You see, after a while, I knew they had me on my knees, and that if I wasn't able to take a dose of sleeping pills, I would have to let myself slide through the experience, and not try to resist it. So for the first time in my life I had the sensation of being a complete and total whore in the world, and I accepted every blow, every kick, and every gratuitous kindness with the inner gratitude that it could have been a good deal worse. And now I just feel tired, and if the truth be told, pleased with myself, because believe me, Sergius, it was *dirty* work. . . . In the end that's the only kind of self-respect you have. To be able to say to yourself that you're disgusting." (p. 306)

Critic Max Schulz has said that "self-loathing is second only to hatred of others" as the principal emotion in *Deer Park*.[13] This self-hatred is shown in the numerous suicide attempts; Eitel contemplates killing himself, Elena tries suicide several times, and Marion tries to kill both himself and Elena. Yet none of their suicide attempts is successful (neither is that of Rojack in *An American Dream*). These characters seem to derive pleasure out of self-hatred, as we see in Eitel's speech to Sergius: they indulge in anal regression, and then are able to kick themselves for it.

Toward the end of the novel, Sergius undergoes a final self-imposed penance before he is purged of guilt for his sins and ready to follow the pure and demanding road of dedication to art. The punishment he chooses fits the nature of his crime. Even though he has some savings left, he rents a cheap room and takes a hellish job as a dishwasher in a restaurant. He has unconsciously reverted to the existence his dead father led, the wayward failure O'Shaugnessy who abandoned Sergius in an orphanage and used himself up living in dingy rented rooms and washing dishes. Sergius has sinned against the father, so he must suffer as his father did and thereby purify himself. Staring him in the face, like the ghost of his father, is a drunken, broken-down old dishwasher whom Sergius bitterly envies, because his end of the dirty job is easier. The alcoholic old wreck is another version of the destroyed father, like the alcoholic Mr. O'Faye, Martin Pelley, or Eitel. All have been sucked dry; all are emasculated but Sergius.

III

The problem with sex in *The Deer Park* is that it is static, "everything is in the present tense," and the town itself is kept artificially unchanging. Time stands still. People pass their days in dim bars, where they never know "whether it was night or day" (p. 4). All the characters exchange sexual partners, but get nowhere. Desert D'Or is a treadmill, an inferno of endlessly repeated actions that result in no change. Unfortunately, this gives the novel a sense of repetitiousness.

As in *The Naked and the Dead*, relationships appear headed for violent resolutions, but this never occurs. Situations wobble erratically on the brink of violence, but finally stall in impotence. Time itself goes nowhere.

The only one who escapes from Desert D'Or into the supposedly "real world" outside is Sergius, but the critic Robert Solotaroff says that the world Sergius escapes to is really very "contrived."[14] For all of its aura of deception and illusion, Desert D'Or is the arena of conflict in *The Deer Park*. It is the given, and by the end of the novel it has become the "real world"; it is difficult for us to conceive of the alternative that Sergius has presumably found.

The three heroes of the novel—Sergius, Eitel, and Faye—are all seeking autonomy, power over themselves and over the world around them. Eitel advises Sergius at the end to exercise the stubborn defiance of the artist against every power that exists. But Eitel himself cannot maintain this posture; he gives up. None of the three men finds an effective way to cope with power in the totally corrupt world of Desert D'Or, which stands as a microcosm of American society.[15] As Solotaroff writes, "In trying to discern how an expanding life is to be lived, O'Shaugnessy-Mailer must choose between the sloppily generous, compromising liberalism of Eitel and the amoral will to power of Faye."[16] To put this dichotomy another way, Sergius must choose between the anal eroticism of Eitel (sloppy, compassionate, soft, and impotent) and the anal sadism of Faye (disciplined, cruel, filled with hard rage, desiring omnipotent control). Both extremes are self-destructive, and Sergius, who is supposed to mediate between them, is not a convincingly dramatized character.[17]

Thus we are left in *The Deer Park*, as in *The Naked and the Dead* and *Barbary Shore*, with an unresolved and perhaps unresolvable ambivalence. In his fiction that follows, Mailer tries another way to manage the problem. Instead of resorting to multiple characters who represent different aspects of the conflict, Mailer creates in each novel one strong central hero who embodies in himself both the rage for omnipotence and the urge for self-destruction.

Notes

1. Bruce A. Cook, "Norman Mailer: The Temptation to Power," *Renascence* 14 (Summer 1962): 222.

2. Reported by James Baldwin, "The Black Boy Looks at the White Boy," in *Norman Mailer*, ed. Leo Braudy (Englewood Cliffs, N.J.: Prentice-Hall; 1972), p. 76.

3. Norman Mailer, *Of a Fire on the Moon* (Boston and Toronto: Little, Brown, 1970), p. 91.

4. Ibid., p. 440.

5. Joe Flaherty, *Managing Mailer* (New York: Coward-McCann, 1970), pp. 64–65.

6. George A. Schrader, "Norman Mailer and the Despair of Defiance," *Yale Review* 51 (December 1961); 267–80.

7. See Howard Silverstein, "Norman Mailer: The Family Romance and the Oedipal Fantasy," *American Imago* 34, No. 3 (Fall 1977): 279–82.

8. See Stanley T. Gutman, *Mankind in Barbary: The Individual and Society in the Novels of Norman Mailer* (Hanover, New Hampshire: University Press of New England, 1975), p. 47: "Thus Mailer, in *The Deer Park*, turns from revolutionary socialism to artistic creation as a possible vehicle for human redemption."

9. Jonathan Middlebrook, *Mailer and the Times of His Time* (San Francisco, Calif.: Bay Books, 1976), p. 95.

10. Robert Solotaroff, *Down Mailer's Way* (Urbana: University of Illinois, 1974), p. 54: Marion Faye "emerges as much the secret hero of *The Deer Park* as Croft was of *The Naked and the Dead*."

11. Otto Fenichel, *The Psychoanalytic Theory of Neurosis* (New York: Norton, 1945), p. 144.

12. Sigmund Freud, "The Most Prevalent Form of Degradation in Erotic Life," in *On Creativity and the Unconscious* (New York: Harper, 1958), p. 178.

13. Max F. Schulz. *Radical Sophistication: Studies in Contemporary Jewish-American Novelists* (Athens, Ohio: Ohio University, 1969), p. 84.

14. Solotaroff, *Down Mailer's Way*, p. 65.

15. Gutman, *Mankind in Barbary*, p. 52: "Hollywood . . . is America in microcosm. It manifests the competition, violence, and chaos of American society."

16. Solotaroff, *Down Mailer's Way*, p. 70.

17. For criticism of Sergius O'Shaugnessy in *The Deer Park* as an unconvincing character, see, for example, Ibid., pp. 65–66; Gutman, *Mankind in Barbary*, p. 54; and Jean Radford, *Norman Mailer: A Critical Study* (New York: Harper, 1975), p. 21.

6 "The Time of Her Time": He Stoops to Conquer

Playboy Interviewer: Many of your critics accuse you of harboring a good deal of hostility toward women. They point to the classic scene in your story "The Time of Her Time" when the protagonist calls his penis "the avenger" and rapes a girl anally.

Mailer: Let's get something hotsy-totsy. Let's say: takes carnal possession of her posterior territories.

"The Time of Her Time" is critically acknowledged as Mailer's finest short story and one of the best pieces of writing he has ever done. It represents a turning point in Mailer's fiction: the deliberately obscene sexual frankness and the stylistic richness and intensity of the story are characteristic of his subject matter and tone from here on. George Steiner claims that "All of Mailer's obsessions are concentrated and disciplined in this wry tale."[1] This chapter will attempt to pinpoint the nature of these obsessions, which power the tale at its deepest level.

In "The Time of Her Time," Mailer finally approaches one of his goals as a writer: to shock and to provoke outrage. The story is in part a sadistic assault on the reader. Leslie Fiedler, who is generally harsh in his judgment of Mailer's work, admires this particular tale as "a confession of terrifying candor and a parable of our times."[2] The story was outrageous and daringly shameless for its day, as though Mailer felt he could only defeat self-disgust and shame through unabashed self-exposure. It is written in the style of *Advertisements*, in which the shock of brutally candid confession is cushioned by wit, vivid imagery, alliteration, and elegant prose rhythms. The style of "Time" represents a decisive breakthrough in the progression from the relative flatness of Mailer's early prose to the rich metaphorical density and pulsing rhythms of his later writing. In a sense, the real hero of the story is Mailer the prose stylist. This style, which Richard Poirier calls "self-pleasuring,"[3] is consistently hyperbolic and deliberately demonstrative; it has the same quality of athletic exhibitionism as Sergius O'Shaugnessy, the hero/narrator of the tale. The new style, like the new Mailer, advertises itself.

If, under the protective cover of fiction, Mailer evokes some violent, puerile fantasies, still, as Poirier has noted, such fantasies are "an essential part of all of us, of our national and cultural myths."[4] The story is true to the life of the unconscious, and this

113

accounts for its exaggeration and its extravagance. Mailer uncovers and uses his fantasies. He manipulates them in order to expose the raw power plays, the sadomasochistic interplay and the drive for conquest and revenge which he believes underlies modern relationships between the sexes. Sexuality is stripped down to pure aggression.

What sets "The Time of Her Time" apart from *Barbary Shore* and *The Deer Park* is the amount and the intensity of the visceral energy that is concentrated into the short story. "Time" differs from these two novels the way full-scale warfare differs from the cautious maneuvering of international diplomacy. Of course, a short story is by necessity more concentrated in its impact than a novel, but it also seems in "Time" as if Mailer has mined deeper into his own fantasy life and, in the process, liberated energy that he harnesses in fiction. "The Time of Her Time" consolidates his gains and paves the way for *An American Dream*.

There is a very close relationship in subject matter and treatment between the two works, and there are passages in "Time" that are almost identical in phrasing to passages in *Dream*. For example, as Sergius ascends a tenement stairway, he gets "a nose full of the smells of the sick overpeppered bowels of the poor which seeped and oozed out of every leaking pipe in every communal crapper . . ." (*ADV*, p. 480). In comparison, as Rojack goes up the stairs of Cherry's tenement, "The garbage was out on the landings, the high peppery smell of Puerto Rican cooking . . . the door to the latrine was open, moisture seeped off the floor. The stench of slum plumbing gave a terror of old age—how ill is illness, how vile the suggestion of villainous old bowels" (*AD*, p. 116).

In its exaggerated intensity, "Time" can be considered a test run for *Dream*, although in some respects it is more acceptable than that novel because it is more ironic and self-mocking. *An American Dream* is a more earnest and nightmarish plunge into deep fantasies. In both works, however, the melodrama is so overblown that it verges on farce, as if Mailer felt the necessity to transcend all limitations, even if he ran the risk of self-parody.

Moreover, Sergius, the hero of "Time," can be considered a forerunner of Rojack. Like Rojack, Sergius is simultaneously heated participant and coolly detached observer of himself and the action he precipitates, and he evidences the same mixture of self-disgust and clinical fondness of his own hangups. Again, the brutal encounters in bed and the open hatred and rage between the sexes prefigure the explosion into violence in *An American Dream*. The anal rape of Denise by Sergius is an earlier version of the encounter of Ruta and Rojack. Most significant of all, Sergius O'Shaugnessy

is the first of Mailer's *active* narrators. No longer is he Sergius, the
largely passive observer of *The Deer Park*, but instead he is a superstud, a Nordic superman who tackles Denise Gondelman, a Great
Bitch, a "proud, aggressive, vulgar, tense, stiff and arrogant Jewess"
(*ADV*, p. 494), in a sweaty sexual slugfest, a great sporting bout,
just as Rojack takes on Deborah in a match to the death.

The tale is at once a glorification of the power of sex and a *reductio
ad absurdum*. The controlling metaphor is sex as war, and sexual
intercourse takes on the qualities of a championship boxing match,
an encounter between matador and bull or an epic struggle for
survival between two savage beasts in a jungle clearing. The stakes
of each casual encounter are life or death.

The form is mock-heroic. The protagonists, Sergius and Denise,
are blown up into mythic proportions. Their contest is meant to be
symbolic of forces at war in the universe, like the combat of the gods
on Mount Olympus. Sexual encounters as the clash of opposing
mythic forces now become characteristic of Mailer's later works of
fiction, as his characters become less real "human beings" in the
realistic tradition and more superstereotypes, deliberately exaggerated grotesques who belong in a universe of supermeaning and
superrealism. As Richard Poirier says in reference to Mailer's *Prisoner of Sex*: "His chauvinism goes way beyond the war of the sexes.
It becomes a war of the worlds. . . ."[5]

The critic Robert Boyers has written concerning the hyper-
charged sex of *An American Dream*: "There is something faintly
touching and not a little bit absurd in attributing to poor coitus a
burden of such momentous gravity."[6] Various levels of interpretation are possible for the archetypal encounter of Sergius and
Denise. On each level, their sexual warfare represents a different
kind of dialectic: Hipster vs. Square, man vs. woman, Gentile vs.
Jew, or proletarian vs. bourgeois.

One level of interpretation is to see Sergius as a youth in search
of his manhood, or one of Mailer's hipsters on a quest for existential
authenticity. Like all of Mailer's stories, "Time" is a tale of a boy's
initiation into the vicious world of adult sexuality, reflecting that
hopeless confusion of sex with violence we find in Mailer's work.
The initiation of Sergius is also intended as a fictional illustration
of Mailer's theories, evolved in 1957, two years before he wrote
"Time," of the new modern American archetype, the White Negro
or hipster. Sergius is the hipster battling Denise the Square, determined to liberate her from her dead-ass sexual repressions, her
intellectual priggishness, and her obsession with psychoanalytic
jargon; as Mailer would say, from her "totalitarianism." Jean Radford calls Denise the representative of "a group or tendency which

Mailer wishes to see destroyed: the liberal, middle class Jewish intellectuals who have turned their back on the primitive instinctual life and become part of American totalitarianism."[7] In that respect, Denise resembles the jargon-ridden Eleanor Slovoda and Louise Rossman of "The Man Who Studied Yoga." In more general terms, according to Robert Lawler, Denise represents "that part of America which Mailer sees as deadened, overintellectualized and removed from immediate sensual experience."[8]

Sergius' weapon in his crusade is his potent phallus, somewhat comically and self-consciously dubbed "the avenger." He proposes to liberate Denise through the Reichian therapy of a good orgasm, thereby setting himself up as a rival of her middle-class Jewish therapist, "an integrated guy, Stanford Joyce." Of course, Sergius' motives are mixed—probably more revenge than therapy. As one critic aptly puts it, "For a year now, he has been forging his identity out of fifty or more unnamed vaginas."[9]

At the end of *The Deer Park*, Sergius imagines God telling him to "think of Sex as Time, and Time as the connection of new circuits" (*DP*, p. 375)—thus the title of the story, "The Time of Her Time." In the crudest sense, Sergius is trying to "make time" with Denise, but there is also a mystical meaning attached. Richard Poirier claims that Mailer's continuing obsession with the orgasm, which began in *The Deer Park*, stemmed from his feeling that "fucking was a metaphor for mounting time, for giving a measure to history," and the title of the story thus means that Sergius is actually trying to make Denise "'come' into history."[10] In his delusions of grandeur, Sergius sees himself, and only half in jest, as a sexual messiah, just as Mailer sometimes envisions himself as a savior, according to Lawler, who "wants to 'violate' and hence influence America."

Denise is Sergius' toughest case, the taming of the shrew, and bringing her to orgasm is the ultimate test, not only of his manly prowess but of his existential being, his soul itself. If he fails these initiation rites, it will be a permanent setback both for his masculinity and for his quest for salvation. If we see Sergius and Denise as symbols of male and female America, we can also see that Mailer intends Sergius' failure to be a negative commentary on the future history of the country, on the possibilities for future "Time."

In *Sexual Politics*, Kate Millett expresses outrage at the treatment of women in the story. Jean Radford recognizes the complexity of Mailer's own sexual politics, which are an integral part of his battle against "totalitarian" society, but she also feels that Mailer exploits sexual prejudice by making a woman the totalitarian villain of the piece. Radford believes that Mailer, like D. H. Lawrence, harks back

to the supposedly more authentic sexual relationships of more primitive societies. Perhaps the most disturbing feature of the treatment
of Denise is that one is never certain how much Mailer identifies
with Sergius. As Radford writes, "there are no clear signals in the
text—in the form of authorial comment, or in the images and symbols, which denote the author's distance from his narrator's statements."[11] How aware is Mailer, for example, that his sexual
liberator is as obsessed with performance in bed, as cold and manipulative and intellectually removed from immediate sensual experience, as his heroine?

Superficially, "Time" does show some of the characteristics of
pornography: it is grandiose, arrogant, offensive to women, and
in supremely poor taste. If Sergius as fictional construct illustrates
Mailer's theories about sexuality, he also acts out some of Mailer's
sexual fantasies. The author obviously participates in and enjoys his
hero's sexual exploits: the elaboration and energy of the rhetoric
alone would seem to indicate this. Nevertheless, the objectivity of
the story prevents Sergius from becoming merely a fantasy figure for
the author, the heroic superstud of a pornographic novel. Although
Denise uses psychoanalytic tags as a weapon, there is undeniable
truth in her description of Sergius as a "phallic narcissist." What
else could one call a man who refers to his sex organ as "the avenger"? Sergius, like all of Mailer's protagonists, is deliberately created
as an incomplete hero, a man of heroic potential who is weak and
intensely self-critical, struggles to overcome his weaknesses, but
never entirely succeeds. Moreover, the story, unlike that of *An
American Dream*, is a deliberate antiromance, filled with bawdy
gusto. The inflated, mock-heroic style often makes Sergius' strenuous
efforts seem a bit ludicrous, though the reader is uncertain how
much of the comedy is intentional on the author's part.

However, apart from the objectivity about Sergius' weaknesses,
Mailer does rig the terms of the story to justify his hero's behavior.
Given the jungle he lives in and the greedy, emasculating women
he faces, we are meant to feel that Sergius cannot help but be the
way he is in order to maintain his manhood.

A third possible interpretation, espoused by Donald Kaufmann[12]
and Leslie Fiedler, maintains that Sergius and Denise exist only as
stereotypes of the Gentile and the Jew, Sergius the potent Gentile
and Denise the sexually inferior Jew. The confrontation of these two
archetypes is, of course, made comic by our inescapable awareness
of the author standing over the hero's shoulder, playfully indulging
his own hangups at the same time that he maintains a careful fictional distance from his fantasy creations. "She was enthusiastic

about her analyst, he was also Jewish (they were working now on Jewish self-hatred), he was really an integrated guy . . ." (*ADV*, p. 489). Here is Mailer speaking through Sergius, the Aryan hero, expressing contempt and hostility for the middle-class pretensions of a woman who is trying to work out her Jewish self-hatred. The ironies double back on themselves; it is impossible for Mailer, himself a middle-class Brooklyn Jew and self-made bohemian, to claim that he is wholly detached from a personal involvement in these characters. The climax of the story, which is literally a physical climax, occurs when Sergius penetrates Denise in the anus and brings her to orgasm by whispering in her ear these endearing words: "'You dirty little Jew.'" Ironically, this is the same kind of language with which Gallagher baited and destroyed Roth in *The Naked and the Dead*: "'Get up, you Jew bastard!'" (*ND*, p. 661). Fiedler sees the story as a working out of Mailer's Jewish self-hatred, with Denise the stand-in for the passive, intellectual, Jewish-author part of his personality, and Sergius as "the Golden Goy," which Mailer imagines himself to be, a cross between a Hemingway tough-guy hero and a Cossack rapist out of a Jewish nightmare.[13]

Yet another possible level of interpretation is to consider the confrontation of Sergius and Denise as a form of class warfare, with the phallus as the great equalizer. Sergius, inflamed and infuriated by Denise's "college-girl snobbery," sees her as the representative of the aspiring bourgeoisie, and in a flight of fancy imagines himself as

> a primitive for a prime minute, a gorged gouge of a working-class phallus, eager to ram into all her nasty little tensions. . . . I was one of the millions on the bottom who had the muscles to move the sex which kept the world alive, and I would grind it into her, the healthy hearty inches and the sweat of the cost of acquired culture. . . . (*ADV*, p. 488)

The story seems to subscribe wholeheartedly to the myth of the sexual superiority of the working class.

Although all these interpretations are helpful in understanding the manifest level of the story, we can better comprehend the power of "The Time of Her Time" if we consider its strange ambivalence toward sexuality. Sex is depicted as aggressive, violent, gross, crude, and filthy, but it is also glorified as a kind of mystical or metaphysical activity of high existential import.

This duality exists even in the style, which unites elegance with crudity, intellect with sadistic ferocity. For example, in the passage quoted, "I was one of the millions on the bottom who had the muscles to move the sex which kept the world alive," is fairly elaborate and abstract, but "I would grind it into her" is quite the opposite. In the first phrase, Sergius is distanced from himself, he sees himself as only one example of a universal principle at work, but in the second phrase he is direct, active, carnal, and brutal. Moreover, "I would grind it into her, the healthy hearty inches and sweat of the cost of acquired culture" not only expresses sexual assault but also hints at the anal assault to come.

Mailer's characteristic style in all his future work relies upon the incongruity and surprise created by juxtaposing a "high" rhetoric, formal and abstract, with a "low" rhetoric, visceral and colloquial. For example, consider this passage from *An American Dream*: "feeling like a scientist of love whose instruments of detection were either wholly inaccurate or unverifiably acute, I stood up in the middle of my conversation with old friend rogue and simply heaved my cakes . . ." (*AD*, p. 10).

Such a style is a sophisticated literary device to manage an ambivalence of feeling. Anal ambivalence shows up not only in the style, but also in the subject matter, so that sex is debased and degraded even as it is purified and exalted. Sergius admits that he is the type who clings to all the "maternal (because sleeping) sweets of the lady," yet when he wakes up the morning after, he is so disgusted with each new conquest that he can scarcely wait to throw her out:

> the smell of the woman had gone very stale for me, and the arm-pits, the ammonias and dead sea life of old semen and old snatch, the sour fry of last night's sweat, the whore scent of overexercised perfume, became an essence of the odious, . . . I would have liked nothing better than to kick the friendly ass out of bed . . . and start the new day by lowering her in a basket out of my monk-ruined retreat six floors down to the garbage pile. . . . (*ADV*, p. 486)

Nevertheless, the quest of Sergius for apocalyptic sex is also compared, with no embarrassment, to the existential quest of the hero of Kafka's *The Castle*.

Sergius' heroic phallus is crudely labeled "the avenger," but it is also exalted with religious imagery. Sergius calls himself "the messiah of the one-night stand" and "a Village stickman who could master enough of the divine It on the head of his will to call forth more than one becoming out of the womb of feminine Time" (pp. 486, 496). The search for the apocalyptic orgasm becomes equivalent to the quest for the holy grail. There is certainly a strong element of the deliberately mock-heroic in these grossly inflated descriptions, but there is also an unfortunate deadly seriousness behind Mailer's mystical notions of sex, as he proved in *The Prisoner of Sex*. *Prisoner* is a direct exposition of the same attitudes toward sex found in "Time," and without the protective mockery of the fiction, the ludicrous self-contradictions of these attitudes become glaringly apparent. Sex cannot be simultaneously foul, violent, disgusting, degrading, and animalistic even as it is pure, noble, elevating, and spiritualistic. In Mailer's writing, sex mystically connects one to either God or the Devil. He vacillates between the two extremes, yet both are exaggerated and unreal.

It is this anal ambivalence that accounts for the volatile emotional mix in the story of love and hate, gusto and disgust. Sergius has a total contempt for Denise; she arouses him to a kind of rage. She seems to sum up everything he despises: her religion, her class origins, her bohemian and intellectual pretensions, her sexual frigidity, her lesbian indifference to a man. His total disgust, however, resembles the irrational fury of the bigot or the paranoid at the alien, the other. It is not surprising, then, that his rage is converted into perverse and violent lust.

To explain briefly: according to psychoanalytic theory, the paranoid is persecuted by his own introjected image of the parents. He confuses this image with the feces. To rid himself of the foul and threatening power of the image, the paranoid projects it onto a convenient outside object, a person or creature who becomes in his imagination the repository of all that is low, evil, threatening, and dirty. By persecuting this object, he can feel superior to his own dangerous, despised impulses. However, the object has become confused both with the parents and the feces. The paranoid's original ambivalence toward the love objects is transferred onto the new object, and even as he despises and persecutes it, he lusts to possess it. Finally, the two mutually contradictory urges become fused in his mind into a desire to make love to the object by violently raping it in the anus. This is precisely what Sergius ultimately does to Denise, and anal rape now becomes a central concern in Mailer's fiction. Although it is reductive merely to label his heroes "paranoid," it is undeniable that the ambivalence and anxiety of all of them shows certain paranoid features.

Sergius' ambivalence is established in the introductory section, which describes the tough lower East Side slum where he lives and operates a bullfighting school. When he moves into his loft apartment, "it stank of old machinery and the paint was a liverish brown" (p. 479). He reacts by going to the opposite extreme. In his desire for purity, he has the entire place whitewashed, so white that "I used to feel as if I were going snow-blind" (p. 485).

Sergius' pure bachelor's pad, this snow-white monk's cell, is an island of safety in a sea of filth that threatens to engulf him on all sides. The garbage-littered streets outside are ruled by teenage gangs, and

> the worst clue to the gangs were the six-year-olds. . . . They were the defilers of the garbage, knights of the ordure . . . they used to topple the overloaded garbage cans, strew them through the streets, have summer snowball fights with orange peel, coffee grounds, soup bones, slop . . . their pillow fights were with loaded socks of scum. . . . (pp. 479–80)

The description continues at length, detailing their odious activities with great relish and in mock-heroic style, until he arrives at their summer Olympics, when "the streets were so thick with the gum of old detritus, alluvium and dross that the mash made by passing cars fermented in the sun." Then the relatives "cheered them on and promised them murder and the garbage flew all day . . ." (p. 480).

The exaggeration of this description of the environment is integral to the story and sets up the terms for the battle to come between Sergius and Denise. This is a world of filth and violence, a murderous, cannibalistic society where one devours or is devoured:

> here the barbarians ate their young, and any type who reached the age of six without being altogether mangled by father, mother, family or friends, was a pint of iron man, so tough, so ferocious, so sharp in the teeth that the wildest alley cat would have surrendered a freshly caught rat rather than contest the meal. (p. 480)

This world resembles the mental universe of the child depicted in the writings of the psychoanalyst Melanie Klein, in which oral-sadistic tendencies blend into anal-sadistic ones.

> In the oral-sadistic fantasies the child attacks its mother's breast, and the means it employs are its teeth and jaws. In its urethral and anal fantasies, it seeks to destroy the inside of the mother's body, and uses its urine and faeces for this purpose . . . the excrements are regarded as burning and corroding substances, wild animals, weapons of all kinds. . . .

The child then fears "internal attack by a dangerous mother, father, or combined parental figure in retaliation for his own aggressive impulses."[14] The encounter between Sergius and Denise can perhaps best be understood in these terms, as an acting out of oral and anal-sadistic fantasies between a child and an androgynous mother who combines aspects of both parental authorities.

The standard interpretations enumerated—the encounter as a battle between existential Hipster and unenlightened Square, potent male and frigid female, Jew and Gentile, working-class hero and middle-class bitch—are certainly valid. Such polarities dominate the tale on its manifest level, but, as Poirier concludes, Mailer uses metaphysical and other categories as "the safest way to control sex"[15] and has in his writing a difficulty "which is very close to a disability, in bringing together the beauty and the tenderness of love with its violence."[16] What is being enacted on the fantasy level of the tale is very different from the dialectical struggle taking place on the surface.

In the opening section of the story, Sergius is having lunch in a local hashhouse with a black workman he has hired, and he brags to his companion about his prowess in bullfighting, "obeying the formal minuet of the *macho*," and making sure that the hostile neighborhood blacks in the place overhear him.

> I felt the clear bell-like adrenalins of clean anxiety, untainted by weakness, self-interest, neurotic habit or the pure yellows of the liver. For I had put my poker money on the table, I was the new gun in a frontier saloon, and so I was asking for it . . . something was likely to follow from this. (p. 482)

For Sergius, Hemingway's "grace under pressure" becomes equivalent to sphincter control, just as the code of the soldiers in *The Naked and the Dead* is "Keep a tight asshole." Sergius' anxiety is pleasurable because it is "clean" and "untainted."

As Anna Freud writes, "the sexualization and consequent play with anxiety" in obsession-compulsion neurosis is a means of turning a potential threat "into a source of masochistic pleasure."[17] The obsessional plays with the anxiety inside himself as a substitute for playing with feces. Thus, Sergius and Rojack exert their bravado to seek out dangerous situations; as a reaction against this guilty activity, they must persuade themselves that they are actually engaging in something "clean," that they are brave men purifying themselves through this process from any anal "taint" of cowardice. Even sex becomes an anxiety-provoking ordeal for the Mailer hero: fun, but dangerous and dirty, like playing with feces. The hero must persuade himself that he is bravely purifying himself through this vile activity, so he imagines, like Rojack, that he is "plugging a Nazi," or like Sergius, that he is conquering a "dirty little Jew" (that is, defeating the dirty little boy in himself). Paradoxically, they become clean by indulging in dirt. The pleasurable ordeal of the Mailer hero is undergone in the name of both anal purity and phallic prowess. Such physical ordeals and other rituals of purification are central to his fiction.

While Sergius confronts his opposition in the hashhouse, there is in the back of his mind a story about an ex-marine who "believed he was better with a knife than any man in all of New York, and night after night in bar after bar he sang the love song of his own prowess, begging for the brave type who would take on his boast and leave him confirmed or dead" (p. 482). Finally, the knife fighter is defeated by a young Puerto Rican, who humiliates him by engraving "a double oval, labium majorum and minorum on the skin of his cheek" (p. 483). Sergius is a city sophisticate who operates by the strict code of a primitive jungle logic: in his mind, what he faces is either total success or total failure, and the latter possibility carries with it the prospect of being branded as a victim or castrated. If he cannot affirm his masculinity, he is better off dead, because otherwise he would be doomed to be a woman.

In defeating Denise in bed, by the psychological process of displacement, Sergius is really defeating a rival, a fellow stud. Mailer once said in an interview, "You know studs. They're like professional athletes. . . . They think of other studs. They live in the terror that some other dude might be a little better than them. They're like street fighters."[18] The critic Howard Silverstein claims that "Sergius, symbolically turning Denise into a male, buggers her."[19]

Thus there is an obvious, even overstated parallel between Sergius' encounter with the hostile blacks and his sexual encounter with Denise. The neighborhood blacks "stared back with no love" at Sergius (p. 484), and later, when he confronts Denise in bed, "in her eyes there was a flat hatred which gave no ground" (p. 487). He seems to be seeking the same proof of masculinity in both battles. Kate Millett argues that "sexuality is inescapably a case of victimization in Mailer's mind, where the winner 'prongs' or 'brands' the loser, and having defeated the other, consumes the other's power. . . ."[20] As the psychoanalyst Otto Fenichel writes, "For certain compulsive neurotics sexual intercourse unconsciously means a fight in which a victor castrates a victim. Men patients of this kind may have no other interest in sex than to get the reassuring proof that they are not the victim (it seems that they never can achieve a full reassurance)."[21]

Denise, Sergius' sexual combatant, is symbolically equated with his male opponents, for there is a deliberate suggestion of the androgynous in her description. Her breasts are flat and she has "a kind of lean force; her arms and shoulders had shown the flat thin muscles of a wiry boy" (p. 488). She fingers Sergius' biceps "as if in unconscious competition with my strength" (p. 493). Her pants zip in the front, her voice is full of "Lesbian hysterias" and her face has the appearance of a "Village witch" (pp. 487–88). She is also likened to a snake (p. 490). Her description is overloaded with obvious characteristics, making her into a psychoanalytic caricature, as if to defend against her fantasy significance by overstating the case.

Above all, Denise resembles Deborah of *An American Dream*, another cartoon of the "Great Bitch." Denise jabs, "fingernail and all, into the tight defended core of my clenched buttocks" (p. 491), just as Deborah tries to mangle Rojack's root; one attacks from the rear and the other from the front, but it comes to the same thing. It is interesting to wonder why Sergius' buttocks are tightly clenched unless he really *expects* such an assault. It seems as if Sergius is out to penetrate Denise from the rear before she does the same to him; if he does not emasculate her, she will emasculate him. Thus, when he couples with her, she writhes "with the wanton whip-thrash of a wounded snake" and "I wounded her, I knew it, she thrashed beneath me like a trapped little animal" (pp. 490, 501). (In *Vietnam*, wounded animals actually substitute for the parent figures as the objects for a brutal assault and disembowelment.)

According to Leslie Fiedler, Denise is the stand-in for Mailer as intellectual Jewish author, and the encounter of Sergius and Denise is "a mating, brutal as an evisceration, between his [Mailer's] passive self and its more active projection."[22] This would certainly help to explain the overtones of homosexuality in the relationship and Sergius' desire to take her rectal virginity—otherwise, we must assume that he knew *telepathically* the kind of perversion that Denise needed to bring her to orgasm.

However, Fiedler's categorizations are imprecise. Denise can hardly be described as "passive": she partakes as much of the Jewish mother as of the Jewish author. Denise is rather active and mannish; it is just these qualities that make her challenging and attractive to Sergius. Moreover, he knows that she has a Jewish lover uptown, "a very nice guy, passive Arthur" (p. 446), but this only acts as a further challenge and stimulus to his erotic imaginings. By taking on Denise, Sergius is confronting a facsimile of the Jewish mother, and at the same time making love/hate to two Jewish father figures: passive Arthur and active Dr. Joyce, her Jewish analyst. Dr. Joyce is particularly threatening to Sergius; he calls Sergius a latent homosexual. What we have then is nothing so simple as active Mailer versus passive, "Jewish" Mailer. Rather we have Mailer beefing himself up into "the image of the movie male lead" (p. 484), identifying with the aggressor (in this case, the Jewish image of the gentile as Cossack) but still retaining all his private, personal insecurities. In this respect, Sergius is like Rojack, who compares himself to "those particular few movie stars who are not only profiles for the great lover, but homosexual and private in their life" (*AD*, p. 7).

Sergius in "The Time of Her Time" is a sheep in wolf's clothing, a Jewish son in protective disguise who tackles an androgynous authority figure: a phallic, emasculating Jewish mother allied to two Jewish fathers, one meek and passive and the other active and threatening, a homosexual submissive and a homosexual aggressive. They are all projections, shadow figures in Mailer's psychodrama. Denise seems to be the image of both parents, so that, on one occasion, when Sergius is copulating with her after she admits to having just made love to Arthur, he finds his pleasure increased by imagining that he is joining simultaneously with the man in Denise and the mother in Arthur. In other words, in making love with Denise, Sergius is certainly carrying out an "evisceration," but it is against a projected image of the parents, not simply against his passive self.

Moreover, since Denise is a minority figure, both Jewish and a woman, Sergius is able willfully to degrade her, to cast onto her the anality he is eager to possess yet desperate to purify himself from. As Mary Ellmann has noted, Mailer's sexual disgust with women sometimes mounts to "cloacal loathing."[23]

The unconscious desire to attack the parents' insides helps to explain not only the obvious anal sadism in Sergius' desire to penetrate Denise rectally but also the interlinked orally aggressive impulses, which extend into a kind of mutual cannibalism. As Kate Millett has noted, Mailer "converts intercourse to a procedure of absorbing the other's numa as the victorious sits down to digest the spirit which has entered the flesh."[24] Sergius wants "the salts of her perspiration in my mouth. They would be acrid perhaps, but I would digest them, and those intellectual molecules would rise to my brain" (*ADV*, p. 489). Later, he says that victory over Denise "would add to the panoplies of my ego some peculiar (but for me, valid) ingestion of her arrogance, her stubbornness, and her will—those necessary ingredients of which I could not yet have enough for my own ambition" (p. 497). It is interesting that the qualities Sergius wants to ingest—arrogance and stubbornness—are also outstanding characteristics of the classic anal character. In a similar manner, Rojack mines into Ruta's behind, seeking the wit and guile necessary to trick the Devil, and has a momentary fantasy of eating Deborah's corpse to digest her qualities. In Mailer's later writing, unconscious principles are not submerged under the veneer of civilization; for him, the unconscious comes to the surface, as stark and direct and unembarrassed as a fairy tale.

For her part, Denise is no better in her sexual impulses than Sergius; how could she be, since she is tailor-made to complement his oral and anal sadomasochistic fantasies? Her eyes, "bright with appetite, considered my head as if I were a delicious and particularly sour pickle" (p. 489). She kisses with "a muscular thrust of her tongue into my throat, as direct and unfeminine as the harsh force of her voice" (p. 489). She specializes in oral sex. "Her face was rooting in me, her angry tongue and voracious mouth going wild . . ." (p. 500). If Sergius is like Rojack in his impulses to devour and assault from the rear, then Denise, again, is like the carnivorous Deborah.

In creating Denise, it is as if Mailer had created an archetype so overwhelming that he felt he had to recreate her in Deborah in order to "kill her again, kill her good this time, kill her right" (*AD*, p. 50).

As Melanie Klein would explain it, since the child partakes in these anal and oral fantasies in his imagination, he also projects them upon the mother figure and imagines that she will retaliate in kind. Thus, when Sergius defeats Denise by uncovering her secret weakness—a desire to be anally raped—he is, ironically, only revealing his own obsessional fantasies.

Just before Sergius takes "the bridal ground of her symbolic and therefore real vagina" (*ADV* p. 502), he suffers a humiliating defeat, an episode of premature ejaculation which can serve as a summing-up of the fantasy content of the tale. In a sense, this failure of potency is an anal-urethral failure, so his subsequent anal assault on Denise is a form of psychological revenge. And the cycle goes on, until she delivers the final and most telling blow.

In this particular episode, Sergius is unmanned as soon as he can no longer degrade Denise, but instead imagines her directly as the real object of his desires, the parents. Sergius, fired up by the man in Denise and the woman in Arthur, turns into

> a jackrabbit of pissy tumescence, the quicks of my excitement beheaded from the resonances of my body. . . . I spit like a pinched little boy up into black forested hills of motherly contempt, a passing picture of the nuns of my childhood to drench my piddle spurtings with failures of gloom. She it was who proved stronger than me, she the he to my silly she. (p. 499)

This passage is so clinically direct, so overdetermined and diagnostically self-protective, that it provides its own psychoanalytic exegesis.

In the aftermath of this debacle, Sergius remembers being knocked out in the light heavyweight boxing finals in the Air Force.

He wanted to win very much, but as he lay defeated on the canvas, "I watered the cup of my boxer's jock" (p. 500). This confession is more revealing than all of his previous boasting and self-mockery, for it shows the terror that really motivates him. He equates loss of physical or sexual prowess with loss of sphincter and urethral control, with total impotence at the most basic level of bodily functions.

This problem is not just peculiar to Sergius. The episode is similar to incidents in *The Naked and the Dead*, where the soldier Hennessy fouls his pants in terror, or *An American Dream*, where Deborah evacuates her bowels after Rojack has strangled her, leaving behind on the rug a damning piece of evidence, or, in a comic vein, *The Armies of the Night*, where a character named Mailer misses the urinal in the dark and tries to make the most of it by an immediate and public confession of his sin.

The problem of loss of control, loss in the most fundamental, excretory sense, is a central one throughout all of Mailer's fiction. The more his writing becomes psychologically stark, the more the problem becomes unavoidable. It is the problem we are going to face head-on in *An American Dream*: "how vile the suggestion of villainous old bowels." It is as Mailer phrased it in a speech at Berkeley: "And so the men have indeed lost their confidence. They know the thing is out of their control, that something's going on that's larger than them, and they're filled with shame."[25] On one level, Mailer is talking about contemporary man's loss of control over history and the circumstances that control his fate; he equates this with the individual's lack of control over his own bodily processes. Mailer personalizes history by speaking to the private sense of shame and disgust in all of us. Thus "The Time of Her Time" is a story in part about the need to overcome shame.

The achievement of "The Time of Her Time" lies in its assault on the reader through sexual explicitness and energetic style. Mailer is a visceral writer, at his best when his images are rooted in the body, and "Time" stays close to the body. The stylistic intensity and narrative drive are new to Mailer's fiction of the fifties, as if he had found creative release in a fiction of exhibitionism. He takes evident pleasure in exposing his hero and thus indirectly exposing himself. In bringing the unconscious implications, the anal and oedipal tensions of which he could not have been totally unaware, close to the surface of the story—that is, by desublimating them— Mailer's intention seems to be to shock and to stimulate, and thus perhaps to liberate the reader on both the conscious and the unconscious levels. (Of course, in the process he exposes more about himself than he may consciously know.)

The psychological power of the narrative lies in its ambivalence: not simply in the exhibitionism, but in the overpowering sense of shame which that exhibitionism is intended to overcome. If the hero is shameless, we collaborate by listening to him. "The Time of Her Time" is meant to liberate both author and reader temporarily from the endless burden of guilt and shame we all must carry.

Notes

1. George Steiner, "Naked But Not Dead," *Encounter* (December 1961), p. 70.

2. Leslie Fiedler, *Waiting for the End* (New York: Dell, 1965), p. 101.

3. Richard Poirier, *Norman Mailer* (New York: The Viking Press, 1972), p. 71.

4. Ibid., p. 181.

5. Ibid., p. 105.

6. Robert Boyers, "Attitudes Toward Sex in American 'High Culture,'" *Annals of the American Academy of Political and Social Sciences* (March, 1968), p. 39.

7. Jean Radford, *Norman Mailer: A Critical Study* (New York: Harper, 1975), p. 143.

8. Robert W. Lawler, "Norman Mailer: The Connection of New Circuits" (Ph.D. diss., Claremont, 1969), p. 99.

9. Melvyn Rosenthal, "The American Writer and His Society," (Ph.D. diss., University of Connecticut, 1968), p. 113.

10. Poirier, *Norman Mailer*, p. 64.

11. Radford, *Norman Mailer*, p. 143.

12. Donald L. Kaufmann, *Norman Mailer: The Countdown* (Carbondale: Southern Illinois University, 1969), p. 104.

13. Fiedler, *Waiting for the End*, pp. 97–102.

14. Melanie Klein, *Contributions to Psychoanalysis* (London: Hogarth Press, 1948), pp. 272, 382.

15. Poirier, *Norman Mailer*, p. 72.

16. Ibid., p. 31.

17. Anna Freud, *The Writings of Anna Freud* (New York: International Universities Press, 1969), Vol. V, 259.

18. Norman Mailer, "Mailer on Marriage and Women," interview by Buzz Farbar, *Viva*, October, 1973, p. 76.

19. Howard Silverstein, "Norman Mailer: The Family Romance and the Oedipal Fantasy," *American Imago* 34, no. 3 (Fall 1977): 284.

20. Kate Millett, *Sexual Politics* (New York: Doubleday, 1970), p. 334.

21. Otto Fenichel, *The Psychoanalytic Theory of Neurosis* (New York: Norton, 1945), pp. 276–77.

22. Fiedler, *Waiting for the End*, p. 100.

23. Mary Ellmann, *Thinking about Women* (New York: Harcourt Brace, 1968), p. 40.

24. Millett, *Sexual Politics*, p. 328.

25. Norman Mailer talking about Women's Liberation in a speech at the University of California, Berkeley, 24 October 1972. The quotation is not a paraphrase but is transcribed from a tape recording.

_____

I

It would be useful at this point in our review of Mailer's works to look back over the distance Mailer has traversed. Let us return for a moment to the opening of *The Naked and the Dead*.

> *Nobody could* sleep. When morning came, assault craft would be lowered and a first wave of troops would ride through the surf and charge ashore on the beach at Anopopei. All over the ship, all through the convoy, there was the knowledge that in a few hours some of them were going to be dead.
>
> A soldier lies flat on his bunk, closes his eyes, and remains wide-awake. All about him, like the soughing of surf, he hears the murmurs of men dozing fitfully. "I won't do it, I won't do it," someone cries out of a dream, and the soldier opens his eyes and gazes slowly about the hold, his vision becoming lost in the intricate tangle of hammocks and naked bodies and dangling equipment. He decides he wants to go to the head, and cursing a little, he wriggles up to a sitting position, his legs hanging over the bunk, the steel pipe of the hammock above cutting across his hunched back. He sighs, reaches for his shoes, which he has tied to a stanchion, and slowly puts them on. His bunk is the fourth in a tier of five, and he climbs down uncertainly in the half-darkness, afraid of stepping on one of the hammocks below him. On the floor he pushes his way through a tangle of bags and packs, stumbles once over a rifle, and makes his way to the bulkhead door. He passes through another hold whose aisle is just as cluttered, and finally reaches the head.
>
> Inside the air is steaming. . . .

The mood of the opening passage is one of dull, repressed anxiety expressed as a kind of agitated depression. The anonymous G.I. is isolated among a mass of men who are stuffed like cattle into the hold of a ship, uncomfortable, trapped, stifled, and scared. The bottled-up tension surfaces in the outcry of the sleeping man, " 'I won't do it.' " As he nervously awaits combat, the soldier tries to relax, but leaves his bunk only to find a repetition of the same oppressive conditions that surround him.

The opening paragraph focuses on a mass consciousness and then

129

moves in for a close-up of one man. The soldier is deliberately made anonymous; his private fear is only an instance of the general anxiety. He is one small unit ("fourth in a tier of five"), a cog in the great machine. The men are not even united by their common anxiety, which isolates them further. They sweat out their anxiety alone in the darkness, heat, and claustrophobia of their environment. The men are like sheep bound for slaughter. There is no relief, no dignity, no camaraderie, and seemingly no hope for any of them. Many of the "naked bodies" sweltering in the hold are soon "going to be dead." The opening of the novel thus sets the mood for all that follows.

This depressing emotional tone is coped with, however, by deliberate depersonalization on the part of the narrator. The author is omniscient, removed, and aloof. He moves from the general to the particular, thereby placing the anxiety of his soldier in a larger social context. The language is workmanlike, spare, and restrained, restricted almost entirely to realistic description. There is only one metaphor (the men murmur in their sleep "like the soughing of surf"), but it is not just verbal decoration. Quite efficiently, the metaphor reminds us of the title of this first section ("Wave") and of the conception of the men not as individuals but as a mass, an impersonal force like the assault "wave" on the beach.

The immediacy of the present tense and the impingement of anxiety as we are placed inside the soldier's mind are allayed by the mechanical efficiency of the style and the formality of the overall intellectual and aesthetic structure. Our omniscient guide is tough, frank, and unembarrassed; there is no area of human experience he will shrink from. He lets us know right away that this is gritty realism, not for the tender-minded; he does not refrain from conducting us in the opening paragraphs to the latrine. Nevertheless, the style and the omniscient narration give us formal reassurance. This guide may expose us to some grim sights, but he will shield us; we are willing to place ourselves in his competent hands.

Now let us take a jump forward seventeen years in time and several light years aesthetically to the opening of *An American Dream*.

> *I met Jack Kennedy in November, 1946. We were both* war heroes, and both of us had just been elected to Congress. We went out one night on a double date and it turned out to be a fair evening for me. I seduced a girl who would have been bored by a diamond as big as the Ritz.
>
> She was Deborah Caughlin Mangaravidi Kelly, of the Caughlins first, English-Irish bankers, financiers and priests; the Mangar-

avidis, a Sicilian issue from the Bourbons and the Hapsburgs; Kelly's family was just Kelly, but he had made a million two hundred times. So there was a vision of treasure, far-off blood, and fear. The night I met her we had a wild ninety minutes in the back seat of my car parked behind a trailer truck on a deserted factory street in Alexandria, Virginia. Since Kelly owned part of the third largest trucking firm in the Midwest and West, I may have had a speck of genius to try for his daughter where I did. Forgive me. I thought the road to president might begin at the entrance to her Irish heart. She heard the snake rumble however in *my* heart; on the telephone next morning she told me I was evil, awful and evil, and took herself back to the convent in London where she had lived at times before. I did not know as yet that ogres stand on guard before the portal of an heiress. Now in retrospect I can say with cheer: that was the closest I came to being President.

Our omniscient narrator is replaced by someone who grabs us by the elbow and bends our ear with a lurid, high-powered, intimate confession, like the Ancient Mariner at a cocktail party. Who is this hero? He tells us nothing about himself directly; he seems to exist only in relation to Jack Kennedy, a real person, and Deborah Caughlin Mangaravidi Kelly, a fictitious character whose name sounds suspiciously like that of Jacqueline Bouvier Kennedy.

Our narrator, Rojack, speaks in the tone Mailer had perfected in *Advertisements for Myself*, a blend of boasting and self-depre-cation, overstatement cut by apology ("Like many another vain, empty, and bullying body of our time, I have been running for President these last ten years in the privacy of my mind. . ." [*ADV*, p. 17]). Such a narrative tone is a perfect strategem for a character whose grandiose self-love is matched only by his immense self-loathing.

Rojack is insecure. Even as he tries to seize our attention by invoking big names and big power, he asks our forgiveness for his own overweening ambition. His guilty fascination with power is equaled by his fear and awe of it. Whatever Kennedy does with his date that November evening in 1946 is never mentioned, but we can be certain he is cooler about it than our narrator. Rojack (called at Harvard "Raw-Jock") is obviously not to the manner born. He is a usurper: rather than wooing power and following an assured course like Kennedy, he must force the issue and grab power—in this instance, by immediately seducing Deborah.

Although our hero is insecure, ambitious, power-conscious and power-hungry, driven and impulsive, we cannot wholly dismiss him. He relates his adventure in retrospect, from the safe distance of time. He speaks about himself with self-conscious detachment, but with some articulate wit and charm. He holds nothing back; he confesses to everything and even begs our forgiveness. Rojack's foibles appeal to the underdog and the impossible dreamer in all of us. After all, this is America, and everyone is supposed to have the possibility to grow up to be President. If Rojack is arrogant, ambitious and a seducer, still his minor transgressions do not seem to merit Deborah's prissy, schoolgirl judgment that he is "evil, awful and evil." Mailer must get us to side with Rojack at this early stage; if we can forgive the hero now for this venial sin, we will be more likely to side with him as his crimes increase in seriousness. Rojack's plea for absolution puts us as readers in the position of father-confessor; at the same time, it is an open invitation for us to participate in the most extreme of fantasies.

Mailer is trying, first to strong arm us, and next to charm us into a phantasmagoria, a nonstop, unexpurgated orgy of fantastic and dangerous dreams, egotistical, free from the demands of logic and conventional morality. *An American Dream* deliberately defies taboos. It is a voyage into the id, intended to renew the self and the society by exposing us to extreme experiences, releasing the powers that lie within us. Like the New York party Mailer wants to attend in *The Armies of the Night*, the trip with Rojack has "every promise of being wicked, tasty, and rich" (*AN*, p. 84). Many of the original reviewers of the novel were understandably aghast. *An American Dream* is not everyone's cup of blood.

Taking the trip along with Rojack involves a good deal of risk along with the artistic and fantasy gratification. In *The Naked and the Dead*, we were protected by an aloof and efficient omniscient narrator and a slow-moving action. Here we are presented with an individual who tries to make direct contact, to impress us with his personality and his style, and then to plunge us immediately into his raw fantasies. Things move fast; before we are five pages into the novel, Rojack has killed four Germans in a grotesque and graphically violent scene. By the end of thirty pages, Rojack has murdered his wife.

Mailer, however, has a new set of defenses to offer us against all this violence. *The Naked and the Dead* opened in the present tense, with the men facing the uncertainty of possible death, and we must face that anxiety along with them. Although the narrative quickly switches into the past tense, throughout the novel we never know what is going to happen to the characters, and each new death comes as a shock. *An American Dream*, on the other hand, offers us the formal reassurance of retrospect. We know that whatever Rojack tells us is behind him, and he has survived.

A second line of defense against the rawness of the fantasies is sublimation through style. The rhythm of the language, the alliteration, and the profusion of metaphor all entertain the reader and deflect some of the anxiety of the subject matter.

Finally, the use of fairy-tale symbolism in *American Dream* distances our perspective on the action. There are enough clues in the first page of the novel to let us know that we are entering a fairy-tale world: the reference to snakes, to hidden treasure, to "evil," to "a diamond as big as the Ritz," to the "ogres" that guard the magic portals, and to Deborah as a kind of fairy princess. Jack Kennedy, of course, is a figure out of American myth; in our dream life, he is forever associated with "Camelot."

Between his writing of *The Naked and the Dead* and *An American Dream*, Mailer's conception of history had become radically altered. The passage from *The Naked and the Dead* perceives historical reality as a force that can be observed, measured, and analyzed, just as one can take apart a machine or separate out the vectors of force that make up the movement of a wave. In the opening of *American Dream*, historical reality is perceived entirely in magical, even paranoid terms. It can no longer be analyzed systematically or rationally; strange and awesome forces are at work. Mailer now finds historical reality so threatening and overwhelming that it is not enough just to analyze it—he must actively compete with it. He establishes his own hyperbolic, surreal myth through the seductive power of fiction: the fable of Rojack, pretender to the throne of the legendary Prince Jack.

Mailer now finds that only the symbolic language of fairy tale and dream is sufficient to suggest the forces at work in reality. The opening of *The Naked and the Dead* deals with the surface appearance of things, but the opening of *American Dream* ignores surfaces in order to plunge directly into the level of unconscious meaning: "so there was a vision of treasure, far-off blood, and fear" and "ogres stand on guard before the portal." The first page of the novel compresses enough material to provide a novel in itself; it merely skims over the events in order to extract the mythic content.

The psychological process of condensation, so central to the imagery of dreams, becomes a central device of the style here. For example, Deborah, with her mixed ancestry, is both the all-American girl and a royal princess. Her name is filled with ominous overtones: Mangaravidi suggests "mangle" and the Italian for "avid to eat"; Deborah sounds like "devourer," Caughlin like "coffin," and Kelly like "killer." Again, the language of the opening is extremely suggestive. "Far-off blood" has multiple meanings: the royal blood of her distant ancestors, the spilled blood that covers the hard-earned treasure, or the blood of defloration or menstruation. Finally, it also hints at Deborah's violent death to come. "A vision of treasure" suggests not only her family wealth but also "the chaste treasure," or virginity. Mailer reinforces this suggestion by references to "the portal" and "the entrance"; doors as vaginal symbols are psychological commonplaces. The imagery is copious, deliberately overloaded and hyperbolic.

The idea of breaking through the portal to get to the buried treasure is repeated in several later scenes: when Rojack breaks Deborah's neck, he conceives of it as pushing against an enormous door to get to a jeweled city. When he invades the "verboten" portal of Ruta's rear, he thinks of it as a raid on "pirate's gold" (*AD*, p. 45). Finally, in the novel's climatic scene, Rojack quakes as he faces Kelly's door.

The grouping of images at the opening of the novel—the portal, the snake, the treasure—provides a symbolic cluster that accrues meaning as the images are repeated throughout the story. They deliberately call attention to themselves as standard fairy-tale or dream symbols. Ironically, by making what is latent into the manifest content, by incorporating it into the surface of the work, this style may also defend against dangerous levels of unconscious meaning.

The opening of *The Naked and the Dead* is compared with the opening of *An American Dream* to indicate the radical alteration in Mailer's aesthetics: form, style, and everything else seems to have changed. What, if anything, remains that might indicate that the two novels were written by the same author?

First, the unnamed soldier and Rojack both face traumatic situations at the opening of their respective works; both novels are programmed by an unceasing series of extreme and traumatic events. Paradoxically, life for the Mailer hero does not seem to begin until the moment when he confronts death. Mailer's short story of 1942, "A Calculus at Heaven," ends as the protagonist, Captain Hilliard, waits for dawn and the certain death by Japanese machine gun it will bring. The rendezvous with death is also like the moment of birth. As Mailer's unknown soldier in *The Naked and the Dead* lies stuffed into the hold, he thinks of how he

will lie there waiting for the dawn and he says to himself, I wish it was time already, I don't give a damn, I wish it was time already. . . he is thinking of an early morning in his childhood when he had lain awake because it was his birthday and his mother had promised him a party. (*ND*, P. 4)

Mailer's hipster also does not begin to live until he faces death, and in the same way Rojack first comes into being for himself as he courts suicide in his murderous assault on the Nazis.

The Naked and the Dead and *An American Dream* are also similar in the isolation of the hero. Rojack, like the soldier, is a loner, scared and cut off from any outside support, and dwarfed by an awesome and threatening power. In *The Naked and the Dead*, the force is the machinery of war; in *American Dream*, political, religious, financial, and sexual power are linked together in a conspiracy, a magical network of forces. Both the unknown soldier and Rojack are playing in the big leagues, and they don't even know the rules. Their sense of being isolated and threatened (when Rojack takes the hill occupied by the Germans, he does it all alone) is like the insecurity of a child in the face of angry parents.

Rojack's attempt to control his own fate seems similar to that of Croft in *The Naked and the Dead*. Both deny danger by courting danger and deny impotence by trying for omnipotence. Croft's assault on Mount Anaka leaves a trail of dead bodies behind him and is ultimately useless; Rojack also leaves a collection of corpses behind him and he is defeated just when he seems about to make it to his goal.

We are supposed to admire Rojack for his boldness and daring, his try for the treasure in the face of blood and fear, just as we are supposed to admire Croft's heroic but misguided and doomed effort. Yet the attitude toward power in *American Dream* is ultimately ambivalent: fascination and excitement spiced with guilt but sometimes tinged with self-disgust. The attitude toward power in this novel reminds one of Mailer's attitude toward sex: "sex to Mailer's idea of it was better off dirty, damned, even slavish! than clean and without guilt" (*AN*, p. 24). Indeed, sex and power are hopelessly confused with sodomy and dirt in *American Dream*. Mailer makes it obvious that, in seducing Deborah, Rojack is ripping off power and vicariously raping her influential and awesome father. Yet Mailer seems to applaud this sublimated buggery as one step better then the ultimate evil: actual homosexuality. "Onanism and homosexuality were not, to Mailer, light vices—to him it sometimes seemed that much of life and most of society were de-

signed precisely to drive men deep into onanism and homosexuality
. . . you earned manhood provided you were good enough, bold
enough" (AN, pp. 24–25). Conscious acting out becomes a way to
deny the terrible unconscious wishes. The unembarrassed candor
of The Naked and the Dead is transformed into the unabashed exhibitionism of An American Dream: Mailer shows the courage of his
bad taste.

II

Ultimately, then, what The Naked and the Dead and An American
Dream have in common are certain underlying psychological
attitudes: ambivalence toward power and a deliberate confusion
of power with sex and with dirt. The aesthetic transformation in
the later novel represents a shift in emphasis in the system of defenses. By the time of writing American Dream, Mailer had allowed
his repressed conflicts to rise to the surface; he makes the latent
content more manifest, though without necessarily entirely understanding or admitting the unconscious roots of these conflicts in
his own psyche. He makes intuitive, metaphoric connections between sodomy and power, but projects them outward and converts
them into working principles not only for the motivation of his
hero but for the operation of the society at large, even for the cosmos.
True, the novel is "a burlesque treatment of the obscene version
of the American Dream that possesses the unconscious mind of
America at the present time," as John W. Aldridge says,[1] but it
is also a denial of the paranoid fantasies that possess the unconscious
mind of Mailer. He really does see society as a conspiracy "designed precisely to drive men deep into onanism and homosexuality." This is not to say that this perception invalidates the novel.
A work of art consists of compromise formations; it is capable of
expressing simultaneously multiple, even mutually contradictory
impulses. Robert Solotaroff sees Dream as Mailer's attempt both
to purge himself from his tyrannical system, which had created
turmoil in his private life and forced him to stab his wife, and also
to justify that system by converting it into art. The book represents
both public penance and artistic redemption for its author.[2]

" 'God owns the creation, but the Devil has power over all waste,'
Mailer writes in . . . The Presidential Papers; and this anal-genital
struggle underlies the narrative strategies of An American Dream.
Rojack wages titanic battle against the anal demonism of Deborah-
Ruta-Kelly . . . to win . . . a glimpse of the 'heavenly city,' " writes
Max F. Schulz.[3] Richard Poirier concurs, finding the core of the

novel in Rojack's continual war between "creative sexuality and a destructive perversity, God and the Devil, the Devil's hideout being associated in this book with the anus and the destruction of it with buggery." Poirier believes that *An American Dream* reveals Mailer's increased revulsion from all kinds of sexuality that are, in the literal sense of the word, degenerate, that express what he takes to be the de-creative impulse, the turn toward death in American society."[4]

Yet ambivalence is the key to understanding this battle, an ambivalence that neither of these critics fully takes into account. Rojack must fight against degeneracy, against anal diabolism only because it is so appealing to him. Both his love and his hate, his attraction to and repulsion from anality are pushed to extremes. Mailer makes the intestinal mode into a primary source of power and of meaning in his private cosmology, an essential mode for constructing metaphor and comprehending all the processes of reality.

According to Aldridge, *American Dream* dramatizes "the various ways a man may sin in order to be saved, consort with Satan in order to attain to God."[5] As Mailer claims in his movie, *Beyond the Law*, one can pursue evil for good reasons or for evil ones; some people sin only in order to defeat evil. By this kind of ingenious reasoning, Rojack's repressed homosexual impulses are willfully converted into honorable and manly aggression, as when he kills four German soldiers or imagines that he will steal the secrets of the Devil out of Ruta's anus. Rojack's desire to waste, destroy, and mire himself in corruption is paradoxically viewed by him as a "clean," moral act, the route to salvation, the way to free himself of impurity. Like Marion Faye, he believes that "to be pure one must seek out sin itself, mire the body in offal so that the soul may be elevated" (*DP*, p. 329).

Allan J. Wagenheim, in his discussion of the mythic significance of *An American Dream*, says that Rojack is on a quest for manhood, "another of the countless heroes taking journeys to specific places where some most desirable object of power or wealth is to be obtained, but not before he surmounts a series of obstacles, and slays an ogre or a dragon."[6] When Rojack has intercourse with Deborah, "I used literally to conceive of a snake guarding a cave which opened to the treasure, the riches, the filthy-lucred wealth of all the world" (p. 34). The desirable object of wealth or power in the novel is associated with excrement, and the vagina is associated with the anus. Rojack's journey, like that of the soldiers in *The Naked and the Dead*, can be considered a symbolic progress through a series of tunnels or caves, passageways that represent the anus.

In *St. George and the Godfather*, Mailer describes the fascination of a walk on the floor of a political convention as equivalent to "a promenade through vales of malignity or a passage through corridors of vested bile."[7] In the same manner, when Rojack stands in the lobby of the Waldorf, he considers ascending the back stairs to Kelly's lair, "through locks and ambushes, up through vales of anathema exuding from the sleep of the wealthy" (p. 207). The imagery re-creates the magical world of fairy tales, where the hazards are as much supernatural as physical. Just as inanimate objects take on a life of their own in Dickens, so the environment comes alive in Mailer's writing, charged with mental force. Mailer and Rojack both make daring journeys through supercharged rectal passageways crammed full of psychic dangers.

When Rojack ascends to Kelly's suite in the elevator, he has the sensation of "moving through a tunnel rather than rising in a shaft" (p. 208). When his father-in-law enfolds him in a smothering embrace, "I could feel the beating of Kelly's heart, some mighty sense of the powers in a cavern" (p. 217). Elsewhere, Rojack asks us, "Do you know psychosis? Have you explored its cave? I had gone out to the end of my string" (p. 133). Kelly is the foul beast whose power Rojack must overcome, symbolically the Devil or the Minotaur. Unconsciously, however, all these journeys into caves can represent the desire to homosexually rape the father.

So beneath all the anal anxiety in the novel, we find repressed Oedipal desires. The clinical term that describes such a syndrome is *compulsion* or *obsession neurosis*. "The typical compulsion neurotic, experiencing a conflict between his phallic, Oedipal wishes and his castration fear, substitutes anal-sadistic wishes for his Oedipal demands . . . regression is a means of defense," writes Otto Fenichel.[8] "The superego . . . becomes more sadistic and rages against the anal and sadistic demands not less than previously against the genital ones."[9]

In *The Presidential Papers*, Mailer compares the national consciousness to a river that has diverged into two incompatible streams: a surface that is "concrete, factual, practical and unbelievably dull" and "a subterranean river of untapped, ferocious, lonely and romantic desires, that concentration of ecstasy and violence which is the dream life of the nation."[10] The surface is anally repressed, holding back a potential explosion of dangerous desires. The world of coexisting yet incompatible extremes is the world of the obsessional. Mailer's theory of the America of the two rivers presents us with a nation obsessed.

Thus, we can begin to see what *American Dream* is really about: "that concentration of ecstasy and violence which is the dream life of the nation." In unconscious terms, the novel acts out the explosion to the surface of all those repressed Oedipal and anal desires. We can see in Rojack all the traits that Fenichel ascribes to the obsessional: the split between order and chaos, the intellect and the irrational, creation and destruction, good and evil, God and the Devil. "Am I good now? Am I evil forever?" Rojack asks himself after he murders Deborah (p. 38). Rojack allows himself no middle ground between the two extremes; he sees things only in terms of artificially rigid dichotomies. Just as Mailer, as one critic notes, is fond of "antinomies or simple opposites,"[11] so Rojack's thought is based on a series of bipolar schematizations.

Rojack exhibits the classic symptom of obsession neurosis: he hears commands that compel him to do strange things. "In analysis," explains Fenichel, "it turns out that the actions that have to be counteracted or avoided have an objectionable instinctual significance; as a rule they represent the tendencies of the Oedipus complex, distorted, it is true, in a very characteristic way."[12] Melanie Klein writes that "the obsessional mechanisms are a defense against paranoid anxieties";[13] when the compulsions fail to work, the underlying paranoia threatens to take over. It is interesting to note that after Mailer stabbed his wife in 1960, the police surgeon reported that Mailer showed "homicidal and suicidal tendencies . . . delusional thinking . . . symptoms of paranoid breakdown."[14] In any case, Mailer has created in Rojack a portrait of a driven, obsessed man whose defenses have begun to disintegrate. He must reassert control, or else the "return of the repressed" will overwhelm him.

Just as "control" was one of the words that appeared with the most frequency in *The Naked and the Dead*, so it is a central concern of *An American Dream*. Shago Martin imprisons the wildness and savagery in his singing "to something complex in his style, some sense of irony, some sense of control, some sense of the way everything is brought back at last under control" (p. 182). This could also describe Mailer's own style in the novel. Rojack says, "There was nothing so delicate in all the world as one's last touch of control" (p. 196). Kelly tells Rojack to control the *mess* he has created: " 'it doesn't matter whether people think you killed Deborah, it matters only whether people are given the opportunity to recognize it's been swept under the rug, and you and I together are in control of the situation' " (p. 233). Finally, when Rojack beats up Shago, "My rage took over. . . . I was out of control . . ." (p. 193).

Along with the fear of losing control, Rojack is terrified of losing his balance, both in the physical sense of falling down and in the psychological sense of becoming unbalanced. Rojack confesses, "Probably I did not have the strength to stand alone" (p. 18). Later, when Rojack faces up to Shago, the singer says admiringly to Cherry, " 'I be damn . . . you got yourself a stud who can stand' " (p. 184). Balancing on the thin line of the parapet without falling into certain death is Rojack's finest hour; he must accomplish this without shaming himself before Kelly, the father figure. Rojack's attempts to be autonomous, to stand alone, re-create a crucial stage in human development, a stage whose trials the anally fixated are doomed to repeat endlessly. This is not to say that the novel can only appeal to readers who are similarly obsessed: the terrors of shame and doubt and the struggle for self-sufficiency are universal concerns.

Nevertheless, Rojack is caught in the bind of his own ambivalence. The ego (and for that matter, the guts) of the compulsion neuotic is both overmanipulated and out of control, a piece of disputed territory in the endless warfare between the obtrusive commands of his tyrannical id and the cruel imperatives of his superego.[15] Rojack cannot control his urges: he does not know whether to hold on or to let go. He forces both modes into incompatible extremes: holding on means murder (strangulation), but letting go means suicide (dropping from a height). When he balances on the parapet, Rojack is walking a thin line between holding on and letting go, between his rage to kill and his urge to punish himself.

Finally, the novel is a dream become a nightmare. Rojack achieves self-control, but only through the extreme solution of eliminating the parents. Incest, suggests Mailer, is a route to power, a tool of the Devil: " 'Incest is the gate to the worst sort of forces,' " says Barney Kelly (p. 246). An American Dream is filled with repeated references to overtly incestuous relationships (between Cherry's brother and sister, between Kelly and his daughter Deborah, and between Kelly, Bess Trelawne, and her daughter) and the central conflict is symbolically incestuous, the most undisguised family romance Mailer had yet written.[16] One critic asserts that "at the center of this novel is an inverted Oedipal compulsion," that is, Rojack's desire to murder the mother figure in order to possess the father.[17] However, Rojack seems instead to want symbolically to make love to and kill both parents. At the end, not only is Deborah strangled and Kelly whipped but Shago and Cherry also lie dead. This is a terrifying version of the Oedipal drama in which both mother and father are destroyed; neurosis gives way to psychosis. Rojack tries to retain the image of the "good mother" in the form of Cherry, but not even this is permitted. His destructive impulses win out over his need for love. He perceives all the authorities as alike: buggers who want to take control of his bowels. Rojack wants autonomy, but to attain that power he must eliminate the parents.

The almost total avoidance of any reference to the hero's childhood or his family is a clue to the anxiety that is being repressed here. The first ten pages offer a capsule history of Rojack's career from his entrance into the army, a raw youth fresh out of Harvard, through his battle with the Nazis, his political career, his life as an intellectual and celebrity, and his marriage, until we find him in middle age, a self-confessed failure and potential suicide. Or murderer. Only the hero's parents and childhood have been eliminated. Rojack gives the illusion of being a self-made man; his life begins for him with the moment of bloody initiation into manhood. Brief references elsewhere establish the fact that he has a Jewish father and a Protestant mother, but these are merely nominal parents, overshadowed by Kelly and Deborah, his substitute parents.

As in *Barbary Shore* and *The Deer Park*, references to childhood and the original parents have been almost eradicated and the story focuses instead on the crucial moment of initiation into manhood. This test comes when Rojack confronts the four Nazi soldiers. Even though he kills them and is awarded the Distinguished Service Cross, he feels a sense of failure. "I had scored, but no football in my belly at the end, just six points. And those blue eyes kept staring into the new flesh of my memory" (p. 6), the ice-cold eyes of the last German that haunt him for years afterwards, and unman him.

The novel moves with the scrupulous logic of the unconscious from the encounter with Deborah in the back seat of a car to his encounter on the battlefield, from Rojack's initiation into the sexual big leagues to his initiation into killing and death. In both, success is thwarted. *An American Dream* is a novel of initiation into manhood, an initiation that fails and must be repeated again and again through continual risk taking.

III

Viewed in this way, the first chapter of the novel divides into four separate encounters: first the struggle with Deborah, which involves a defiance of the father, Kelly; next the murder of the Germans, an explicitly homosexual assault, and on an unconscious level patricidal; third, attempted suicide; and finally, the murder of Deborah, the symbolic, evil mother, which takes the place of

142   An American Dreamer

the failed suicide attempt and re-enacts the murder of the Germans.

Let us look closely at that battlefield scene, which, in its hallucinatory vividness, is the most remarkable thing in the opening chapter. The assault on the German soldiers is paralleled by an assault on the reader with a non-stop barrage of high-powered metaphors.

In Rojack, the young Harvard intellectual thrown into a position of leadership in combat, we have another Lieutenant Hearn, but a Hearn who is ready to kill to maintain power. "Like Stephen Rojack in *An American Dream*, whom he foreshadows," says critic Raymond A. Schroth, "Croft makes a religion of power and a ritual of courage."[18] Kate Millett finds that "in Stephen Rojack . . . the intellectual Hearn does at last manage to become a Croft," a killer-hero.[19] The secret admiration for the energy of the fascist mentality, that "identification with the aggressor" evidenced in *The Naked and the Dead*, now surfaces in the personality of Rojack, a "tough-guy intellectual"[20] in whom Croft and Hearn are subsumed into a single unified sensibility. This incongruous joining of images reflects the contradictions in Mailer's own personality, and also mirrors the contradictory myths of masculinity in the American Dream.

The mood of the battle scene is "fear and funk and a sniff of the grave" (p. 3), recalling the "vision of treasure, far-off blood, and fear" (p. 1) with Deborah, implying that, unconsciously, the two scenes have much in common. The enemy is dug in on a "modest twin dome, a double hill with a German machine gun on one knoll and a German machine gun on the other" (p. 3), a deliberate parody of the maternal breasts, the nipples delivering death instead of sustenance.

Whereas the sexual scenes in the novel are described with metaphors of combat, the war scene is depicted with sexual metaphors, revealing the interchangeability of the two for the author. When Rojack hurls his grenades to wipe out the machine-gun nests, "I was exploded in the butt from a piece of my own shrapnel, whacked with a delicious pain clean as a mistress' sharp teeth going 'Yummy' in your rump" (p. 4), a hint of the voracious, cannibalistic sex that follows in the novel, with the attack on the rump suggesting a kind of masochistic, homoerotic pleasure. This simile is followed by another image mixing sex and violence: "I pulled the trigger as if I were squeezing the softest breast of the softest pigeon which ever flew, still a woman's breast takes me now and then to the pigeon on that trigger, and the shot cracked like a birth twig across my palm, whop!" (p. 4). We are back with the suggestive "twin domes" of the machine-gun nest, the breasts giving death instead of life, only now labor pains and birth itself are viewed as a kind of death.

The first German soldier Rojack kills is described as a repulsive young homosexual. The adjectives are piled on, as if to emphasize Rojack's extreme disgust: "a great bloody sweet German face, a healthy spoiled overspoiled young beauty of a face, mother-love all over its making, possessor of that overcurved mouth which only great fat sweet young faggots can have when their rectum is tuned and entertained from adolescence on, came crying, sliding, smiling up over the edge of the hole, 'Hello death!' blood and mud like the herald of sodomy upon his chest . . ." (p. 4). Rojack takes sadistic pleasure in destroying that face: "the round went in at the base of his nose and spread and I saw his face sucked in backward . . . he looked suddenly like an old man. . . ." As he dies, he cries " 'Mutter' " (p. 4).

The description of the first German's face resembles the image later on of Deborah's head after it hits the pavement: "swollen . . . like a fat young girl," the face "filthy," and "the back of her head, like a fruit gone rotten . . . the center of a pond of coagulated blood" (p. 59). The description of the young German as "spoiled" with "mother-love" (p. 4) also brings to mind Mailer's depiction in *The Prisoner of Sex* of the young D. H. Lawrence as "a momma's boy, spoiled rotten" and "arrogant with mother-love." The resemblance between the killings of Deborah and of the German begins to become clear; the unconscious logic behind both acts is the same. In both murders, Rojack is attempting to eradicate the part of himself that he cannot tolerate: the momma's boy, weak, soft, and rotten as a piece of spoiled fruit, and the image that he always connects with the momma's boy, that of the foul, anal homosexual.

Rojack projects the things he most fears in himself onto the first German. He does not know the soldier is a homosexual; he merely takes him for one, just as, later, he takes Ruta for a Nazi. Paradoxically, however, his destruction of the German is described like an explicitly homosexual assault: the carbine is "a long fine antenna" pointed at the machine-gun "hole," and the bullet enters at the base of his nose, substitute for the anus. The murder is also symbolic castration; the German is turned into a "toothless" old man (p. 4).

Mailer does not try to evade any of this. All of his repeated and heavily weighted imagery brings the psychological meaning to the surface of the tale. As Kate Millett says, again and again in his novels, Mailer openly "demonstrates the violence of his characters as springing directly from their stifled homosexuality."[21] The truism that repressed homosexuality yields violence is repeated so often in Mailer that it seems a way of neutralizing the violence by giving it a psychological justification, even a kind of nobility, as when he speaks of D. H. Lawrence choosing to become a man "by an act of will" although he was "blood and bone of the classic family stuff out of which homosexuals are made."[22]

The conscious overelaboration of homosexual images in the murder of the soldier may be the author's way of reassuring the reader and himself, "I have it all under control." It is a sublimation of anxiety to the force of intellect and style. The overwhelming imagery also counters this anxiety through an all-out assault (both anal and phallic) on the reader. Moreover, the repetition of images such as "the momma's boy, spoiled rotten," not only throughout this novel but throughout Mailer's works, suggests that it is not so much a thematic concern as an obsession. Beneath the conscious, sophisticated manipulation of highly charged images, there seems to be an unconscious logic at work that is beyond the novelist's control.

After the death of the first German, the second comes up, "timed like the interval in a shooting gallery":

> his hole mate, a hard avenging specter with a pistol in his hand and one arm off, blown of, rectitude like a stringer of saliva across the straight edge of his lip, the straightest lip I ever saw, German-Protestant rectitude. *Whap*! went my carbine and the hole was in his heart and he folded back the long arm with the pistol, back across the chest to cover his new hole and went down straight and with a clown's deep gloom as if he were sliding down a long thin pipe. . . .(p. 4)

Whereas the first German soldier was characterized as an anally "loose" personality, the second, in contrast, is as anally retentive as is humanly possible. Significantly, he is "the hole mate" of the first; if the first was a masochistic, passive homosexual, then the second is a sadistic, aggressive one.

Along with his anally retentive aspects, the second German is the father as a stern, punishing figure, a totally phallic threat: "the long arm with the pistol," "the straightest lip I ever saw," "hard avenging specter," and the twice-repeated "rectitude," with its suggestions of both "erection" and "rectum." His symbolic castration ("one arm off, blown off") by Rojack is not enough; this father figure must be destroyed a second time, given a "new hole," yet he still goes down "straight . . . as if he were sliding down a long thin pipe."

If the first murder was the murder of himself, Rojack the son as passive homosexual, then the second is the murder of the father as homosexual assailant. Rojack is compelled to reenact the combat again and again, as if he were gunning down targets in a shooting gallery. The man of "rectitude," the father as "hard avenging specter," is reincarnated in the Irish detective Roberts, mixed with a touch of the corruption of the first German. "He had never looked more like a cop. The dedication of his short straight nose hung above the confirmed grin of corruption at the corner of his mouth. Rectitude, cynicism, and greed threw off separate glints from his eyes" (p. 160).

The third German is knocked off easily, but the fourth is the worst of all; he seems to sum up all the previous opponents.

> then the last stood up straight with a bayonet in hand and invited me to advance. He was bleeding below his belt. Neat and clean was his shirt, level the line of his helmet, and nothing but blood and carnage below the belt. I started to rise, I wanted to charge as if that were our contract, and held, for I could not face his eyes, they now contained all of it, the two grenades, the blood on my thigh, the fat faggot, the ghost with the pistol, the hunchback, the blood, those bloody screams that never sounded, it was all in his eyes, he had eyes I was to see once later on an autopsy table in a small town in Missouri . . . eyes of blue, so perfectly blue and mad they go all the way in deep into celestial vaults of sky, eyes which go back all the way to God . . . and I faltered before that stare, clear as ice in the moonlight . . . and now I had no stomach to go, I could charge his bayonet no more. So I fired. And missed. And fired again. And missed. Then he threw his bayonet at me. It did not reach. He was too weak. It struck a stone instead and made a quivering whanging sound like the yowl of a tomcat on the jump. (p. 5)

This last section of the episode receives the strongest emphasis and the greatest length, which is appropriate since it increases the suspense. Certain elements, however, are markedly set off. After the three extraordinarily long sentences describing the first three encounters, the rhythm breaks with this short sentence: "He was bleeding below his belt." Because the break occurs at this point, the sentence receives double emphasis. It is central, summing up what all four encounters are about: emasculation. Rojack had easily taken care of the first three, but on the fourth, the castration is too clearly visible. He begins to identify with the figure . This man is more *real* than the other grotesque soldiers; he is rotten but dignified, like "a noble tree with rotten roots" (p. 5). Rojack is literally unmanned before him. Despite his massive wound, the German is a phallic threat still. He invites Rojack to advance, and then hurls his bayonet, which misses, but still makes the potent sound of "a tomcat on the jump."

The reference to the ice-blue eyes of the figure on the autopsy table foreshadows the last image of the destroyed father in the novel, the farmer dead of cancer whose stench haunts Rojack. The man with the ice-blue eyes, the malevolent yet impotent father, is echoed once again in Detective Roberts, who has "the sort of cold blue eyes which live for a contest" (p. 60).

The deliberate overtones of homosexual assault in the scene continue when Rojack's men cheer him, and one even kisses his mouth. Later, Deborah caricatures the incident, belittling Rojack's manhood with an accusation of homosexuality that is vicious and accurate: " 'It must have been quite a sight. You whimpering and they whimpering, and you going pop pop pop with your little gun' " (p. 23).

The eyes of the fourth soldier never leave Rojack. They represent for him a fear of castration, and they lead to a special compulsion. He connects the destruction of the Germans with the full moon, and so he carries on a "secret frightened romance with the phases of the moon" (p. 7). His bondage to the timetable of lunar cycles is a form of feminization, as though he suffered from a menstrual cycle.

The moon is the central, unifying symbol of the novel: the major events, both the sex and the murders, are equated because they all take place under a full moon. The moon is thus a rich, ambiguous symbol, associated with both life and death. More than a symbol, it is a totemic object of worship: a goddess. It comes to stand in the novel for the power of the female for both creation and destruction, a seductive and lethal lady with whom Rojack is carrying on a dangerous romance: he must court death to get to her. The moon, in other words, is the mother. It becomes associated with the maternal womb, death, and incest: the first dying German cries "'*Mutter*,' one yelp from the first memory of the womb" (p. 4); Cherry says, "'the moon is out, and she's a mother to me'" (p. 264); the moon is called "princess of the dead" (p. 259); life in the unreal, air-conditioned, desert world of Las Vegas is compared to "life in a submarine, like in the safety chambers of the moon" (pp. 268–9); and Kelly's incestuous liaison with Deborah is termed a voyage "to the tar pits of the moon" (p. 254).

Several critics have noted the association of Deborah with Diana, goddess of the hunt and of the moon, who rules in earth, heaven, and hell under various names: Hecate, Persephone, or Luna.[23] When Deborah, the moon-lady, the evil mother, is killed, the moon becomes connected instead with Cherry, the good mother.[24] If the moon is a "platinum lady with her silver light" (p. 12), Cherry is a blonde with a "silvery cunning in her features" (p. 61) and "an elusive silvery air" (p. 89).

Robert Solotaroff sees the moon in *Dream* as a positive symbol of all Being, "a triggering device which enables Rojack to hear his being, the proclaimer of the pure truth about himself. . . ."[25] Nevertheless, Rojack is like a werewolf in thrall to the moon, and he wishes to be free of its terrifying power. It forces him to do horrible things. The moon has power in his private system of superstition; it is connected to the compulsion to commit murder and incest. The voice of the moon is seductive: incest calls, but death stands in the way. To fulfill her commandments, Rojack must kill someone or else kill himself.

He says, "There are times when I like to think I still have my card in the intellectual's guild, but I seem to be joining company with that horde of the mediocre and the mad who listen to popular songs and act upon coincidence" (p. 2). Psychoanalytic theory might be able to shed some light on Rojack's condition: "The overvaluation of intellect often makes compulsion neurotics develop their intellect very highly. However, this high intelligence shows archaic features and is full of magic and superstition. The ego shows a cleavage, one part being logical, another magical."[26]

All of Rojack's fears—of failure, homosexuality, castration, and death—have come to center on his wife Deborah and their unsuccessful marriage. As Allan J. Wagenheim writes, "Deborah is depicted not as a normal adversary but as supra-human, a monster, and always in animal terms—a Great Bitch, a lioness, a bull!—always a ferocious and predatory animal. . . ."[27] She is nothing less than the "overpowering, castrating mother," and Rojack's marital war is connected with "the need to free himself from the Oedipal triangle."[28]

We have met Deborah's type before, in Dorothea O'Faye and Lulu Meyers of *The Deer Park*. Deborah is a higher-class, bettermannered version of Dorothea. Dorothea, like Deborah, "had her court, she had money in the bank . . . she was violent too . . . she used up people and time . . . A really drunken evening had to end with Dorothea screaming 'Get out, get out you son of a bitch before I kill you!'" (*DP*, pp. 8–9). Like Lulu, Deborah goads her man and then belittles him. Lulu dares Sergius to jump a fence on horseback and then calls him a baby for taking a stupid dare (p. 132), and she stops him from boxing a rival for her, calling Sergius brutal (p. 236).

This is reminiscent of the scene in which Rojack boxes with an obnoxious friend of Deborah's at a party, hoping for her approval, and finds that she has quit the room. "'Of course I left,' she said later, 'it was a sight, bullying that poor man'" (*AD*, p. 16). Nothing that Rojack does will please Deborah; she systematically cuts away his confidence. Everything he has is little in her eyes: his "little girls" (p. 30) and his "little gun" (p. 23).

But Deborah is a far more formidable opponent than Lulu or Dorothea—Rojack believes her to be a witch. "She had powers, my Deborah, she was psychic to the worst degree, and she had the power to lay a curse" (p. 22). She even has the evil eye, the lone green eye that haunts Rojack after her death. Like the Nazis, she is a phallic threat, represented particularly by her seductive voice, which "leaped like a deer, slipped like a snake" (p. 20).

She reeks of various odors which make her more menacing. *An American Dream* operates on an elaborate system of vapors and smells; each person has a characteristic odor and each emotion its specific aroma. "Evil expresses itself less in acts than in odours. Mailer uses smells to symbolize the absolute wrong that is an aspect of final reality," writes Anthony Burgess.[29] When she drinks, Deborah emits "a stench of sweet rot" (p. 24), and when she becomes angry, "a powerful odor of rot and musk and something much more violent came from her. It was like the scent of the carnivore in a zoo" (pp. 29–30). From the time of writing *The Naked and the Dead*, Mailer has had the most hyperdeveloped sense of smell in American letters. He incorporates that sense into the metaphysical structure of *An American Dream*. Later, he even posits a "science of smell" in *Of a Fire on the Moon*. The use of smell puts his images on a more primitive, gut level. Smell is the most evocative of the senses; it acts as a trigger for memory associations. Smell is also the most atrophied sense in man, and it is associated with the early stages of development and with lower animals such as canines. The olfactory orientation of anal-erotic children, which is lost in most adults, frequently returns in compulsion neurosis.[30] The reliance on his nose turns Rojack into more of a savage, and it gives him an extra set of clues to guide him through the jungle of carnivorous beasts that is *An American Dream*. One sniffs out the enemy.

Deborah is characterized as a man-eating beast. Rojack carries the mark of her teeth on his ear (like D.J. in *Why Are We in Vietnam?*, who is bitten on the rear by his father). Deborah's maternal grandfather, Mangaravidi, ran a meat-packing plant. As mentioned before, that Italian name roughly translates as "avid to eat." It suggests gluttony and greed. The taste for flesh is in her blood. After he has murdered her, Rojack has a momentary fancy of digesting her corpse, thereby vitiating her cannibalistic propensities. As we have seen, this impulse to kill rather than be killed, to castrate rather than be castrated, and to eat rather than be eaten runs through all of Mailer's work.

According to John W. Aldridge, Mailer earns the liberty to deal with cannibalism and numerous other perversions in *An American Dream* by operating within the tradition of the gothic romance, "in which fantasy and fact, witchcraft and melodrama, myth, allegory, and realism combine."[31] The prose romance was the genre favored by such nineteenth-century American authors as Cooper, Melville, and Hawthorne because of its flexibility.

In this superreal atmosphere, a creature of superhuman evil such as Deborah could naturally exist, and there is a dream-logic for Rojack to murder her to solve his dilemma. Certainly, after her final performance, where her every maneuver is calculated to taunt and belittle him, who could blame Rojack? Deborah seems to deserve her fate. Because this is a first-person narrative, we are drawn into sympathy with Rojack, and in fact, feel remarkably comfortable with the murder. In a novel that begins with a scene of such hallucinatory vividness as the murder of four Nazi ogres, a graphically bloody scene that moves with all the gory beauty and slow-motion precision of a nasty psychedelic vision, we can hardly be disturbed by yet one more murder. Deborah is another ogre, another Nazi, and she even attempts to mangle the hero's root. Moreover, the elaboration and elegance of the figurative language in the descriptions remove the brutalizing effects of the violence, and instead tend to invigorate the reader, who admires the rhythm and snap of the sentences and the barrage of images. In this context, wife-murder is completely justifiable, and no moral qualm can disturb the reader, especially when the wife in question is as totally evil and life-destroying as Deborah, like a stepmother from the Brothers Grimm. Questions of guilt and remorse play little part in this novel of crime and punishment; instead, the dominant emotions are shame and rage.

The murder of Deborah, which concludes Chapter One, is climactic in every sense of the word. The description of the murder refers back to the slaughter of the Nazis, and sums up all the metaphoric (and unconscious) concerns of the chapter.

As Rojack strangles Deborah, he says, "I had the mental image I was pushing with my shoulder against an enormous door which would give inch by inch to the effort" (p. 31), as though he were taking her maidenhead. Mailer makes it obvious when Rojack feels "some desire to go ahead not unlike the instant one comes in a woman against her cry that she is without protection . . ." (p. 31). The murder is equivalent to rape. The series of four "cracks" breaking her neck echo the "whap" of his carbine as it kills the Germans; the fourth "crack," in a sense, makes up for his cowardly inability to kill the fourth soldier.

At the same time that murder equals orgasm, it also seems to equal excretion: "pulse packed behind pulse in a pressure up to thunderhead; some blackbiled lust . . . I was through the door, hatred passing from me in wave after wave, illness as well, rot and pestilence, nausea, a bleak string of salts" (p. 31) He is purging himself of his wastes in a kind of bowel movement or regurgitation. Later, in the police station, Rojack says, "I was letting go my grip on my memory of the past . . . Surrendering the hard compacted anger of every hour when she had spoiled my need . . ." (p. 80). This excreting or vomiting up of aggression occurs in two other places in the novel: when Rojack "heaves his cakes" over his friend's balcony at the cocktail party, and later when he vomits in the bathroom at Cherry's nightclub.

IV

After the murder, Rojack has passed through a threshold, and is symbolically reborn. "I opened my eyes. I was weary with a most honorable fatigue, and my flesh seemed new. I had not felt so nice since I was twelve" (p. 32). In the next chapter, he says, "I was feeling good, as if my life had just begun" (p. 39). However, he must still undo the murder. If it had been like a bowel movement, his first action after murder, appropriately enough, is to wash his hands, and even to wash the place on his shoulder where Deborah had touched him during the struggle. Now, purged and cleansed, Rojack feels the equal of the father: "my eyes had the blue of a mirror held between the ocean and the sky—they were eyes to equal at last the eyes of the German who stood before me with a bayonet . . ." (p. 38).

In the scene of copulation and sodomy with Ruta that follows, Rojack unleashes the new potency which the murder has liberated in him, and takes further revenge on Deborah. There is little freedom in this encounter, however—it is another of Rojack's compulsions. A mental command tells him he must go to the maid's room.

Ruta, the party girl from Berlin, is a totally erogenous creature, his inferior, a sex object for the expression of Rojack's will. Her name functions as a sexual pun on several levels: first, to rut or copulate; and second, as Kate Millett mentions, her name in German "refers both to the switch or birch of chastisement as well as to the penis."[32] "Root" is also a favorite Mailer term for the male genitals ("she reached with both hands, tried to find my root and mangle me"). So Ruta is a sexually ambiguous creature, a bisexual to please Rojack's contradictory sexual impulses. In the midst of making love to her, he imagines that she is a Nazi, calls her one, and even convinces himself of the fact against all reason, another instance of Rojack's projecting onto others the attributes that he wishes them to have. When he says, "There was a high private pleasure in plugging a Nazi, there was something clean despite all" (p. 44), he is back again with the murderous, homosexual assault on the German soldiers, still fighting desperately against his own castration. He converts Ruta mentally into a man, and then buggers her, justifying the buggery by the fact that she is a Nazi, so that his assault is no longer anal but somehow clean.

A quotation from Ernest Jones's analysis of *Hamlet* might illuminate the psychic mechanisms in operation here:

A feminine attitude toward the father presents itself as an attempted solution to the intolerable murderous and castrating impulses aroused by jealousy. These may persist, but when the fear of the self-castration implied gains the upper hand, i.e. when the masculine impulse is strong, the original aggression reasserts itself—but this time under the erotic guise of active homosexuality.[33]

Deborah had taken the place of father and mother for Rojack. Up until the murder, Rojack's relationship to her has been primarily subservient and masochistic. He adopted the role of a passive homosexual, submitting to anilingus from Deborah. Now his aggression reasserts itself, and he takes to buggery, or active, sadistic homosexuality, but in a disguised and ambivalent form with Ruta. As Denise tells Sergius in "The Time of Her Time," repeating the wisdom of her analyst, "'He told me your whole life is a lie, and you do nothing but run away from the homosexual that is you'" (*ADV*, p. 503).

Rojack's ambivalence toward the vagina and the anus is subsumed under the metaphysical construct of God and the Devil, good and evil. The vagina "leads to the creation" (*AD*, p. 44), and so presumably to God, but he associates the anus with the Devil: "there was canny hard-packed evil in that butt . . ." (p. 44). Rojack desires to associate with evil now, for he wants to absorb Ruta's guile, "the wit to trick authority" (pp. 44–45), which he will need to evade punishment for the crime he has just committed. As Deborah says,

"'I'm evil if truth be told. But I despise it, truly I do. It's just that evil has power'" (p. 36).

Beyond this concern with good and evil, however, is the notion of the vagina, and consequently lovemaking with a view toward procreation, as the penultimate good, and the anus, along with sodomy, as the acme of evil. In this respect, Mailer is quite conventional, even puritanical. The Devil is a homosexual villain. Rojack believes in "the swish of the devil" (p. 35), and his flirtation with Satan, with illicit power, and with the anus, is tantamount to homosexuality. When Rojack has his orgasm with Ruta, and chooses her anus over her vagina, he "comes" to the Devil. The final judgment on the encounter with Ruta is negative; it is infertile sex.

Chapter Two ends with Rojack pushing Deborah's body out the window. He experiences a sadistic, vicarious orgasm as she falls, "feeling the weight of her flight like a thrill in my chest, and heard a sound come up from the pavement all ten stories below, a flat, surprisingly loud and hollow thump . . ." (p. 52). There is a sublimated sexual, even excremental thrill in the drop for him (the elimination of dirt). Through Deborah, Rojack also reenacts the suicidal leap he was unable to take himself from his friend's balcony earlier in the evening. Moreover, Deborah had announced to Rojack during their quarrel that she was going to have him cremated after death and drop his ashes on the East River Drive. Now he retaliates by dropping *her* on the East River Drive.

One of Rojack's deepest anxieties is the fear of falling. This fear also operates in *The Naked and the Dead*, most notably in the scene in which Roth falls to his death. Fear of falling is symbolically equivalent to a fear of sexual activity (orgasm equals death) and to a fear of losing one's balance, one's mental self-control. "I had one of those anxieties which make it an act of balance to breathe," Rojack tells us, "too little air compresses the sensation of being throttled, but too much—one deep breath—and there is a fear of a fall" (p. 48). Waiting in the police station, he imagines death by the electric chair as the "long vertigo of a death which fell down endless stone walls" (p. 87). Confronting Shago's switchblade is likened to "standing on the edge of a high cliff, one's stomach sucking out of one, as one's eyes went down the fall" (p. 186). But by the logic of counterphobia, which commands him "That which you fear most is what you must do" (p. 203), he finds his last and most deadly test walking the stone parapets of his father-in-law's balcony, teetering above a thirty-six story fall. Like Marion Faye in *The Deer Park*, Rojack is *compelled* to do those things he most fears: the anxiety substitutes for sex.

After telephoning the authorities to report Deborah's "suicide," Rojack once more makes love to Ruta, as if to compensate her for the anal intercourse they had earlier. Since everything that his body emits he believes is holy (or diabolic), Rojack feels certain that every woman desires to be impregnated by his sperm, and must feel cheated when their lovemaking does not result in a child. This narcissistic overvaluation of bodily products is yet another characteristic of his anal eroticism. To his disappointment, he never had a child by Deborah to prove his potency, and his possible child by Cherry dies when she does. In the course of the novel, the restoration of Rojack's potency becomes an issue of symbolic, indeed almost cosmic, importance.

When he arrives on the street below, Rojack finds that Deborah's body has collided with a car, resulting in a mysterious chain of events. Those in the car detained by the police are Eddie Ganucci, a Mafia chief long sought by the law, his nephew Tony, operator of a nightclub, and Cherry, a blonde singer from that nightclub. Ganucci is later revealed to have close connections with Barney Kelly, Rojack's father-in-law. Cherry, with whom Rojack will have an affair, has also had intimate associations with Kelly—she had been his mistress. The characters in *Barbary Shore* and *The Deer Park* were connected by a daisy chain of sexual relationships, and so are those in *An American Dream*, but there is an added element now. Like the characters in a Dickens novel, the people in *An American Dream* are linked together by a vast and magical web of coincidences,[34] an interlocking system of events that seems to have cosmic significance. Mailer utilizes the patterns of irrational, even paranoid thought to give the novel all the magical reverberations of myth, dream, or fairy tale. The plot of *An American Dream* is a cosmic conspiracy in which every thread ties Rojack to Kelly, the ogre father.

Now that Deborah is dead, Cherry shows a maternal concern for Rojack: "'You poor man, your face is covered with blood,' she said . . . she took out a handkerchief and dabbed at my cheek. 'It must have been so awful,' she said. A subtle hard-headed ever-so-guarded maternity lay under the pressure with which she scrubbed the handkerchief at my face" (p. 61). Yet there are disturbing signs in this first encounter. Her eyes are "an astonishing green-golden-yellow in color (the eyes of an ocelot)" (p. 61). Deborah also had green eyes. Is Cherry yet another predatory mother, this time an ocelot instead of a snake, lion, bull, or boar? Cherry also has an "almost masculine voice" (p. 61), and her nose turns up "with just the tough tilt of a speedboat planing through the water" (p. 61).

In the same episode, Rojack meets Roberts, the detective. Significantly, Roberts comes upon him from behind, while Rojack is kneeling over the body of Deborah. Allan J. Wagenheim notes how Rojack sees all authorities as alike, all corrupt and out to get him.[35] Now Roberts also takes the place of Deborah. "I had an uneasy sense of Roberts which was not unlike the uneasy sense I used to have of Deborah" (p. 60). And "sitting next to me Roberts gave off the physical communion one usually receives from a woman" (p. 62). O'Brien, another detective, smells reminiscent of both the fat Nazi homosexual and Deborah. "A sort of fat sweet corruption emanated from him" (p. 67). Again, like the "faggot," his odor is "oversweet" (p. 74). Deborah fights "like a prep-school bully" (p. 30), and O'Brien has "the funk a bully emits" (p. 74). The character descriptions tend to fall into stereotypical patterns. Their repetition suggests that they are all components of a single authority figure—bisexual, rotten, and murderous—and that it is really this central fantasy figure who is Rojack's persecutor. Furthermore, because this is very nearly a monodrama, with the other characters existing primarily as projections of Rojack's unconscious fears and desires, it is also possible that this malevolent figure is only a paranoid re-creation of everything that Rojack most fears in himself: the violence, the filth, and the homosexuality.

When Roberts questions him, Rojack projects all his motives into Deborah. He feels suicidal, he believes he is possessed by vile demons inside himself, he fears cancer and wants to jump, and he unhesitatingly gives these as Deborah's motives for suicide. Rojack puts his own words in Deborah's mouth—"'I didn't have cancer before. But in that hour I stood by the window, it began in me. I didn't jump and so my cells jumped'" (p. 70).

This strange cancer phobia may be related to Rojack's other unconscious concerns. Erik Erikson believes that an anal fixation "finds its adult expression in paranoiac fears concerning hidden persecutors and secret persecutions threatening from behind (and from within the behind)."[36] Psychoanalytic theory relates cancer phobia to an internalized conflict: the psyche punishes itself, which is safer than punishing the hated person. This is felt by the neurotic as a generalized fear of being attacked from inside, that is, eaten by cancer.[37]

In someone fixated at the anal state, the unconscious equation becomes: retained feces = retained hatred = cancer. Retention of feces (emotion) results in cancer; excretion becomes symbolically equivalent to acting out hatred. Both are dangerous: on the one hand, there is emotional impotence and the conversion of the insides into rot; on the other hand, there is the violent expulsion of hatred.[38] In *An American Dream*, Mailer *reifies* unconscious processes, so that the psychic equation becomes real, as when Rojack witnesses the autopsy of an old man who has died from cancer:

> Some take the madness and stop it with discipline. Madness is locked beneath. It goes into the tissues, is swallowed by the cells. The cells go mad. Cancer is the growth of madness denied. In that corpse I saw, madness went down to the blood—leucocytes gorged the liver, the spleen, the enlarged heart and violet-black lungs, dug into the intestines, germinated stench. (p. 267)

Just as Rojack projects his cancer phobia onto Deborah, there are a disproportionate number of characters in *An American Dream* plagued with internal disorders: characters like Ganucci suffering from cancer of the bowels; ulcerous detectives, belching and farting. Besides the numerous threats from outside, there is also the danger of rebellion from inside. Ganucci symbolizes for Rojack the terrors of old age, impotence, and rot from within. On one occasion, as he is climbing the stairs to Cherry's apartment Rojack says, "the stench of slum plumbing gave a terror of old age—how ill is illness, how vile the suggestion of villainous old bowels. . . . 'Fail here at love,' said the odor, 'and you get closer to subsisting like me'" (p. 121–2).

Failure in love is still Rojack's primary fear as he pursues Cherry. He decides not to confess in the police station, because he has "a horror of appearing feeble before that young blonde girl" (p. 87). Listening to her sing in the nightclub, Rojack confesses, "I had a fear of the singer," for he believes that "women must murder us unless we possess them altogether . . ." (p. 100). He has a "dread of the judgment which must rest behind the womb of a woman" (p. 119), so in retaliation he sends a psychic arrow into her womb.

Allan J. Wagenheim believes that his arrow is an attempt by Rojack to destroy Cherry's threatening and destructive power as a woman and mother, "whereas the qualities in Cherry which attract him point up the correlative condition which usually accompanies fear of the castrating mother-wife: the homosexual alternative. . . . Rojack is unconsciously seeking the ultimate orgasm with a non-woman."[39] This assertion seems plausible, considering the sexual ambiguity of the encounter with Ruta, and the suggestions of masculinity in the description of Cherry earlier. Now in the nightclub, the suggestion is reinforced. Cherry looks a bit "like the little boy next door. A clean tough decent little American boy . . ." (p. 97). She has a "delicate boy-girl face" (p. 99), a hint of the androgynous in her character. At various times, her face takes on the look of "a rock-hard little jockey" (p. 124) and a soldier (p. 110). The dichotomy is further defined by Rojack. "I seemed to feel not one presence in her, but two, an ash-blonde young lady of lavender shadows . . . a woman with a body one might never be allowed to see in the sun, and then the other girl, healthy as a farmer . . ." (p. 108). Wagenheim identifies the lavender lady, "the unattainable woman of mystery whose body will never be seen" as "the mother, that part of the female he fears." The other part is "more boy than girl—'healthy as a farmer'—and therefore less threatening."[40]

Roberts warns Rojack away from Cherry, saying, "'Know who she is?'" Rojack replies jestingly, "'Poison, pure poison'" (p. 112). Ironically, this remark reminds us of Deborah, whose poisonous fangs seemed to inject venom into Rojack at the moment of orgasm (p. 34). Cherry is the mother as deadly snake, the mother confused with the father once again.

Rojack pursues Cherry because she provides a new challenge to his courage, and he constantly requires new challenges. He is compelled to pursue the mother, even though in courting her he knows he is courting death. He justifies the hunt to himself as a masochistic affirmation of his manhood. Now he must fight off several men to get to her, as in a fantasy of rescuing the mother from peril. Throughout the nightclub sequence, Rojack acts compulsively and feels a manic exhilaration in the omnipotence of his thought. He shoots mental arrows at people and registers the results. "Something" in Rojack's mind decides that he must face down Cherry's prizefighter boyfriend, so Rojack butts into the conversation in a pushy way guaranteed to get him into trouble. Grace Witt writes that Rojack "thrives on a sense of danger; if that danger does not exist, it must be created. . . ."[41] This necessity to create a threat makes critic Leo Bersani wonder "to what extent Mailer's own sense of himself has depended on his ability to provoke attack,"[42] that is to say, on counterphobia.

In the nightclub scene, and the other scenes with Cherry, Mailer is at his most romantic, sophomoric, and embarrassing, and the narrative sags. It is difficult to believe that Rojack's drunken witticisms would enchant Cherry, and it is also difficult to believe in Cherry as a character, the whore-with-a-heart-of-gold. Maybe Mailer is better as a woman-hater, creating females who are masterpieces of meanness and bitchery, such as Denise Gondelman, rather than wallowing in daydreams of love at first sight. Or perhaps his excessive romanticism about women is only the other side of his excessive hostility.

After making love with Cherry, Rojack must return to the unending warfare of the city streets, that paranoid vision in which "there was ambush everywhere" (p. 131). In a passage in the *Esquire* magazine version of the novel, Rojack compares his affair with Cherry to love on a three-day pass. As one critic writes, "The grace to which Rojack aspires was first revealed to him—as it was lost—in the Second World War, and much of Mailer's dreaming is the creation of a civilian landscape as energetic and dangerous as the military one. . . ."[43]

On his way from Cherry's to his apartment, traveling uptown in a cab, Rojack fights the compulson to go drinking again. He seems to need alcohol to fuel him for each new stage of his adventures. Probably not since Charles Jackson's *The Lost Weekend* has there been an American novel with more continuous boozing than *An American Dream*. As Mailer once asserted, "You drink to fill yourself up . . . I drink when I feel empty."[44] Liquor is "blood" to Rojack (p. 14), a transfusion, a sort of oral acquisition of potency. He must constantly steel himself by refueling, because all the anxiety of his encounters is draining him dry. There is "ambush everywhere" for Rojack, traps both external and internal. Each bar seems to have been placed there for his personal temptation.

The next assault that Rojack receives is a series of phone calls, first from the television station and next from the chairman of his department at the University, terminating his connection with these institutions. Both authorities are treated satirically, as apologetic, equivocating, and essentially corrupt conformists. Arthur, the television official, is another version of Collie Munshin of *The Deer Park*, a comic, phony, shameless hustler. Since Mailer's heroes are usually consumed with shame, they cannot help but admire the apparent shamelessness of their enemies.

On the unconscious level, these conversations represent another homosexual assault on Rojack by the authorities. He feels like "the French had felt when the Nazis invaded the Maginot line from the rear . . ." (p. 141). Rojack is now cut off from all institutional, societal (that is to say, parental) support, stripped of all the status he had used to define himself before. He is a free agent who must exist on his own, nourished by raw, elemental instincts and defenses. The question remains: will he have the strength to stand alone?

Following his conversation with these impotent and yet menacing authorities, Rojack goes to a meeting with Detective Roberts. Thus far, Roberts has been the kindly father. He stopped the beating of a suspect in the police station, and when Rojack was threatened in the squad car by Detectives Leznicki and O'Brien, Roberts heeded Rojack's request to "call off these hoodlums" (p. 75). This last scene is remarkably reminiscent of an incident in *The Naked and the Dead*, when Lieutenant Hearn evidences his "father-dependency" by relying on General Cummings to rescue him from the two colonels who are menacing him.

But like Cummings, Roberts is ambivalent and also has his dark, violent, and aggressive side. This particular afternoon, Roberts has taken on some of the oversweet smell of his bully O'Brien (p. 152), which means that Rojack can expect another disguised homosexual assault. Roberts proceeds to browbeat Rojack, presenting him with the evidence of his guilt in Deborah's death and demanding Rojack's immediate confession. Rojack is terrified of prison, which represents for him a final surrender to his homosexual potentialities. In a passage from the *Esquire* version Rojack imagines himself in prison: "I would lie in a cell at night with nothing to do but walk a stone square floor and dream through heats of desire for one of the girls in the men's wing of the prison, one of those girls with all but a woman's body (and a man's organs). . . ." [45]

The last and most damning piece of evidence that Roberts presents to Rojack is the state of Deborah's large intestine. The autopsy had shown a relaxation of her sphincter muscle, indicating her strangulation prior to the fall, and the detectives later discovered traces of fecal matter on her clothes and on the bedroom carpet. Rojack has prepared a flimsy alibi that Deborah was "unbalanced" (p. 157), soiled herself and the carpet while he was in the room, and then jumped out the window because of shame. He even halfway believes this himself: "this imaginary account now had the vividness of the real" (p. 157). In the *Esquire* version, Rojack has Deborah saying "'I can't control anything any more.'" He also refers to the "infantile reversion, the fecal horror," and "the hysteria of strength with which I cleaned the carpet as if I must protect her good name." [46]

In earlier scenes, Rojack projected his own worst fears, such as his fear of cancer, onto Deborah as motives for her suicide. The terror that Rojack projects now onto Deborah is his fear of losing his balance, of a loss of self-control evidenced in the loss of sphincter control. All this reinforces the notion that one of Rojack's deepest fears is an anal anxiety, a primitive, childlike terror of having no control over one's body: "the infantile reversion, the fecal horror."

Indeed, it is on the basis of the "fecal horror" that Rojack is about to be convicted. As if by magic, Kelly chooses this moment to phone police headquarters, ordering the pressure lifted from Rojack. The all-powerful father is protecting Rojack, or perhaps only preserving him for a grimmer fate, just as General Cummings in *The Naked and the Dead* toyed with Lieutenant Hearn.

V

Now Rojack must see Kelly at midnight, and he dreads this assignation more than any other encounter in the novel—even more than the interrogation by the police. There is a strange displacement of anxiety in this novel onto irrational causes, so that what Rojack fears most is not a guilty verdict for murder but the moon, falling from a height, or getting cancer. Aside from these phobias, he is scared of his wife and his father-in-law, who obviously must be stand-ins for the real objects of his fear, the parents. But in the self-contained, irrational logic of this novel, magic rules and metaphors become real. The action really takes place inside the mind of the narrator, and so we accept Rojack's vivid fears as real to him. In a cab on the way downtown from the police to Cherry's, Rojack hears a wind outside, "and it had the long ripping round of a voracious wind at sea which tears off the water and snatches at the roots of the grass . . . I could all but sniff the sour rot of clotting blood in the pits of this wind" (p. 162). Even the wind, the environment itself, is another foul, emasculating predator, another embodiment of Deborah and Kelly.

Once Rojack returns downtown, Cherry reveals to him that Kelly had been her "sugar-daddy" for several years. We have already discovered that Ruta is Kelly's mistress, and there are hints of incest (later confirmed) between Deborah and Kelly. The pattern is becoming clear: every woman that Rojack becomes involved with has already been possessed by Kelly. Rojack seems doomed to play second-string to the father figure. A. Alvarez notes this "curious, undiscussed thread in the narrative," and sees in it some explanation for Rojack's sexual exhibitionism, which "has about it a compulsive desperation that flows pure from infantile sources: as who should say, 'However omnipotent and overpowering Daddy is, you *shall* take notice of me.'"[47]

Rojack has been long enough without a threat; as if on cue, Shago Martin enters and attempts to evict Rojack from Cherry's apartment. Shago is a man to fear, a black stud (in line with the sexual puns in the nomenclature of the novel, there is the suggestion of "to shag" or copulate). He even had the strength to defy Deborah once.

Rojack and Shago have followed reverse routes: Rojack is becoming more of a "White Negro" whereas Shago is turning into a negroid white. Ironically, Shago has earned a television program on the same channel and in the time slot vacated by Rojack. Since killing Deborah, Rojack has dropped out of the world of the Square into the psychic underworld, and one of his prizes is Cherry, Shago's ex-mistress.

Allan J. Wagenheim feels that Shago is symbolically the Devil (he speaks in tongues, he is a prince in his territory, prince of darkness), and that Rojack "must possess Shago, just as he possessed Deborah, and thus acquire his power," the supposedly primitive, phallic power of the black man.[48] (Sexist and racist myth rules in this novel, as Mailer presumes it rules the American unconscious.) In another sense, Rojack and Shago are psychic doubles. Both are anally sadistic. (Shago's initials "S. M.," suggest sado-masochism). Both stand up to Deborah, and both woo Cherry. Finally, it is Shago who is murdered at the end in place of Rojack.

The confrontation with Shago, like the battle with the Germans, had deliberate overtones of overt homosexuality: "I took him from behind" (p. 192). As Rojack tosses Shago down the stairs, he catches "a smell of full nearness as if we'd been in bed for an hour" (p. 193). Wagenheim says that "Rojack is painfully close to the truth about himself which he still cannot accept—that he is a latent homosexual, and that Shago is the lover he desires."[49]

Beneath this scene is the "regressive fantasy" which Leslie Fiedler accuses Mailer of indulging in *An American Dream*: "flirting with the possibility of getting into bed with papa."[50] In Fiedler's opinion, Shago is not the lover Rojack desires, but merely a projection of Rojack, one of his "Bad Brothers."[51] If so, then all the violent acts that are facsimiles of homosexuality are only sublimations of the latent desire to submit homosexually to the power of the father. This is a theme developed in Mailer's works from the very beginning, in the ambivalent relationship between General Cummings and Lieutenant Hearn, with its implications of homosexual overtures. It is an aspect of all the power relationships between men in Mailer's novels. As Fenichel theorizes, "Vacillation between the original masculine attitude, now reinforced and exaggerated by the active-sadistic component of anal eroticism, and the feminine attitude represented by the passive component of anal eroticism forms the most typical conflict in the unconscious of the male compulsion neurotic."[52] Both the desire to submit to the father and the desire to rebel against the father are exaggerated in Rojack into a tremendous ambivalence and constant anxiety about homosexuality. Paradoxically, he seems to be trying to deny his homoerotic urges even as he acts them out in the murder of the Germans, the rape of Ruta, and the battle with Shago.

This brings us to the encounter with Kelly: the entire action has been moving toward this confrontation; Rojack has been avoiding facing his father-in-law throughout the novel. The sustained dread now rises to a fever pitch in Rojack, and he is swayed by contradictory impulses, one voice telling him to go to Harlem and take his punishment there for what he has done to Shago, another voice commanding him to keep the appointment with Kelly at the Waldorf Towers. Rojack is torn between two hells, but decides to visit Kelly's inferno, drawn by the authority of counterphobia: "That which you fear most is what you must do" (p. 203). He had committed symbolic incest with the mother and murdered her, cuckolded the father a second and a third time with Ruta and Cherry, and he had managed to evade the father's underlings; now he must do battle directly with the ogre himself.

The lobby is filled with policemen, and even the elevator operator studies Rojack "like a police matron" (p. 207). Rojack feels flooded with panic. The visit to Kelly is laden with overtones of a descent into the inferno, the lobby of the Waldorf as "the antechamber of Hell" (p. 206).

Kelly's coat of arms is also redolent with symbolic meaning: a lion rampant and a serpent devouring an infant. Snake and lion metaphors are used throughout the novel to suggest Kelly's and Deborah's predatory instincts, and the symbol of the serpent eating the naked babe is an overloaded castration image. When Kelly greets Rojack, he wraps him in his arms like a serpent coiling itself around its prey, and the embrace even reminds Rojack of making love with the treacherous, man-eating Deborah.

There follows a succession of images in which Kelly is likened to Deborah, father to mother, Dracula to "Dracula's wife" (p. 214). His smell, with "a hint of a big foul cat," mixed with "a witch's curse" is "all of Deborah" for Rojack. His face is like Deborah's, and his presence is more real to Rojack "as an embodiment of Deborah than of himself" (p. 217). Father and mother seem to merge into a bisexual authority figure who threatens Rojack, just as Roberts earlier appeared to metamorphose into Deborah.

Kelly as ogre father has certain resemblances to General Cummings of *The Naked and the Dead*. Mailer writes about Cummings, "His expression when he smiled was very close to the ruddy, complacent and hard appearance of any number of American senators and businessmen" (*ND*, p. 81), whereas Kelly "gave off the fortified good humor which is to be found in the company of generals, tycoons, politicians, admirals, newspaper publishers, presidents, and prime ministers" (*AD*, p. 219). Both men have cold, gray eyes. Both Kelly and Cummings have frigid, bitchy wives, both are enormously successful, and both seem to be latent homosexuals. Both tempt and dare the young heroes, Hearn and Rojack. Mailer's attitude toward those in power in American society has not changed very much over seventeen years; they are still conceived in Faustian, romantic terms, only now their demonic power has increased. From the exaggeration in the depiction of Cummings, Mailer has taken the leap into the super-realism of Kelly, who operates by magic and telepathy. Nevertheless, both are omnipotent and corrupt Father Figures, variations on the same character.

Just as thoughts of Deborah brought out the impulse to suicide in Rojack, so the meeting with Kelly forces him once more to flirt with jumping. The urge to suicide is still in Rojack. According to psychoanalytic theory, sometimes "an obsession does not provide the avoidance of what was originally feared but compels the person to do just that which he was originally afraid of. . . . Fear of high places may be supplanted by the obsessive impulse to jump down."[53] The original, terrifying impulse in Rojack is incest and parricide. In order to suppress that desire, whenever it occurs Rojack forces himself to think of the most incapacitating terror he knows, acrophobia. As the original impulse to murder the parents grows stronger, the defense against that impulse, the urge to jump to suicide, also grows stronger.

Rojack leaves Kelly's apartment to stride along the parapet on the terrace while Bess and Ganucci are inside conversing. Bess, an evil and powerful old witch, aged and yet still handsome, and Ganucci, the corrupt old Mafioso dying of cancer, are another set of symbolic parents for Rojack, another seductive and dangerous mother and another powerful and foul old man. Rojack cannot stand being in the same room with them; some impulse he does not comprehend makes him retreat to the terrace, and yet another impulse brings up the notion of jumping. The unconscious thought that is the basis of this compulsion seeps through: "I had a thought then to get up and stand on the parapet, as if to dare the desire by coming closer to it would be logical, and the dread which followed this thought had a pure thrill like the moment in adolescence when one realizes one is finally going to get it—get sex—but what a fear! I was trembling" (p. 224). It is possible now to trace the unconscious logic behind the obsession that has been troubling Rojack all along. First, he thinks, "I could make love to my mother, and possibly also my father." Then the mind instantly responds with terror—"No, they would destroy me! And making love to my father means being a homosexual. I must protect myself by killing them." To prevent him from killing them, his mind orders him to kill himself instead.

The final line of defense against incest is cancer. If Rojack fails to jump, he is positive he will get cancer, that is, the repressed aggression will turn against him and his very insides will rebel. As Mailer writes in *The Presidential Papers*, "the right to destroy oneself is also one of the inalienable rights. . . . It is possible that many people take heroin because they sense unconsciously that if they did not, they would be likely to commit murder, get cancer, or turn homosexual."[54] He puts these three ideas together as if they are somehow linked.

In Rojack, the whole convoluted process of logic that leads from incest to parricide to suicide by jumping to cancer is designed to conceal and defend against the original impulse. Consequently, the command that emerges at the end of this chain of unconscious logic is isolated, treated as though it were delivered into his mind by some alien messenger. Nevertheless, when he likens jumping to the thrill of his first sexual experience, Rojack leads us back along the tortuous chain of thought to the original basis in incestuous desire.

The strange commands that Rojack hears inside his head represent the superego acting as a cruel tyrant against the impulses of the id by regulating the actions of the ego. Both superego and id are cruel tyrants, so Rojack is never sure whether he is being possessed by the Lord or the Devil. There is actually little difference between them. There is a war going on for control of Rojack's mind; no wonder he feels as if he is living in a battlefield and exhibits all the symptoms of combat fatigue.

Kelly's extended monologue, in which he all but admits to incest with Deborah, is another instance of Rojack's projecting his anxieties. Just as Shago was a kind of double for Rojack, Kelly proves to be much like Rojack, ambitious and extremely power-hungry. Both are sons of immigrants, and both rise in social status by marriage to wealthy debutantes.

In particular, both men are obsessed by incestuous desires. In a scene that parallels Rojack's death wish on the balcony, Kelly describes how he felt visited by the Devil, who urged him to commit incest with Deborah. Kelly begged the Lord to deliver him, and immediately felt a powerful impulse to go to the window and jump. Unable to jump, in fear and trembling, he decided instead to send Deborah back to the convent, and the compulsion disappeared.

The father, in other words, acts out the incestuous desires of the son. Kelly's compulsion to jump is the same as Rojack's. The parallelism is so obvious that it seems deliberately built in, like the phallic symbolism of Shago's umbrella. It is impossible to say, however, how far this conscious choice, control, and awareness of the material go below the manifest, thematic levels. The regularity and repetition of the themes and metaphors show that, far from being carelessly thrown together, as some critics suggest, *An American Dream* is a very carefully planned and elaborated work. If anything, it is overdetermined and overcontrolled, even schematic at times, but this may be a defense against the sex and violence of the subject matter.

Kelly's confession of incest allows Rojack to feel morally superior: he has only murdered, but the father has committed incest. " 'Yes, I killed her,' I said, 'but I didn't seduce her when she was fifteen, and never leave her alone, and never end the affair' " (p. 253). Of course, this does not account for Rojack's ambivalent feelings toward his stepdaughter Deirdre, whom he is afraid to see because he loves her too much. Against his will, Rojack finally visits Deirdre in her bedroom at Kelly's apartment.

Again, Rojack projects his evil desires onto Kelly when he imagines that Kelly is inviting him to

> bring Ruta forth, three of us to pitch and tear and squat and lick, swill and grovel on that Lucchese bed, fuck until our eyes were out, bury the ghost of Deborah by gorging on her corpse, for this had been the bed, yes, this Lucchese had been the bed where he went out with Deborah to the tarpits of the moon. . . . (p. 254)

Wagenheim mentions that Kelly never says this; Rojack thinks it is on Kelly's mind and attributes the invitation to him.[55] The appeal is to participate in the primal scene, and indulge in all the perversions that have been on Rojack's mind throughout the novel: incest with both father and mother, parricide, coprophilia, and cannibalism, the contents of his id spilled out in a single vision of an uninhibited family orgy where all his oral, anal, and genital desires can be released with the blessings of a benevolent father.

The rational part of Rojack rebels against all this, however. "For I wanted to escape from that intelligence which let me know of murders in one direction and conceive of visits to Cherry from the other, I wanted to be free of magic, the tongue of the Devil, the dread of the Lord . . ." (p. 255). According to Karl Abraham, the obsessional neurotic carries on a constant struggle against unconsciously wishing to commit the primal crime of killing and eating the father: "His morbid anxiety bears witness on the one hand to the impulse to do that deed, and on the other, to the yet more powerful inhibition of his criminal impulses."[56]

Now Rojack picks up the umbrella-phallus he won from Shago and the message comes through to walk the parapet or else Cherry is dead. Once more, the only way he can conquer his desire to commit incest and murder is by countering it with the fear of heights and thoughts of suicide.

Rojack's trip along the parapet thirty-six stories up is one of the most intense and anxiety-provoking scenes in a work laden with fear and trembling. Robert Langbaum calls the scene " a triumph of narration. Because we sweat it out with Rojack as wind, rain, and psychologically sensed supernatural forces . . . threaten to dislodge him, we believe in the importance of this ordeal, that it is his Purgatory, his penance and way to salvation."[57]

As a religious allegory, since Kelly is the Devil, Rojack's ordeal relates to the temptation of Christ by Satan to cast himself from the heights and thus prove his power. This is in line with other Christian symbolism in the novel—it takes place in March and concerns a hero who is persecuted and reborn. Mailer translates psychic warfare into metaphors of spiritual warfare.

In terms of the plot structure, this stroll along the parapet toward the end of the novel balances against the first suicide attempt on the balcony toward the beginning of the novel.

In terms of the struggle between Rojack and Kelly, Rojack has now surpassed the father both sexually and morally, so the walk supposedly serves as the ultimate proof of his autonomy.

Finally, on the unconscious level, the description of the walk on the parapet is filled with the same images of anal and phallic impotence that dominate all of Mailer's novels. Rojack feels "exposed" as if he is "naked," he shivers "out of control" and almost weeps "like a child." The only thing that keeps him going is self-disgust and the memory of "revolting failure" (p. 257).

When Rojack is about to succeed, Kelly tries to push him off by poking him with Shago's umbrella. Rojack retaliates by whipping him across the face with the umbrella, symbolic of homosexual assault and patricide, once again justified as self-defense. Just as Rojack's sexual desire for Deborah was transformed into a murderous rage that was justified as self-defense, so his homosexual ambivalence toward Kelly is also converted into homicidal rage. Kelly does not die from the assault, but for Rojack it seems sufficient that he has proved himself more potent. Now Rojack tosses the guilty instrument, the umbrella, over the parapet. It is his substitute for either murdering the father or destroying himself.

The confrontation between Kelly and Rojack can best be understood, not as the contest of two fictional characters or even as the clash of two symbols but rather as one more episode of Rojack's inner warfare. The novel has been interpreted here as an account of Rojack's struggle for self-control. Kelly is then a part of Rojack, just as all the main characters are projections of the hero's fears and desires. Kelly is yet one more part of himself with which Rojack is unable to come to terms. Psychoanalytic theory postulates that in paranoid delusions the persecutor is equivalent to the homosexual object or the "narcissistically hypercathected and projected organ (feces, buttocks)" or the projected superego.[58] The superego itself has its basis in the internalized image of the parents. Kelly is thus at once persecutor, father figure, homosexual love object, and, symbolically, fecal matter. The ambivalence of Rojack's love/hatred for his own substance is projected onto Kelly; this helps to explain his fear and ambivalence toward Kelly.

The problem with the anal neurotic is that he treats others like shit because he treats himself like shit. Kelly manipulates Rojack throughout the novel as Rojack would like to manipulate others: excrementally. Consider how Kelly toys with Rojack, maintains his grip on him, and makes it quite clear that Rojack is in his power, that, as in the police station episode, he can put the squeeze on Rojack or release him at will. Kelly's power reaches very far; he can clamp down on people from a distance. When Rojack tries to set the time for an appointment, Kelly maintains control by naming the hour. As Rojack approaches the Waldorf Towers, he feels as if he were making a progress through a tunnel. When Kelly suggests that Rojack take a stroll around the parapet, Rojack feels a sense of compulsion. Kelly's tones "pushed me to answer. . . .and I only knew I was in some difficult all but inextricable situation in which he would succeed to push me further, and then further again . . ." (pp. 251–52). Rojack feels trapped in a tunnel or cavern, in some sort of inextricable situation, and imagines that he is being pushed. Kelly's final way of asserting his mastery is to order Rojack to balance on a point where he is in imminent danger of dropping to destruction. What Kelly really wants to do with Rojack is to control him and then *eliminate* him.

Now Rojack rushes downtown only to discover that his precognition has magically come true: both Shago and Cherry are dead. "By means of another murder (this time by proxy)," writes Wagenheim, "Rojack is free of another wife-mother who will someday, surely, make a grab for his sex-organs."[59] Shago, the Bad Brother, dies in Rojack's place, as punishment for incest and murder. Cherry must be killed off because Rojack never really wanted a clear field to her; he is terrified of the mother as much as he desires her. Possession of Cherry would only begin the cycle all over again, just as the Germans kept popping up like targets in a rifle gallery. As Melanie Klein writes:

> The pressure exerted by this early superego increases the sadistic fixations of the child, with the result that it has constantly to be repeating its original destructive acts in a compulsive way. Its fear of not being able to put things right again arouses its still

deeper fear of being exposed to the revenge of the objects whom in its imagination, it has killed and who keep on coming back again. . . .[60]

When Rojack entreats the police to let him see Cherry he says, " 'She's my wife, officer' " (p. 263), the same words he had used before when he demanded to see Deborah's corpse. The echo is deliberate; it gives the work the eerie reverberations of a recurrent nightmare. It also suggests an unconscious equation between the two women, for Rojack feels as responsible for the murder of Cherry as he was for that of Deborah. He seems to have the "kiss of death."

The scene with Roberts which follows reinforces all the underlying psychic themes of the novel. Roberts was first introduced as a threatening authority figure, a replacement for Deborah. Roberts is alternately protective and intimidating, but now he is a feminized father, "kind as a mother" to Rojack (p. 264). Under the influence of liquor, Roberts falls apart, cries, and confesses to cheating on his wife and beating up his mistress. He is yet another double for Rojack, corrupt and trapped in a cycle of failure and violence.

Measured against Roberts, Rojack now seems a man of integrity who has broken out of the trap of mediocrity by indulging to the full all the desires Roberts represses. Whether one takes Roberts as Rojack's double or as defeated father, Rojack seems triumphant by comparison, just as Sergius seemed stronger at the end of *The Deer Park* by comparison with the fallen idol Eitel.

At the beginning of the novel, Rojack destroys his persecutors, the German soldiers, who unconsciously stand for his own fears of anal and phallic impotence and for the revengeful father. Nevertheless, they continue to haunt him. At the end of the novel, Rojack sees the corpse of a cancer patient eviscerated on the autopsy table. This man has the same symbolic power as the Germans, and he too haunts Rojack: "he came back from phosphate fertilizer in every farmer's field, he rose out of every bump of a dead rabbit on the road, from each rotting ghost in the stump of a tree, he chose to come back later at every hint of a hole in emotion or a pit of decay . . ." (p. 266). The entire novel is a testimony to the power of the repressed, which must always return. For Rojack, there is no final escape from the rot.

VI

Just as the old man's corpse is the dead end of corruption in America, Las Vegas is the dead end for Rojack's vision of the jeweled city, an American paradise as a hell in the desert. Here, as else-where on his journey, Rojack is supernaturally lucky, but still he is denied the possibility of the love that will give his existence meaning. After a last flirtation with suicide and a fantasized phone call to Cherry, Rojack abandons the United States entirely, and flees south, beyond the desert to the primitive jungles of Guatemala and Yucatán in hope of a new life. He ends as a thwarted hero, who escapes from the pit of corruption and survives after all the other characters are destroyed and defeated, but who still is denied what he really wants. As the novel concludes, his long trip is just begin-ning.

Besides being the anxiety dream of an obsessional neurotic named Rojack, who can never possess both autonomy and the mother love he wants, *An American Dream* is a particularly American odyssey about a nation whose myths hold out infinite promise that can never be delivered, infantile delusions of power that can never be fulfilled.

At the beginning of the novel, Rojack has attained "The American Dream," but he is still totally dependent for his power on Kelly and Deborah, the Devil and his mate, father and mother: "probably I did not have enough strength to stand alone" (p. 18). It is, as he admits, "a devil's contract" (p. 18), a Faustian bargain. Deborah controls his very "substance"; when he leaves her, it is as if "all of my substance fell out of me" (p. 19). This very undependable substance is symbolically fecal matter, that original and most ambivalently loved object. Deborah as mother regulates his move-ments; in his struggle for autonomy, Rojack retaliates by treating her like feces, as something valuable, to be held onto as long as possible, and then as something hateful and vile, to be constricted (strangled), and then eliminated.

Mailer once said in an interview that "a great writer has to be capable of knowing the rot, he has to be able to strip it down to the stink, but he also has to love that rot."[61] In *An American Dream*, *everything* stinks, including the American dream and the hero himself. But Rojack secretly loves that rot. How is one to attain self-control and purity in a uniformly corrupt world? A total purga-tion is impossible for Rojack, for that would mean self-destruction. The substitute is the destruction of the love objects. As Shago Martin tells him, " 'That's S.M. Shit on Mother' " (p. 184).

Mailer puts us inside Rojack's mind as he battles for self-control and autonomy, battles to free his soul from its contract with the Devil (to escape from the parents), using diabolic wiles in order to overpower Satan. But the heroic contest is also an internal struggle of Rojack against himself: he must excrete the Devil within himself by acting out his most powerful instincts.

In the psychological monodrama that is *An American Dream*, Rojack is a sort of war correspondent reporting on the civil war inside himself. He feels compelled to push his obsessions to the limits and beyond in order to test himself, gaining masochistic pleasure from his own anxiety. Like Rojack on the parapet, the novel maintains unslacking tension, a dynamic balance on the narrow borderline between pleasure and pain, love and hate, heaven and hell. As in *The Naked and the Dead*, Mailer manages by the end of the novel to exhaust both hero and reader from combat fatigue.

And so Rojack tries and fails, because ultimately the struggle is within, a struggle for total control of the self. This chapter began with the beginning of *The Naked and the Dead*; now we return to the close of that novel:

> Croft kept looking at the mountain. He had lost it, had missed some tantalizing revelation of himself.
> Of himself and much more. Of life.
> Everything. (*ND*, p. 709)

Toward the end of *American Dream*, we also find Rojack looking up at a goal he cannot win:

> The night before I left Las Vegas I walked out in the desert to look at the moon. There was a jewelled city on the horizon, spires rising in the night, but the jewels were diadems of electric and the spires were the neon of signs ten stories high. I was not good enough to climb up and pull them down. (*AD*, P. 269)

Notes

1. John W. Aldridge, "The Energy of New Success," in *Norman Mailer: A Collection of Critical Essays*, ed. Leo Braudy (Englewood Cliffs, N.J.: Prentice-Hall, 1972), p. 118.

2. Robert Solotaroff, *Down Mailer's Way* (Urbana, Ill.: University of Illinois, 1974), pp. 131–33.

3. Max F. Schulz, *Radical Sophistication* (Athens: Ohio University, 1969), p. 30–31.

4. Richard Poirier, "Morbid-Mindedness," in *Norman Mailer: The Man and His Work*, ed. Robert F. Lucid (Boston: Little, Brown and Company, 1971), pp. 164–65.

5. Aldridge, "Energy of New Success," p. 118.

6. Allan J. Wagenheim, "Square's Progress: *An American Dream*," *Critique* 10 (1966); 53.

7. Norman Mailer, *St. George and the Godfather* (New York: New American Library, 1972), p. 86.

8. Otto Fenichel, *The Psychoanalytic Theory of Neurosis* (New York: Norton, 1945), p. 160.

9. Ibid., p. 306.

10. Norman Mailer, *The Presidential Papers* (New York: Putnam's, 1963), p. 38.

11. Leo Braudy, "The Pride of Vulnerability," in *Norman Mailer*, ed. Braudy, p. 14.

12. Fenichel, *Neurosis*, p. 270.

13. Melanie Klein, *Contributions to Psychoanalysis* (London: Hogarth Press, 1948), p. 318.

14. Benjamin DeMott, "Docket No. 15883," *The American Scholar* 30 (Spring 1961): 234.

15. See Fenichel, *Neurosis*, p. 297. Typical conflicts of compulsion neurosis are "conflicts of masculinity versus femininity (bisexuality), of love versus hate (ambivalence), and especially of id (instinctual demands) versus superego (demands of conscience)."

16. Howard Silverstein, "Norman Mailer: The Family Romance and the Oedipal Fantasy," *American Imago* 34, No. 3 (Fall 1977): 284–86.

17. Timothy Evans, "Boiling the Archetypal Pot: Norman Mailer's American Dream," *Southwest Review* 60 (Spring 1975): 160.

18. Raymond A. Schroth, "Mailer and His Gods," *Commonweal*, May 9, 1969, p. 227.

19. Kate Millett, *Sexual Politics* (New York: Doubleday, 1970), p. 318.

20. Peter Shaw, "The Tough Guy Intellectual," *Critical Quarterly* 8 (Spring 1966): 13–28.

21. Millett, *Sexual Politics*, p. 332.

22. Norman Mailer, *The Prisoner of Sex* (Boston: Little Brown and Company, 1971), pp. 137, 153–54.

23. Evans, "Boiling the Archetypal Pot," 163–64.

24. Robert Langbaum, *The Modern Spirit: Essays on the Continuity of Nineteenth and Twentieth-Century Literature* (New York: Oxford, 1970), p. 156.

25. Solotaroff, *Mailer's Way*, p. 155.

26. Fenichel, *Neurosis*, p. 300.

27. Wagenheim, "Square's Progress," 48.

28. Ibid.

29. Anthony Burgess, *The Novel Now* (New York: Norton, 1967), p. 51.

30. Fenichel, *Neurosis*, p. 278.

31. Aldridge, "Energy of New Success," p. 118.

32. Millett, *Sexual Politics*, p. 12.

33. Ernest Jones, "The Death of Hamlet's Father," in *Art and Psychoanalysis*, ed. William Phillips, (Cleveland: World Publishing Co., 1967), p. 150.

34. Donald L. Kaufmann, *Norman Mailer: The Countdown* (Carbondale: Southern Illinois University, 1969) p. 36.

35. Wagenheim, "Square's Progress," p. 52.

36. Erik H. Erikson, *Childhood and Society*, 2D. ed. (New York: Norton, 1963), p. 254.

37. Fenichel, *Neurosis*, p. 398.

38. The impulse toward coprophagia, the secret desire to reincorporate one's evil substance, is an outgrowth of this ambivalence and anxiety toward feces. See the chapter on *Why Are We in Vietnam?*

39. Wagenheim, "Square's Progress," 55.

40. Ibid., p. 54.

41. Grace Witt, "The Bad Man as Hipster: Norman Mailer's Use of the Frontier Metaphor," *Western American Literature* 4 (Fall 1969): 215.

42. Leo Bersani, "The Interpretation of Dreams," *Partisan Review* 32 (Fall 1965): 604.

43. Jonathan Middlebrook, *Mailer and the Time of His Times* (San Francisco, Calif., Bay Books, 1976), p. 123.

44. On "The Dick Cavett Show," 14 January 1971.

45. *Esquire* (March 1964), p. 148.

46. *Esquire* (May 1964), p. 150.

47. A. Alvarez, "Norman X," *Spectator*, May 7, 1965, p. 603.

48. Wagenheim, "Square's Progress," 59.

49. Ibid.

50. Leslie Fiedler, "The New Mutants," *Partisan Review* 32 (Fall 1965): 518.

51. Leslie Fiedler, "Master of Dreams," *Partisan Review* 34 (Summer 1967): 353.

52. Fenichel, *Neurosis*, p. 277.

53. Ibid., pp. 268–69.

54. Mailer, *Presidential Papers*, p. 12.

55. Wagenheim, "Square's Progress," 63.

56. Karl Abraham, *Selected Papers of Karl Abraham* (London: Hogarth Press, 1949), p. 475.

57. Langbaum, *The Modern Spirit*, p. 154.

58. Fenichel, *Neurosis*, p. 429.

59. Wagenheim, "Square's Progress," 65.

60. Melanie Klein, *The Psychoanalysis of Children* (London: Hogarth Press, 1959), p. 236.

61. See Harvey Breit, "Talk with Norman Mailer," *New York Times Book Review*, 3 June 1951, p. 20. See also *Why Are We in Vietnam?*, p. 34: "D. J. has ideas like nobody else. He sees through to the stinking roots of things. . . ."

I

One of the last images Mailer leaves us with in _An American Dream_
is of a corpse dead from cancer, lying gutted on the autopsy table.
Rojack is an unwilling witness to the autopsy; not only his eyes but
also his nose are assaulted. "Cancer is the growth of madness denied," says Rojack. "In that corpse I saw, madness went down
to the blood—leucocytes gorged the liver, the spleen, the enlarged
heart and violet black lungs, dug into the intestines, germinated
stench" (_AD_, p. 267).

In _The Naked and the Dead_, the soldiers wander onto a field
after a battle looking for abandoned treasure. Instead, they gradually

> become aware of a familiar stench. . . . It was a smell of decay
> not exactly sweet but a good deal like ordure leavened with
> garbage and the foul odor of a swamp. The smell varied . . . some-
> times it struck their noses with the acute loathsome scent of
> rotting potatoes, and sometimes it was more like the lair of a
> skunk. (_ND_, p. 210)

The smell comes from the bodies of dead Japanese soldiers that
litter the battlefield. This careful orchestration of foul odors and the
choice of specific details—the sickly sweet smell of decay, the
swamp, and the rotting potatoes—makes the description resemble
numerous passages in _An American Dream_. One Japanese corpse
in particular is similar to the body Rojack sees on the autopsy table.
"His legs and buttocks had swollen so that they stretched his
pants. . . ." He lies on his back.

> He had a great hole in his intestines, which bunched out in a thick
> white cluster like the congested petals of a sea flower. The flesh
> of his belly was very red and his hands in their death throe had
> encircled the wound. He looked as if he were calling attention
> to it. (p. 211)

This brings us to a scene in _Why Are We in Vietnam?_, in which
M.A. (for Medium Asshole) Pete has wounded a caribou in the rear
and has tracked him in a helicopter to finish the kill. "M.A. Pete
sends a Nitro Express up into his gut from the rear, right into the
red mask of the old wound . . . the .600 900-grain blasted through
his intestines, stomach, pancreas, gallbladder, liver and lungs, and

left a hole to put your arm in, all your arm, up to the shoulder if you are not squeamish, entrail swimmer . . ." (*WV*, p. 97). Big Luke, the guide for the hunt, guts the entrails and feeds the caribou meat to the party, and "it tasted loud and clear of nothing but fresh venison steeped in bile, shit . . . it was so bad you were living on the other side of existence, down in poverty and stink wallow with your nose beneath the fever . . ." (p. 98).

These are more than recurring images of emasculation, though that suggestion is unmistakeable; they are images of evisceration. In *Why Are We in Vietnam?* D.J. delivers a mock self-diagnosis in the person of a jargon-ridden Jewish therapist named Rothenberg, called Rottenbug. Rottenbug is intended as a burlesque on contempory therapy, yet the analysis that D.J. renders through him is ironically accurate. Among other dangerous symptoms, Rottenbug finds D.J. obsessed with "disembowelment diagrams" (p. 14). If we decode the "disembowelment diagrams" scattered throughout the novel, we get a clue to some of the central concerns of *Why Are We in Vietnam?* and, incidentally, to much of Mailer's thinking. To track the truth we must, like shamans, read the message written in the entrails.

The passage quoted from *An American Dream* contains two linked concepts, cancer and madness, which are inseparable concerns of Mailer's in his later works. The problem of sanity versus insanity that plagues Rojack (he believes that he will get cancer if he doesn't go crazy) can also be seen as a problem of retention versus elimination, too fierce a control as opposed to going completely out of control. All of Rojack's bodily processes—ejaculation, regurgitation, even *cogitation*—are projective processes he equates with defecation. Rojack is like an infant with unruly bowels; his bodily processes create problems of control for him, and their products, like the feces of an infant, are narcissistically overvalued. His willpower, his very thought processes, are extremely dangerous, like some lethal brand of excrement that poisons internally (is cancerous) or else explodes violently, killing someone else or recoiling and wounding him. Rojack's dilemma, in microcosm, is precisely that of an auditor mentioned in *Why Are We in Vietnam?* who visits a prostitute. "Well, the audit got it up but he would not let it go, there was a knot of congested fatigue in his heart, he was afraid he would blast himself if he ever blew it into her . . ." (p. 115).

Rojack allows himself no middle ground between the dangerous and violent extremes of retention or elimination, holding on or letting go: either you hold back your madness under the strictest discipline and risk suicide by cancer, or you work out your madness in action and take the corresponding risk of running murderously amok.

One thing that connects the images from the three novels is the emphasis on stench; not surprising, for they are predominantly anal images. The suggestion of castration is present in each passage (the incision in the corpse, the wound in the soldier, and the hole in the caribou), but the hole that is so violently blasted out suggests the anus as well as the vagina ("the lair of a skunk" and "stink wallow"). Finally, all three passages are linked by their overwhelming sense of putrefaction and decay, of the insides turned into excrement. In *The Armies of the Night*, Mailer confesses that "he had been suffering more and more in the past few years from the private conviction that he was getting a little soft, a hint curdled, perhaps an almost invisible rim of corruption was growing around the edges" (*AN*, p. 58). Uniting the passages from the three novels is an underlying fear of feces and the asshole, of "the rim of corruption."

What Rojack witnesses in the corpse on the autopsy table is a *revolt of the insides*. Taken in this context, the recurrent scenes of disembowelment in *Why Are We in Vietnam?* become perhaps more comprehensible. Fenichel claims that "as a retaliation for anal sadistic tendencies, fears develop that what one wished to perpetrate anally on others will now happen to oneself. Fears of physical injury of an anal nature develop, like the fear of some violent ripping out of feces or of body contents."[1] Thus when D.J. runs his father Rusty's "middle-aged ass into the Dallas lawn fertilizer" in a game of touch football, Rusty retaliates in a singularly appropriate manner—he bites D.J. in the ass (*WV*, p. 40).

Later in the novel, this assault by Rusty on D.J. is replayed in the very scene where M.A. Pete kills the caribou with his comically oversized gun. The caribou is a buck, but it is decribed as effeminate, "to wit the ass of the caribou is white, its stumpy tail is white, soft as a white ruffle at Milady Hightits throat" (p. 94). D.J. also played a woman's role in his father's assault, specifically the role of his mother, Alice Hallelujah. "D.J.'s here to say that Rusty bit his ass so bad because he was too chicken to bite Hallelujah's beautiful butt. . . . D.J., as you may have divined, is a manly clean-featured version in formal features of his mother . . ." (p. 41). Rusty wounds D.J. in the rear, and M.A. Pete hits the caribou in the hindquarters. As D.J. limps off, Rusty repeats the assault, biting him over and over again in the same location. M.A. Pete shoots the crippled animal "right into the mask of the old wound," this time blasting out his insides. D.J. claims that the scars on his butt were produced "by the slivers of a horn shattered on a fighting bull" (p. 42), whereas M.A. Pete asserts that the scars on the face of his trophy, caused by the bullet fragmenting as it exited, are actually "the fighting marks of a big buck caribou fighter" (p. 98).

In both scenes, the desire to assault the father homosexually and kill him ("run his ass into the ground") is expiated by a reversal of roles, in which D.J. is forced to play the part of the mother who is murderously assaulted by the father. D.J. even conceptualizes intercourse between his parents in terms of assault by feces and disenbowelment. He plays on an old dirty limerick:

> Mum's first name is Alice. They found her vagina in North Carolina and part of her gashole in hometown Big D. Why? Why was her parts metaphorically blasted? Because, man, she used a dynamite stick for a phallus. . . . D.J.'s father, big Daddy, old Rusty, has got the dynamite. He don't come, he explodes, he's a geyser of love, hot piss, shit, corporation pus, hate, and heart, baby, he blasts, he's Texas willpower, hey yay! (p. 13)

As in all Mailer novels, love turns into hate and sex into anal sadism and murder. The only way Rusty can express his "excess of love" for D.J. is by biting him on the ass. When a similar attack is launched against D.J.'s proxy, that emasculated caribou, the result is total evisceration, a creature "blasted" just as his mother is metaphorically exploded. No wonder D.J. feels such empathy for the animals even as he kills them; the hunt acts out the raging violence and fears of violence that are in his own mind. "You could smell the anger in that wolf's heart (fucked again! I'll kill them!) . . ." (p. 70).

All of the animals in the novel are facsimiles of D.J., his father Rusty, or his mother Alice. The same traumatic scenes of disenbowelment are enacted over and over again, animals shot in the rear or the intestines and then butchered. Hunts have been described in literature before, but few so drastically visceral. Rusty describes to D.J. the evil habits of the American eagle, the worst of which is "they even pull the intestine out of a carcass like a sailor pulling rope with his mouth" (p. 132).

In another episode, D.J. and his buddy Tex witness a huge old bear tearing out and eating the guts of a little calf. When the bear bites into the bark of a tree, it is "a deep easy bite, mean and pleasurable, like a businessman copping a goose on a bare-ass nightclub waitress, yum!" (p. 190). "Businessman" suggests an unconscious equation of the beast with Rusty, the Texas tycoon. This particular bite not only conjures up the scene where Rusty assaults D.J. from the rear but is close in phrasing to a passage in *An American Dream*, where Rojack is "exploded in the butt with a piece of my own shrapnel, whacked with a delicious pain clean as a mistress' sharp teeth going 'Yummy' in your rump" (*AD*, p. 4). For all the apparent psychoanalytic candor of *Why Are We in Vietnam?*, with violent Oedipal and anal conflicts seething right on the surface, this repetition of images from one novel to the next implies that the choice of metaphor is not entirely under the author's conscious control.

The businessman bear that Tex and D.J. spot attacks a herd of caribou, getting "one calf who stumble in fright and griz right down on young beast and with one paw at the neck and the other on the flank, goes in with mouth open to rip her belly and get the living blood and taste of live entrail" (*WV*, p. 192). To add insult to injury, after having disemboweled the calf and chewed its guts for awhile, the bear "contents himself by taking a piss at the head and a big bear drop of baubles at the tail" (pp. 192–93). Then the mother caribou returns to mourn over the body of her dead calf.

This particular scene repeats the pattern of the earlier one in which Rusty bit D.J. on the rear, and D.J. was protected by his mother, and another incident later in the novel when D.J. recalls being almost beaten to death by his father when he was five years old, and again being rescued by rushing into his mother's arms. The attack of the bear on the calf only plays the scene out to its violent conclusion. D.J. secretly fears that his father will homosexually assault and disembowel him, eat his insides, and then shit upon him. D.J. has such fears because this is precisely what he wishes to do to his father: "D.J. was in such a murder ball of sick disgusted piss-on-dad . . ." (p. 157). As in *An American Dream*, feces and murder, "mud and blood" are conjoined, though here the connection is more openly avowed.

The world of *Why Are We in Vietnam?* is a savage, predatory environment similar to the "tenement jungle" of "The Time of Her Time," where "the barbarians ate their young." Every environment in Mailer's novels is a decaying jungle where carnivores stalk their prey; he started with a jungle in *The Naked and the Dead*, and he has stayed in that jungle, only penetrating with each new foray closer to the horrifying mysteries that lie at the heart of its darkness.

The barbarians eat their young, and because of this D.J. cannot really trust his mother, and is afraid of his own dependence upon her. Like Mailer's notion of D. H. Lawrence in *The Prisoner of Sex*, D.J. is a male "feminized" through an excess of mother-love, and he battles against the "feminization."

In truth, D.J. secretly desires to disembowel his mother as well as his father. Early in the hunt, D.J.'s alter ego, Tex Hyde (Mr. Hyde to his Doctor Jekyll), takes down a wolf "with a shot into the gut" (p. 68). Afterwards, D.J. is "half-sick having watched what Tex had done, like his own girl had been fucked in front of him and better..." (p. 69). His reaction seems to imply that a shot in the guts is equivalent to intercourse. D.J. smells the wolf's mouth, and it is "a crazy breath, wild ass odor, something rotten from the bottom of the barrel" (p. 69). Elsewhere, D.J. talks of his mother's breath being "big! like the bottom of a burnt-out bourbon barrel" (p. 12). There is an unconscious connection between the wolf and the mother; D.J. is envious because Tex, his alter ego, can enjoy the incestuous pleasure of shooting the mother in the gut, a desire that sends D.J. himself into a guilty sweat. Later, when the hunting party shoot their first grizzly, a "female bear her belly half demolished" (p. 119), D.J. is too nervous even to pull the trigger.

Finally, when Rusty and D.J. search for bear together, the hunt turns into a form of intense masculine competition, really an unconscious rivalry for the possession of the mother. Between the two of them, they blast the creature apart, turning the insides of the bear into "a rocket of exploded works" (p. 144). It is Rusty, however, who gets off the last shot and claims the animal as his own, thereby cheating D.J. out of the kill. "Final end of love of one son for one father" (p. 147). It is not the bear for which D.J. cannot forgive his father, only the act that the destruction of the animal symbolizes: final possession of the mother in the form of disembowelment, a sexual act which in this novel goes beyond the murderous potential of mere intercourse, beyond even anal assault.

In a way, since the enemy is within, and since D.J. identifies himself so strongly with his mother, what he is trying to do involves both incest and a masochistic attempt to eviscerate the female part of himself. " 'Why, shit,' " says Shago Martin to Stephen Rojack, " 'you just killed the little woman in me' " (*AD*, p. 194).

Because disembowelment is the central concern of *Why Are We in Vietnam?*, the overriding obsession and anxiety, the word *guts*, with all of its different significations, is one that crops up with almost as much frequency as those much-used obscenities every critic has noted. The word *guts* offers an ideal way to combine the anal with the phallic, and also suggests anxieties concerning disembowelment. In ordinary speech, *guts* expresses admiration for someone's masculinity or courage ("That took guts"). A euphemism for the word is *intestinal fortitude*. *Guts* is almost synonymous with *balls* whereas *gutless* has come to mean "castrated." Analogous with this is the concept of the guts as the locus not only of fear and courage but of all the emotions, the center of things human, like the heart. At the same time, because of their association with excrement, the entrails are thought of as rotten, a particularly nauseating part of the body (*rot gut*). There is also the phrase, *I hate your guts*, which expresses an intense loathing, along with the implied desire to disembowel the hated object. A whole chain of unconsciously related ideas centers upon this single highly charged word.

Using its first meaning, D.J. employs *guts* interchangeably with courage or potency. "Rusty was sick. He had to get it up. They had to go for grizzer now. Well, he was man enough to steel his guts before necessity . . ." (*WV*, p. 107). Later, during the hunt for bear, D.J. says, "It's amazing what waiting can do to a man's guts. . . . Rusty scurries about in his gut and reamasses his cool. He is getting to feel taut" (p. 121). When Rusty refuses to turn back from the hunt, D.J. says "he's not there to have his lust blooded and placated, he is up, his guts are there" (p. 123). One can see here a deliberate confusion between the concepts of masculinity, courage, and erectile capacity.

D.J. takes the meaning of *guts* one step further, muddling its phallic connotations with its anal ones. For D.J., the fecal column is synonymous with an erection, whereas diarrhea is synonymous with detumescence. When they are tracking the bear, he describes his fear by saying, "D.J. feels shit yellow between his toes, his bowels slosh internal bilge, every bit of hard shit in him has broken down to squirts like spit and dishwater rumblings" (p. 142). Since the entrails are the center of potency, diarrhea is tantamount to cowardice and impotence, just as in *The Naked and the Dead*, where the soldiers' motto was "Keep a tight asshole," and loss of sphincter control always signaled oncoming decay or death.

According to D.J., Rusty is even equipped with the supernatural power (symbolically situated in his nose) to dissolve excrement in the guts of other men: "any flunky taking to Rusty and not knowing what to say cause he's hiding some fuckup is going to find all that hardpan constipated Texas clay in his flunky gut turning abruptly to sulfur water and steam. Not to mention specks of zipping around deepsea shit" (p. 36). Big Luke, Rusty's backwoods counterpart, has the same awesome, magical power: "if you even a high-grade asshole and had naught but a smidgeon of flunky in you . . . it would still start in Big Luke's presence to blow sulfur water, steam, and specks of hopeless diarrhetic matter in your runny little gut, cause he was a *man*!" (pp. 46–47). One may say that D.J. is merely speaking hyperbolically—he is always speaking hyperbolically—but the unconscious belief behind such statements is a fear of internal attack, based on the notion that others can literally affect your insides, touch your very substance. When D.J. claims for himself the power to see "right through shit . . . right into the claypots below the duodenum of his father" (p. 49), he is not just speaking metaphorically.

Throughout the narrative, D.J. habitually characterizes others in terms of their lowest common denominator: the excretory functions. For D.J., everyone else is a lower or higher grade of asshole. Ironically, however, D.J., that self-confessed "shit-oriented late adolescent," "marooned on the balmy tropical isle of Anal Referent Metaphor" (p. 150), is only projecting, confusing the world with his own conception of himself. At the center of D.J.'s excremental vision is the inescapable fact that he also sees himself as an asshole. In the scene between Hallelujah and her analyst, which D.J. fantasizes, his mother says that D.J. is "so big and dark and mysterious and he goes all the way back to Egypt" (p. 17). But as D.J. has already told us, it was "the asshole belonged to Egypt" (p. 8). D.J.'s fear that he has been feminized through an overdose of mother-love is right out on the surface, but just beneath this anxiety is the belief that his feminization lies in the anus, which is for him a kind of masculine vagina, and that he himself is nothing but a walking anus, ripe for invasion by others. "Huckleberry Finn is here to set you straight, and his asshole ain't itching, right?" (p. 8) he is quick to tell us.

Perhaps D.J.'s self-conception as an asshole open to attack creates the style of the narration, its unique form of verbal harangue. John W. Aldridge calls D.J.'s talk "lingual bowel movement."[2] D.J. flings everything at the reader, like one of Swift's Yahoos pelting his enemies with excrement.

He gleefully hurls insults and challenges at the reader, belittling the reader's presumed masculinity, daring the reader to castrate or sodomize him. This is counterphobic activity. D.J. counters fears of exposure by absurd overexposure, just as he counters his fear of the asshole by constantly evoking it, in an overwhelming barrage of scatological obscenity. Fenichel writes, "A combination of coprophilia, exhibitionism, and sadism is expressed in coprolalia, that is, in the joy of uttering obscenities. . . . Obscene words retain remnants of the old magical power which language in general originally had. They force, or are intended to force, the listener to visualize with hallucinatory clarity the objects they denote."[3] Moreover, "anal words bring anal pleasure."[4]

In the first sentence of the tale, D.J. calls the reader "Braun-schweiger," a brown liver sausage which resembles the elemental substance that fascinates him. The strategy seems evident: turn the reader into feces. Mailer has chosen a method of narration that is new to him, one which delves even further into the confessional mode than *An American Dream*. Mailer gains gratification (purgation) through a kind of psychic striptease. He defuses his personal obsessions by having the reader associate them with his fictional creation instead, as John W. Aldridge has noted.[5] The talent of the obsessional lies in endlessly elaborating his own symptoms, often structuring them into systems. From a distance, it can even look like self-knowledge when it is really self-obsession.

At the same time, precisely because all the submerged conflicts are brought to the surface in *Vietnam*, desublimated, Mailer leaves the narrator more exposed than ever. The anxiety about internal attack is countered by an obsessional technique—disemboweling everything in sight in the novel—and also by a direct assault on the reader. D.J. alternately woos and attacks his audience, expressing the same ambivalence toward them that he feels toward his parents and toward Tex Hyde, or, what is closer to the heart of the matter, the same ambivalent love-hate relationship he has with himself. The reader-as-feces can be dealt with in the same manner as the excremental love object, held onto or cast aside at whim, loved or hated. The members of the audience as love object cannot respond, cannot talk back, which makes them much more satisfactory than loved ones who are present, and also much more subject to control.

D.J.'s attitude toward the reader-as-feces is another aspect of the war within himself, the battle that he conceptualizes in terms of assault from the rear against his behind and his insides. The superego, or the Lord, attacks in the rectum in order to gain control of him, inserting a tape recorder into "the bowels of Creation" to spy on his most personal and private bodily processes (p. 24). But if the Lord is in his asshole, he "must be Satan" (p. 26). The superego, or the internalized identification with the parental authority figures, becomes confused with the feces. The superego (parents or feces) exercises a control over him that he cannot tolerate. But, ironically, if the tyranny is within, he must stage a revolution against himself, extirpate the Lord/Satan and the "little woman" within himself, even if it means disembowelment and self-destruction. If in real life Mailer has turned the knife against others, perhaps it is his only alternative to turning it on himself.

Mailer's concern with being attacked internally can be traced back to *The Naked and the Dead*, where the soldier Wilson undergoes protracted agony before dying of a stomach wound. Sergius in "The Time of Her Time" feels he is suffering the appropriate punishment for his way of life; he is certain that "the sore vicious growl of my stomach was at least the onset of an ulcer and more likely the first gone cells of a thoroughgoing cancer of the duodenum" (*ADV*, p. 479). In *An American Dream*, Rojack is continually vomiting, that is, in a sense being disemboweled, "the food and drink I had ingested wrenched out of my belly and upper gut" (*AD*, p. 11). In the same novel, the obsession with cancer of the gut is epitomized in the body on the autopsy table and in the decaying old Mafioso, Eddie Ganucci: "Death had already invaded him" (p. 223). Finally, in *Why Are We in Vietnam?*, excrement is equivalent to "defeat" (*WV*, p. 151) in D.J.'s metaphysics, and defeat is equivalent to "dying inside" (p. 49).

If one of the paramount anxieties in *An American Dream* is cancer of the guts, this is merely displaced in *Vietnam* into fear of disembowelment. The focus of the cancer shifts from the guts to the brain, which for D.J. is synonymous with the asshole.[6] In one of his incarnations, D.J. is a crippled Harlem genius suffering from a tumor in the brain, "gone ape in the mind from outrageous frustrates wasting him" (p. 58), just as Rusty goes "insane" with "frustration" (p. 40). The tumor is equivalent to feces, and the cancer is equivalent to constipation. "Think of something black-ass and terrible, black as a tumor in your brain . . ." (p. 57). In this sense, *An American Dream* is a more psychologically optimistic novel than *Vietnam*: the former offers the choice of insanity or cancer; in the latter, since the cancer has shifted to the brain, there is no choice at all— the tumor will drive one insane. Excrement is the instrument of the devil; it is bound to waste you ("hot damn!") and leave you "unbalanced." The only solution that D.J. sees is "to avoid all frustration of impulse . . . if D.J. makes it through a day without a single impulse held back, he should not need to piss a drop" (p. 153).

In *Vietnam*, the anxiety concerning insanity and cancer is intricately connected with the fear of disembowelment. In the "Terminal Intro Beep and Out," D.J. has a vision of North America destroyed by the white man, "all gutted, shit on, used and blasted" (p. 205), like the caribou calf slaughtered by the bear. It is the punishment D.J. wishes to enact on his parents, and the one he fears will be carried out on himself.

John W. Aldridge writes that Mailer envisions himself as a "symptomatic consciousness," symptomatic of America in all its contradictions, "mediating between his personal micro-hells and the major disasters of his age."[7] The critic Tony Tanner says that the continent itself in *Vietnam* seems plagued with "periodic dark rages of annihi-

lation . . . a compulsion to waste substance. . . ."[8] What happens is
that D.J. *becomes* America, and his violent obsession with disembowelment, his "micro-hell," is projected onto the continent itself
as an explanation for the "major disaster" of Vietnam.

This obsession with disembowelment helps to explain the place
in the novel of one of the more grotesque minor characters, Gottfried
Hyde, a mortician known as "Gutsy" to his friends. Gutsy's business
is in guts—the legal disembowelment trade. He is "in his element
when up to the elbows in intestinal slime" (p. 162). According to
D.J., he is extraordinarily fertile, satyrlike—he "comes more often
than anybody in the whole fucking state." "Gutsy comes all over the
place out of a vast enthusiasm for life (or some such disease of un-
balance as the fucked-out cynics would say) . . ." (p. 164). This
ability, so D.J. claims, is attained by Hyde's constantly dredging
through corpses. Later D.J. and Tex engage in this same necrophilia,
gaining mysterious "powers" by conducting "private autopsies"
(p. 157). Similarly, Rojack was tempted to absorb Deborah's power
by cannibalizing her dead body. The driving urge behind all this
necrophilia and cannibalism is actually coprophilia. If you unconsciously fear that someone will gain power over you by disemboweling you, removing your beloved bodily substance, then you retaliate
by disemboweling him and absorbing the magical power of his
substance.

One image that is repeated throughout the novel is of weeds
thriving on a dungheap: marijuana, the devil weed, grown on human
shit; Tex Hyde as "a malevolent orchid in a humus pile" (p. 19). This
culminates in the last chapter with the image of "all those fucking
English, Irish, Scotch, and European weeds, transplanted to North
America" and then converting the continent to excrement, "cause
a weed thrives on a cesspool, piss is its nectar, shit all ambrosia"
(p. 205). America is powerful, fertile, and thriving, but only as a
weed (or a cancer) is powerful, growing on waste, both product
and process diabolic. "Get a man greedy enough and he got the guts
to go—go, go, Gutsy Hyde—" (p. 206). Gottfried, or Gutsy, is one
of these successful immigrant weeds, and he gains his potency by
gutting others—bodies "all gutted, shit on, used and blasted." He
is, as the common expression goes, a "greedy guts." Vietnam is then
a natural extension of American expansion; having thoroughly
blasted this continent, we insanely "waste" and gut another country
so that the American weed can continue to thrive.

Just as the hunters despoil the Alaskan wilderness, so America
indiscriminately dumps its "technological excrement" (*AN*, p. 114)
all over Vietnam. Like a cancer, the nation destroys the body that

houses it and then feeds on the waste it creates. Mailer once said in an interview, "I have a funny mystical feeling about evil . . . you have to pursue it to the end. . . . America had to pursue it to the end in Vietnam, eating its own waste, its own filth, to see how evil it was."[9] It is this horrific vision that underlies *Why Are We in Vietnam?*, a vision of a nation that cannot help being what it is, of a nation foully obsessed, of "the growth of madness denied" (*AD*, p. 267).

For Mailer, Vietnam is symptomatic of the plague that must rage and run its course in America, but it is at once symptom and cure, both a symbol of our evil and the punishment for our crimes. We are in Vietnam because we have no choice. Karl Abraham writes, "In one of my patients the idea of eating excrement was connected with the idea of being punished for a great sin. Psychologically speaking, he was correct." The patient was atoning for "the deed of Oedipus."[10] Finally, this helps to explain why D.J. must go to Vietnam at the end of the novel: it is because he cannot help himself, because he is *compelled* to go.

II

There is a great similarity between the unconscious content of *Why Are We in Vietnam?* and *An American Dream*. Like Rojack, D.J. is threatened inside by the play of hostile forces and controlled by telepathic voices. Rojack wants to be "free of waste and guilt and gutting of the earth" (*AD*, p. 253); D.J. wants to "get the fear, shit, disgust and mixed shit tapeworm out of fucked-up guts" (*WV*, p. 176). Both D.J. and Rojack are anally obsessed, concerned with waste and buggery. Both are ambivalent and alternate between love and awe for the parents and murderous hatred of them. Both novels deal with the unconscious desire to destroy the parents through buggery and disembowelment.

American Dream, however, moves toward the acting out of the fantasies and then a reparation for them. Rojack is torn between the anal-sadistic urge to eliminate the parents and the desire to destroy himself. Finally, he achieves a kind of perilous balance between his ambivalent impulses as he teeters on the parapet like an infant taking his first steps. D.J. never advances even that far, because he lacks most of the dynamism of conflict. One critic notes that *Vietnam* has only "a bare minimum of dramatic tension or external conflict" and "the characters are significant primarily on a symbolic plane."[11] In *American Dream*, conflicts are defended against through action; in *Vietnam*, they are defended against primarily through the sexualization of language. Everything is subordinated to the power of the word: in particular, to the supposedly magical restorative power of the four-letter word.

Vietnam is an excessively manic and anally sadistic novel, but much of its aggression is directed against the reader. D.J. wants purification for his sins, for the "animal murder" (p. 7) that symbolizes the destruction and disembowelment of the parents, but he accomplishes his purgation by expelling a lot of words, by repetitious and compulsive talk. D.J. casts out his evil impulses onto the reader through compulsive obscenity. He feels damned, so the reader must be cursed. The language of *American Dream* may have been lavish and hyperbolic, but the verbiage here even takes precedence over the action. Despite the virtuoso eloquence of certain passages, such as the lyrical descriptions of nature, the novel is freighted with excess rhetoric. With his elaborate word play and incessant obscenity, D.J. turns language itself into excrement and buries the reader under a flow of "lingual bowel movement." [12]

Nevertheless, *Vietnam* possesses a redeeming quality of humor that is notably lacking in *American Dream*. Anna Freud writes:

> For the obsessional . . . it is as natural to be at cross-purposes with himself as he invariably is at cross-purposes with his objects. Aggressive argumentation and hostile attitudes to the environment run parallel with the torturing relationships which exist between his inner agencies. [13]

Through D.J., the aggressive argumentation of the obsessional is converted into witty diatribes and the hostility toward the self is spiced with self-mockery. In this respect, *Why Are We in Vietnam?* leads the way toward what may be Mailer's finest comic novel (though some do not consider it a novel at all): *The Armies of the Night*. If ever there was a hero at cross-purposes with himself and with his environment, it is the "Norman Mailer" of that narrative. As John W. Aldridge writes, "the secret of Mailer's appeal, the very essence of his heroism" is that he is "guts at war with all his unmastered contradictions and fears. . . ." [14]

Notes

1. Otto Fenichel, *The Psychoanalytic Theory of Neurosis* (New York: Norton, 1945), p. 68.

2. John W. Aldridge, "From Vietnam to Obscenity," in *Norman Mailer: The Man and His Work*, ed. Robert F. Lucid (Boston and Toronto: Little, Brown, 1971), p. 189.

3. Fenichel, *Neurosis*, p. 350.

4. Ibid., p. 296.

5. John W. Aldridge, "The Perfect Absurd Figure of a Mighty, Absurd Crusade," *Saturday Review*, 13 November 1971, p. 46.

6. Note in *Vietnam*, among multitudinous examples: "shitheads" (p. 206); "my brain in the deep of its mysterious unwindings. Maybe there will be a day when they discover how to dig it out" (p. 24); and "America is run by a mysterious hidden mastermind . . . who's got a plastic asshole installed in his brain whereby he can shit out all his corporate management of thoughts" (p. 36).

7. Aldridge, "Absurd Figure," p. 43.

8. Tony Tanner, "On the Parapet: A Study of the Novels of Norman Mailer," *Critical Quarterly* 12 (Summer 1970): 171–72.

9. In an interview on "Newsroom," KQED-TV, San Francisco, 5 February 1971.

10. Karl Abraham, *Selected Papers of Karl Abraham* (London: Hogarth Press, 1949), p. 444.

11. James Toback, "Norman Mailer Today," *Commentary* (October 1967), pp. 74, 75.

12. See n. 3.

13. Anna Freud, *The Writings of Anna Freud* (New York: International Universities Press, 1969), Vol. v, pp. 246–47.

14. Aldridge, "Absurd Figure," p. 48.

•

I

In *The Armies of the Night*, that anal ambivalence, called "schizo-phrenia" by Mailer, which has been an implicit pattern in all his work, moves from background to foreground, becoming the manifest subject matter. *Armies* is another Mailer tale of "guts at war," valuable for the radical candor of its self-analysis. By looking at himself as a literary character, Mailer is able to gain psychological distance to investigate the irresolvable ambivalence that lies at the core of his personality and his work. He acts out his various roles for his and our benefit, analyzing his performance even as he acts. As a result, he lessens some of the constant strain of his relationship with himself and with his audience. Tenderness softens his rage against himself and against outside objects, channeling it into an ironic, self-mocking wit instead of strident invective. He can accept the possibility of simultaneously hating and loving his America, "tender mysterious bitch whom no one would ever know" (p. 114). He can also accept himself more, with all his contradictions, even if he cannot entirely comprehend the irrational drives that affect so much of his conscious behavior.

The enormous success of *The Armies of the Night*, the book that won more critical and popular success than any of his works since *The Naked and the Dead*, is due to a happy correspondence betwen the man, the moment, and the literary method. At a crucial juncture in contemporary American history, Mailer once more found the appropriate literary form to contain both his vision and his personal ambivalence as well as the hopes and the uncertainties of the nation. Throughout the fifties and sixties, he had been delivering jeremiads against the repressive, deadly, totalitarian nature of American society; by 1968, at the height of the Vietnam War, a larger segment of the populace than ever before was alienated enough to agree with some of his criticism, which finally seemed to have been borne out by the pressure of events.[1]

Moreover, as mentioned before, Mailer has from the beginning of his career been a writer at war, battling continually against both external and internal threats. At the time of the 1967 March on the Pentagon, the country was undergoing both a war abroad and a political and cultural civil war at home. Mailer, whose psyche had always been in a state of civil war, was supremely qualified to describe the agony of a nation being torn apart.

He found the ideal form in which to convey both his and America's "schizophrenia" (the term is Mailer's; he uses it loosely). First, he had a single clear, unified action that took place over a span of four days: the events preceding the March on the Pentagon; the March itself; his arrest and imprisonment; and his release. Second, he offered himself as the protagonist of the action, an ambivalent hero who could stand as a microcosm of the divided loyalties of the nation. Such a hero acted out the conflict in an intensely subjective, personalized fashion. Third, he gained an objective perspective on the action by relating it in the third person. The aesthetic distance also allowed him a comic, ironic view of his hero, converting a character who would otherwise seem egotistical and overbearing from a pretentious ass into a flawed but sympathetic protagonist, "a simple of a hero and a marvel of a fool" (p. 216). This is a comic epic about a hero in spite of himself—a hero at odds with himself who nevertheless comes through all right in the end.

The Armies of the Night, like all of Mailer's novels, is concerned simultaneously with the initiation of a man and the crisis of an American nation poised between two possible futures, one totalitarian and the other free.[2] The actions of the hero and the future of the country are related by analogy; the manner in which the man passes or fumbles his initiation rite stands as a measure of how the nation may fare. After a gap of twenty years, Mailer had once again encountered a subject—combat and history—large enough for him to put to use his talents as a fictional General. As in *The Naked and the Dead*, here was a single battle representative of a much larger war to determine the shape of the future. Mount Anaka is tranformed into the great symbol of the Pentagon. Lives are at stake: "in a few hours some of them were going to be dead" (*ND*, p. 3) opens *The Naked and the Dead*; "how incredible if in two days one was going to be dead!" Mailer ponders near the beginning of *Armies* (*AN*, p. 11). For once he would not have to struggle so much to impart grandiose meanings. The Pentagon March was a subject Mailer had long been hungering for, a heroic subject in an age scarce in heroes.

The fact that the hero of this particular novel happens to be named "Norman Mailer" merely reaffirms who had been the model for the heroes of his previous novels. *Armies*, says Jean Radford, "is another chapter in the muted autobiography of Norman Mailer which runs throughout his work. . . ."[3] But never before had the reader seen Mailer in action in all his complexity. The book aroused so much interest because Mailer brought all his gifts to bear on examining himself, and because his crisis of identity and that of the

nation happened for a moment to intersect. Mailer boldly seized
the opportunity and appeared temporarily to have mastered both
himself and history; his self-affirmation expressed our own cravings
for identity and control.

Seen in the light of his previous works, *The Armies of the Night*
seems the inevitable culmination of Mailer's long search for a way
of dealing with himself in print. If he began his career by removing
himself from the narrative through use of the omniscient point of
view in *The Naked and the Dead*, his subsequent books show an increasing attempt to write himself into the work, first in the first-
person narratives of *Barbary Shore* and *The Deer Park* and then in the
self-mythologizing of *Advertisements for Myself*. As a consequence,
the fictional mask begins to wear a bit thin in the narrators of the
two novels that follow *Advertisements for Myself*. In *An American
Dream*, one is constantly aware of how much Rojack's career parallels Mailer's own life and fantasies, and how much Rojack's theories
and obsessions duplicate Mailer's. Next, in *Why Are We in Vietnam?*, D.J. seems not an actual American teenager but an implausible freak: a foul-mouthed existential philosopher speaking in
tongues, a mouthpiece for Mailer.

In his earlier fiction, Mailer deals indirectly with his insecurity,
ambivalence, and confusion of identity by splitting himself into different characters, multiple heroes who express different and often
warring tendencies in himself. These multiple heroes battle it out
among themselves for supremacy in their fictional worlds, and also
compete for the interest and sympathy of the reader.

In his work of the sixties, Mailer's identity confusion is expressed
in images of splitting or what he calls "schizophrenia," as in Mailer's
idea of the "two rivers" of American life, or in D.J. and Tex Hyde
(Doctor Jekyll and Mr. Hyde), or in the Mailer of *The Armies of the
Night*, who is both modest individual and shameless "Beast."

The theme of uncertainty of identity is also built into Mailer's
experiments in point of view. For example, the anonymous narrator
of "The Man Who Studied Yoga" is a floating ghost who says, "I
would introduce myself if it were not useless. The name I had last
night is not the same as the name I have tonight" (*ADV*, p. 157). The
anonymous narrator of "Advertisements for Myself on the Way
Out" (a rather turgid and pretentious story included at the end of
Advertisements for Myself, and intended, like "The Man Who
Studied Yoga," as the prologue to a long novel or projected series
of novels) is also a floating ghost of no fixed identity. Again, the
deliberate confusion of identity is built into the point of view of
Vietnam: D. J. claims to be either a rich white Texas teenager, or

a crippled young black genius in Harlem, two opposing sides of the nation ("You never know what vision has been humping you through the night" [*WV*, p. 208]).

The return to third-person narration in *The Armies of the Night* allowed Mailer psychological distance and control in examining the ambivalent nature of his own shaky identity, and by analogy, the identity of the nation. Jean Radford mentions that "He is able to write about the problems of America as he sees them with a new flexibility and irony—the stridency that marks so much of his essay work is absent from *The Armies of the Night*."[4] One might add that the point of view also permits him an aloof and ironic playfulness in dealing with the problems of Norman Mailer, softening the stridency of his constant self-concern. By shifting from the first to the third person, Mailer still has the satisfaction of exhibiting and advertising himself. But now, by considering himself as a literary character, he balances vanity with self-detachment and objectivity— or at least the *appearance* of objectivity. By making himself into his own toughest critic, Mailer assuages his severe superego, (which always works overtime) and also disarms the critics: "He is funnier and more devastating on the subject of his vanity than anybody else will ever be," wrote one reviewer of *The Armies of the Night*.[5] Mailer's tactic gains him the benefits of both self-exposure and self-protection, for the reader can laugh along with him at the worst excesses of the foolish Mailer while admiring the serene wisdom of the *other* Mailer who tells the story. "Well, he could convert this deficiency to an asset," Mailer thinks in the course of the narrative. "From gap to gain is very American. He would confess straight out to all aloud that he was the one who wet the floor in the men's room, he alone!" (*AN*, p. 31). This is the strategy of the calculated candor of *The Armies of the Night*: to convert deficiency into asset, weakness into strength.

The conflict in the novel is as much internal as it is external; it is not simply Mailer vs. the Pentagon, but Mailer vs. Mailer, battling to resolve his insecurity, his uncertainty about his manhood and his identity. This is a work whose very subject matter is ambivalence.[6] If the hero is not entirely successful in resolving his ambivalence through action, nevertheless the narrator can provide a resolution by being relentlessly in *control*, by transcending the hero's ambivalence. The "Mailer" of *Armies* in part resembles one of his own antiheroes, such as Sam Slovoda, the middle-class, Jewish ex-radical and novelist manqué of "The Man Who Studied Yoga." Both Sam and the hero of *Armies* are ambivalent: vain, finicky, insecure, defensive and neurotically sensitive to criticism, but also intensely self-critical, even self-hating. Both have vast dreams of heroic grandeur that they fear they can never attain. The comedy lies in the disparity between their grandiose visions and their lives. Just as the narrator of "Yoga" looks upon Sam's failings with affection and critical irony, so the narrator of *Armies* contemplates Mailer's foibles with ironic amusement. In both stories there is not only a split within the hero, but also a split between the character of the hero (who cannot control his life) and the character of the fictive persona who serves as a narrator (and who is supremely in control of things).

Mailer as hero of *Armies* is a complex personality who sometimes appears to be an amalgam of two diametrically opposed characters: not just Sam Slovoda alone, but Sam plus his antiself, Sergius the Beast, the big bad wolf of "The Time of Her Time." Richard Levine has argued that Mailer's fiction often involves a battle between the figure of the Jew, like Sam, who is humane, rational, and pacifistic, and the figure of the Cossack, like Sergius, who is instinctual, physical, and violent. In *Armies*, for the first time, Mailer embodies this division in himself rather than in two separate characters: "This national schizophrenia mirrors, or is mirrored by, the schizophrenic division within himself. Sergius, the Cossack in Mailer, fearlessly enters the fray, while Sam, the Jew, watches from the sidelines in terror. . . ."[7]

Mailer tends to see the Jewish side of himself as unmanly, a spoiled weakling, a mamma's boy: "he had on screen . . . a fatal taint, a last remaining speck of the one personality he found insupportable—the nice Jewish boy from Brooklyn. Something in his adenoids gave it away—he had the softness of a man early accustomed to mother-love" (p. 134). This Jewish Mailer is too modest for his taste, "and he hated this because modesty was an old family relative, he had been born to a modest family, had been a modest boy, a modest young man, and he hated that, he loved the pride and the arrogance and the egocentricity he had gathered over the years . . ."(p. 77). One senses in *Armies* how much Mailer has attempted to remake his personality, or at least his image, over the years, to suppress what he views as the loathsomely weak side of himself—Sam Slovoda, overly intellectual, Jewish, effeminate—and defend against it through aggressive action and shameless exhibitionism, qualities he mistakenly associates with manhood. The modest and gentle Jewish man who is also part of him he sees as excremental (tainted) and effeminate. As he writes, "The trouble with being gentle is that one has no defense against shame" (p. 57).

The hero of *Armies* seems to have difficulty managing his aggression, both his hostility toward himself and his aggression toward others (which, as we shall see, is often a projection of his self-hatred). The hero evidences a great deal of aggression in the form of obstinancy, envy, spite, and contempt. Although he claims to be modest, he is, as if in compensation, extremely competitive and domineering. He always pushes to the front rank, always has to have things his own way, and feels slighted when he imagines he has not been given his due. Our protagonist needs to be in control, in charge of things, and therefore he wallows in self-pity at the thought that he may not be a leader of the coming revolution, but merely a martyr, "a future victim" (p. 78). He is also afraid of his aggressive impulses, so that he compensates by an excessive politeness, as in his behavior toward liberal academics: "Since he—you are in on the secret—disapproved of them far more than he could afford to reveal (their enmity could be venomous) he therefore exerted himself to push up a synthetic exaggerated sweetness of manner . . ." (p. 17). Surely he is projecting: there is no evidence in the narrative of "their" venomous enmity; instead Mailer performs a literary hatchet job on the liberal academics. Despite his efforts at overcompensation, sometimes his sadistic and masochistic impulses run out of control, as in his behavior at the Ambassador Theater: "the modest everyday fellow of his daily round was servant to a wild man in himself. . . . he was an absolute egomaniac, a Beast—no recognition existed of anything beyond the range of his reach" (p. 13).

Perhaps as a result of his constant efforts to maintain control of his aggression, his chest is "chronic captive of a mysterious iron vise upon his lungs" (p. 56). In this respect, he reminds one of Rojack, hero of *An American Dream*, who says, "I had my fill of walking about with a chest full of hatred and a brain jammed to burst, but there is something manly about containing your rage . . ." (*AD*, p. 8). The chest tension seems to be caused by bottled-up hatred, and Rojack feels both a confirmation of his manhood and a sort of anal pleasure in holding on to it.

Throughout *The Armies of the Night*, Mailer consistently uses two metaphors to refer to himself: he operates by a principle of "war games and random play" (*AN*, p. 4). Images from the battlefield and the casino permeate the book, often in the form of mixed metaphors ("so strategic choices on the continuation of the attack would soon have to be decided, a moment to know the blood of the gambler in oneself" [p. 29]). Elsewhere in the narrative he speaks of being trapped in the "sarcophagus" of his image (p. 5), yet he does not really acknowledge how much he has contributed to his imprisonment by acting out his own system of metaphors. As a warrior, he is repeatedly compelled to attack. As a gambler, he must constantly take risks, yet he hates above all else to lose. He admits that "Mailer hated to put in time with losers" (p. 8). He admires the Reverend William Sloane Coffin because "our Yale Chaplain had the look of a winner" (p. 67); and when he faces down the Nazi in a staring contest, "the thought of losing had been intolerable as if he had been *obliged* not to lose" (p. 142). Winning becomes a duty, a compulsion for him.

As *Advertisements for Myself* makes abundantly clear, after the enormous early success of *The Naked and the Dead*, Mailer was hurt by years of bad reviews. His response was to become increasingly aggressive in public and in print, to be a warrior and a gambler, to constantly risk more. Nevertheless, the vulnerable and insecure Mailer, the one who secretly fears he is a loser, has not gone away. In *The Armies of the Night*, he is able to soften that harsh, defensive aggression by using the narrator as a buffer between himself and the reader.

During the entire action, the hero seems to be conducting his own private war within the larger demonstration. His behavior with regard to the war protest is characteristically ambivalent: willful, inconsistent, and self-serving. When Mitch Goodman phones to ask him to participate in the protest, Mailer at first balks: "he doubted if he would attend since he had no desire to stand in a large meadow and listen to other men make speeches . . ." (p. 8). Mailer would prefer to make the speeches himself. He is cranky, and scolds Goodman, but checks himself and agrees to go when he realizes he is sounding like "a righteous old toot" (p. 9). Moreover, the interest of the warrior in him has been piqued by the potential for violence in the demonstation. "He felt one little bubble of fear tilt somewhere about the solar plexus" (p. 9); as always, he must confront whatever inspires in him the most fear.

His commitment to the March is at first tentative, but his interest builds when it appears that the event can serve his own ends and provide him with a chance to practice the radicalism he has so long been preaching. For him it becomes the rite of passage of a middle-aged man who is uncertain of his manhood and confused about his identity. Thus, if he begins by refusing to sign a letter supporting draft resisters, and goes to Washington with the greatest reluctance ("It was going to prove a wasteful weekend, he decided with some gloom" [p. 10]), nevertheless, once there he wants to hog the spotlight. He makes the organizer de Grazia promise to let him be the master of ceremonies at the Ambassador Theater. He feels betrayed when de Grazia starts without him ("Traitor de Grazia! Sicilian de Grazia!" [p. 32]) because they are running late and Mailer has disappeared to the bathroom without bothering to let anyone know. Furious, Mailer commandeers the microphone and takes over the show: "The Beast was ready to grapple with the world" (p. 36). Then he is compelled to confess on the spot to the audience that he had accidentally urinated on the floor of the men's room.

At other events that weekend, Mailer feels snubbed every time he is not invited to speak. When the marchers finally begin to move, the notables are shifted

> down from the forwardmost line to what was now no more than the third line, to Mailer's disappointment, for he had been pleased to be in the front rank, in fact had fought doggedly to keep position there, anticipating at the end of the March a confrontation . . . if his head was to be busted this day, let it be before the eyes of America's TV viewers tonight. (p. 107)

He not only wants to be where the action is, but he wants the action to revolve around *him.* After the arrest, we discover that a British camera crew has been following him throughout the weekend, so that his participation in the March and his arrest seem more than ever opportunism and self-aggrandizement. Even imprisonment must be at the hero's convenience: he wants to be among the first arrested, mistakenly imagining he will thereby be among the first released, so that he may attend a cocktail party in New York that same evening.

In the course of the narrative, Mailer confesses perhaps more than he is aware of about himself; all of it would constitute a devastating indictment, except for two factors. First, his candor disarms the reader's own critical instincts.[8] Second, the narrator's strategy is to get the reader to sympathize with his hero's egotism, to root for him as he scores his "touchdown" at the Pentagon. After the disaster at the Ambassador Theater, the reader wants him to succeed. For in the logic of the narrative, egotism is the hero's only defense against almost crippling self-doubt. Thus the reader cheers the protagonist's self-assertion because it pays comic dividends.[9] One identifies with his struggle against enemies both within (his own fear) and without (the faceless Establishment symbolized by the Pentagon).

Finally, Mailer's account of the March completes his attempt during the events to justify himself and to commandeer the March for himself. If he cannot wholly succeed in real life, he will succeed in literature in exerting his control over events. As he admits at one point, "he was off on the Romantic's great military dream, which is: seize defeat, convert it to triumph" (p. 31). And his tactic works. The March on the Pentagon was an ambiguous event; if it is remembered at all today, it is primarily because Norman Mailer was there and wrote about it.

Earlier, it was suggested that Mailer perhaps exposes more than he knows about himself. One of the characters he scores comic points against in the narrative is the famous pediatrician and war protestor, Benajmin Spock; ironically, Dr. Spock could provide an interesting insight into the infantile roots of the protagonist's contradictory behavior. Mailer cites Spock's "perfectly decent speech" before the March, but then confesses

> . . . Mailer had an animus against Spock. Three of Mailer's four wives had used Spock's book on infant and baby care as their bible. Mailer had put his nose in the book once in a while, and . . . it even seem possessed of common sense. Nonetheless, Mailer did not like Spock too much. A marriage is never so ready to show where it is weak as when a baby is ill, and Spock was therefore associated in Mailer's mind more with squalling wives than babies. (p. 99)

If we put our own noses into Spock's book, *Baby and Child Care*, we find a description of a stage of human development commonly referred to as "the terrible twos," that period when a child is still imperfectly toilet-trained and struggling to develop a sense of autonomy. The relevant section is labeled "Contrariness":

> In the period between 2 and 3, children are apt to show signs of balkiness and inner tensions. . . . The 1-year-old contradicts his mother. The 2½-year-old even contradicts himself. . . . He has a hard time making up his mind, and then he wants to change it. He acts like a person who feels he is being bossed too much, even when no one is bothering him. He is quite bossy himself. He insists on doing things just so, doing them his own way. . . . It makes him furious to have anyone interfere in one of his jobs. . . .
>
> It looks as though the child's nature between 2 and 3 is urging him to decide things for himself, and to resist pressure from other people. Trying to fight these two battles without much worldly experience seems to get him tightened up inside. . . .[10]

Although the analogy may at first appear ludicrously reductive, it is nevertheless tempting to apply Spock's common sense explanation to the hero's behavior at the Ambassador Theater ("'I p°ssed on the floor. Hoo-ee! hoo-ee!'" [p. 50]) and to his contradictory feelings and attempts at self-assertion elsewhere in the narrative. Mailer once claimed that Thomas Wolfe wrote "like the greatest five-year-old who ever lived, an invaluable achievement."[11] Similarly, it might be useful to speculate that Mailer writes like the most brilliant two-and-a-half-year old alive. The analogy, if it contains any kernel of truth, is not intended to be derogatory, for Mailer's achievement is likewise invaluable: he speaks for the unregenerate two-and-a-half-year-old in all of us. His erratic behavior evokes contradictory responses: sometimes the reader wants to laugh and cheer him on, and sometimes the parent in the reader wants to spank him.

II

Thus the central conflict of the novel, the hero's ambivalence toward himself and toward external objects, reenacts the anal ambivalence of the childhood struggle for autonomy. Anal ambivalence is built into the system of metaphors of the novel: the hero is the prophet of dirt and happy obscenity, but he suffers from a persistent desire to purge and cleanse himself. Waste is perceived as foul and evil and dead, yet it is also vital, primitive, odoriferous, unmistakable, and true. The hero is sensitized to this ambivalence in America because it also exists in himself, and he uses anal imagery and scatology as a means, if you will, of unearthing buried truth: "Yes, the use of obscenity was indeed to be condemned, for the free use of it would wash away the nation—was America the first great power to be built on bullshit?" (p. 201).

Just as the hero struggles with ambivalent feelings about himself, so he is uncertain about which he hates more: the war protestors, who consist of "the mediocre middle-class middle-aged masses of the left" (p. 96) and their spoiled hippie children; or the Pentagon, symbol of the government war machine. The metaphors pertaining to both forces are similar. One of the ironies of *The Armies of the Night* is that Mailer spends most of the first half heaping contempt on the middle class; the imagery applied to them is biting. By contrast, his treatment of the Pentagon seems routine. He cannot rouse as much hatred for a building, a symbol, as he can for his favorite scapegoat, the much-despised middle class. The fact that the book was so popular among that same group (who are, after all, Mailer's audience) says something about middle-class ambivalence and deep-seated liberal guilt feelings.

The middle-class and the Pentagon are alike in being characterized as inhuman, deathlike, machinelike, impotent or sterile, and excremental. For example, the "Liberal Party" is described in Chapter 4 as "programmatic" (p. 14), "servants of that social machine of the future" (p. 16). They will be "natural managers of that future air-conditioned vault where the last of human life would still exist," on "Utope cities" on "dead planets" like the moon (pp. 15–16). Their houses are "institutional" colors and remind him of "the scent of the void which comes off the pages of a Xerox copy" (p. 15). Punning on the term "interior decoration," Mailer suggests that the furnishings of their homes reflect the state of their psyches. Their mechanical decor neglects the "true powers of interior decoration," the essential furniture of the psyche: "greed, guilt, compassion and trust" (pp. 15–16). And just as they are psychically desensitized, so they are sexually incomplete: their lap is "undernourished," their loins "overpsychologized" (p. 15).

As he sees it, the middle-class left cuts itself off from its roots, denying its humanity, its animal, carnal, excremental nature. They are simply too *clean* for Mailer: "The super-hygiene of all this mental prophylaxis offended him profoundly. Super-hygiene impregnated the air with medicated Vaseline—there was nothing dirty in the damn stuff; and sex to Mailer's idea of it was better off dirty, damned, even slavish! than clean and without guilt" (p. 24).

Mailer does not want to be identified with these super-clean people, even if an accident of history has them temporarily fighting on the same side with him. For this urban middle class, "by the sheer ineptitude, the *kinks* of history, were now being compressed into more and more militant stands, their resistance to the war some hopeless melange, somehow firmed, of Pacifism and closet Communism" (p. 34). The anal metaphor is there in the language of the sentence, although veiled: a mass, a hopeless melange, is passing through kinks, being compressed and firmed. The unspoken implication is that, like feces, the middle class are a hopeless mass, being acted upon by forces against their will. Even their opposition to the war is not, for Mailer, *real* (read "masculine") resistance, but an expression of weakness: "Pacificism and closet Communism." The Pacifists he brands elsewhere as too "gentle" for his taste (p. 68), and "closet" Communism reminds one that it is homosexuals who are forced to live in closets.

Thus, through an elaborate series of allusions and metaphors, Mailer condemns the middle class as sterile and impotent or homosexual, overly clean and yet secretly dirty. These self-contradictory, ambivalent accusations are usually connected in his work; they sum up everything Mailer seems to consider evil. His fundamental loathing of the mediocre, excremental nature of the middle class breaks through clearly in such passages as the following:

> Mediocrities flock to any movement which will indulge their self-
> pity and their self-righteousness, for without a Movement their
> mediocrity is on the slide into terminal melancholia. Most such
> political movements served as piping systems for the brain and
> flushing systems for the heart, bringing in subsistence rations of
> ego and do-it-yourself compassion, all very well as social plumb-
> ing to keep mass man alive, but the Participant wasn't so certain
> that there weren't too many people alive already, certainly in
> America, that hog's trough of Paradise. (p. 96)

The wit of the anal imagery ("movement," "slide," "piping,"
"flushing," "plumbing," "hog's trough") no longer disguises the
nastiness of the feeling. There is an almost fascistic cruelty in the
social Darwinism of this passage: Mailer suggests that mediocrities
should be simply eliminated. Here one sees the kind of extremes to
which excremental loathing can force him; the line between wit
and pure hatred is thin and sometimes difficult to sustain.

If, on the one hand, the middle-class left is anal-retentive, uptight and redolent of deodorant, then, on the other hand, the "spoiled
children of a dead de-animalized middle class" (p. 280) have gone
too far toward the other extreme of anality. They are characterized
by a careless, spendthrift "waste" that displeases the Puritanical,
conservative side of Mailer. Just as the American technologues
have polluted our environment and bombed Vietnam, so the hippies,
Mailer suggests, have wasted their own natures and bombed themselves with an excess of drugs. In the process, the hippies may have
damned themselves and future generations (for Mailer, who likes to
believe in a kind of psychic economy and divine justice, accepted
the scare story that circulated in the late 1960s that LSD affected
the chromosomes):

> It was the children in whom Mailer had some hope, a gloomy
> hope. These mad middle-class children with their lobotomies
> from sin, their nihilistic embezzlement of all middle-class moral
> funds, their innocence, their lust for apocalypse, their unbeliev-
> able indifference to waste: twenty generations of buried hopes
> perhaps engraved in their chromosomes, and now conceivably
> burning like faggots in the secret inquisitional fires of LSD. It
> was a devil's drug—designed by the Devil to consume the love
> of the best, and leave them liverwasted, weeds of the big city.
> . . . drug-gutted flower children. (pp. 34–35)

The same system of anal metaphor Mailer used in his moral in-

dictment of American society in *Why Are We in Vietnam?* is repeated in this passage: "drug-gutted," "waste," "devil's drug,"
"liver-wasted," and "weeds." Aside from the hippies' excrementally
loose nature, the language also hints at homosexuality in the double
meaning of "faggots." Later in the narrative, he charitably decides
that "Mailer's final allegiance . . .was with the villains who were
hippies" over the "corporation-land villains" (p. 93). Nevertheless,
if his final sympathies lean toward the flower children, he still
considers them an excessive reaction to the deodorized nature of
their parents: the parents repress their anality and their sexuality,
whereas the children flaunt theirs, moving toward a diabolic alli-
ance with waste. Nowhere can Mailer find the proper balance to this
anal ambivalence, only a vacillation between extremes, because
nowhere can he find that balance in himself.

Similar anal and sexual imagery is used in the descriptions of
the Pentagon (the central symbol of the work, as Mount Anaka was
the central symbol of *The Naked and the Dead*). Like the middle
class, the Pentagon is inhuman, deathlike, machinelike, sterile,
and excremental, all at the same time. If the sterility seems opposed
to the excrementality, one cannot expect Mailer's system of metaphors to be totally consistent; everything is viewed in terms of
dialectic and is imbued with anal ambivalence. The cluster of
metaphors emerges in the first description of the building:

> . . .they were going to face the symbol, the embodiment, no, call it
> the true and high church of the military-industrial complex, the
> Pentagon, blind five-sided eye of a subtle oppression which had
> come to America out of the very air of this century (this evil
> twentieth century with its curse on the species, its oppressive
> Faustian lusts, its technological excrement all over the conduits
> of nature . . . yes, Mailer felt a confirmation of the contests of his
> own life on this March to the eye of the oppressor, greedy stingy
> dumb valve of the worst of the Wasp heart, chalice and anus
> of corporation land. . . . (pp. 113–14)

This passage comes as Mailer is on the March and attempts to
encompass in a single, convoluted, Faulknerian sentence all his
ambivalent feelings as he rediscovers his love for his mysterious
America even as he nears the symbol of all he hates in the country.
There is a rich stew of metaphor here, an interplay of religious and
excremental imagery. The symbol of the Pentagon serves as a condensation, a summing up of the system of metaphors that Mailer has
been applying interchangeably to the middle class, to America, and
to himself. As he admits here, the Pentagon March serves as "a
confirmation of the contests of his own life."

The anal ambivalence in the metaphors applied to the Pentagon builds. If the Pentagon casts out "technological excrement," it is next described as a "deodorant": "totalitarianism was a deodorant to nature. . . . by the logic of this metaphor, the Pentagon looked like the five-sided tip on the spout of a spray can to be used under the arm . . ." (p. 117). Later, Mailer mentions that "American nightmares which passed on the winds in the old small towns now traveled on the nozzle tip of the flame thrower" (p. 153). Just as the underarm spray suppresses natural odor, so the flame thrower substitutes for healthy "passing wind"; it is only a short step, Mailer seems to suggest, from the deadening deodorant to the lethal purgative of the flame thrower. One is reminded of Marion Faye in *The Deer Park* pleading at dawn in the desert for an atomic blast to purify the earth: "So let it come, Faye thought, let this explosion come . . . until the Sun God burned the earth. . . . Let it come, Faye begged, like a man praying for rain, let it come and clear the rot and the stench and the stink. . . ." (*DP*, p. 161). Just as Faye wanted to wallow in the stench of his corrupt society and alternately wanted to cleanse the world of corruption, so the Pentagon and, by extension, the American people seem possessed by contradictory desires.

In the last image applied to the Pentagon, Mailer compares it to an Egyptian tomb, built out of mud and consecrated to death and mud. America has moved, he says, from the "existential sanction of the frontier" to the worship of the dollar, "filthy lucre." "Nowhere had so much of the dollar bill collected as at the Pentagon, giant mudpie on the banks of America's Nile, the Potomac!" (p. 158). Thus, paradoxically, even as the Pentagon is a sterile, deadening, deodorizing force, it is also a monument consecrated to filth; it sums up our ambivalence.

A set of images repeated throughout *The Armies of the Night*, and also in much of his work since *Advertisements for Myself*, seems to explain some of the paradoxical nature of this ambivalence: in his psychological system, Mailer refers to characters as "greedy" or "stingy," or, worst of all, both greedy and stingy at the same time. Denise in "The Time of Her Time" kisses with "a rubbery greedy compulsion" (*ADV*, p. 452). In contrast, Ruta in *An American Dream* gives off "a thin high constipated smell" (*AD*, p. 46), a "stingy fish-like scent" (*AD*, p. 54). Although she has a "stingy" mouth, she is "greedy" in her lovemaking (*AD*, p. 46). In *Why Are We in Vietnam?*, old greedy-guts "Gutsy" Hyde, the mortician, symbolizes the contradictory nature of the "United Greedies of America" (*WV*, p. 222), powerful and fertile, but turned on by corpses.

Armies explains some of the meanings Mailer attaches to the characteristics of stinginess and greed. He is not opposed to greed itself: he considers greed, along with guilt, compassion, and trust, to be among the "true powers of interior decoration" (*AN*, pp. 15–16); he also mentions that the novelist must be "greedy for experience" (p. 118). However, he is against "outsize greed" (p. 151) unbalanced by those other powers of guilt, compassion, and trust. Worst of all is unadmitted greed, like the destructive "greed and secret lust (often unknown to themselves)" of the corporation-land villains (p. 93). He sees the American pro-war faction as trapped in a bind, caught in a "painful pinch between their stinginess and their greed" (p. 153), and the Pentagon is the "greedy stingy dumb valve of the worst of the Wasp heart, chalice, and anus of corporation land" (p. 114).

In their greed, Americans take in too much, but in their stinginess, they hold on to it. Their psychic equilibrium is disturbed, and this is reflected in the workings of their body and even in the look of their faces. In Mailer's psychological system, which is part Wilhelm Reich and part medieval system of humors, the workings of the body are analogous to the workings of the mind; thus one could call the pro-Vietnam War group either "schizophrenic" or psychically constipated. Instead of intestinal fortitude, they show intestinal impotence. Of course, looking at it not in terms of Mailer's system but from a Freudian point of view, they are not suffering from "schizophrenia" but from the same anal ambivalence which operates throughout the book.

As Mailer reads the faces of the Marshals at the Pentagon, he sees his Army buddies grown twenty years older. But their faces now are stingy, mean, and loveless: "they had the kind of faces which belong to the bad guys in a Western" (p. 150). The tenderness of their youth has given way to rabid hate, "the hatred of failures who had not lost their greed" (p. 154). In contrast to such men are the prison guards, who suffer from the same characteristic American disorder, "the usual constipated mixture of stinginess and greed, blocked compassion and frustrated desires for power" (p. 197), but work out their contradictions in the prison, without violence: "step by step . . . , dealing with prisoners everyday, doling out a kindness here one degree more kind than they had once received, dropping a stinginess there to get the barb of an old stinginess out" (p. 198). Mailer admires them because they are not consumed by hate. He imagines that the guards, like his own "White Negro," are administering self-therapy, resolving through action the contradictions of "their own childhoods . . . a slow solemn process of exchanging psychic equivalents to remake their nervous system" (p. 198). Although the Marshals and the guards are real people, Mailer fictionalizes them, projects qualities onto them so they can be subsumed, as all the characters, incidents, and symbols in *The Armies of the Night* are subsumed, into his private psychology with its organizing system of metaphors.

The same ambivalence that characterizes the people he describes also characterizes the hero, who encompasses such contradictory extremes as virulent hatred for the middle class and tender compassion for his prison guards. His saving grace is that tender streak, along with a degree of objectivity about his own feelings, though he often seems unaware of the irrational basis of his hatreds. Ultimately, many of the hero's responses to other people seem based largely on projections of his own self-love or self-hatred. We often hate most in others those characteristics we despise most in ourselves. The hero comes close to this revelation at two points. First, he confesses, "His deepest detestation was often reserved for the nicest of liberal academics, as if their lives were his own but a step escaped" (p. 15), and next, he admits that the one personality he finds insupportable in himself is that of the nice Jewish boy from Brooklyn.

Although he cannot explain *why* he hates these things, the feelings make some of the hatreds he expresses elsewhere more explicable. If Mailer hates in himself "something in his adenoids" which reveals "the softness of a man early accustomed to mother-love" (p. 136), then it is understandable why he might hate so much the soft middle class with their "proliferated monumental adenoidal resentments" (p. 34) and their "spoiled children" (p. 280): it is partly, as Oscar Wilde puts it in *The Picture of Dorian Gray*, "the rage of Caliban" at his image in a glass. Similarly, the detailed portrait of Robert Lowell also seems to project aspects of the hero's ambivalent self-concept: "Lowell had the most disconcerting mixture of strength and weakness in his presence. . . . physical strength or no, his nerves were all too apparently delicate. Obviously spoiled by everyone for years, he seemed nevertheless to need the spoiling" (pp. 40–41).

Mailer's quest to resolve his ambivalent self-image is built into the split point of view and the plot of *Armies*. When the hero announces to the crowd at the Ambassador Theater, "'Now, you may wonder who I am'" (p. 46), it is Mailer who raises the question of his identity, not his audience. Like Shago Martin in *An American Dream* or D. J. in *Why Are We in Vietnam?*, Mailer at the Ambassador Theater adopts a series of roles and voices. His bizarre, contradictory performance at that event expresses both aggression against the audience and self-aggression. Instead of wooing these fellow protestors, he attacks and alienates them in a self-destructive way, for he sees them as the dreaded, shitty middle class he hates so much in himself.

"'What are you, dead heads?' he bellowed at the audience. 'Or are you all . . . in the nature of becoming dead ahsses?'" (p. 37). When they applaud one of his remarks, he kills the applause in midstream by denouncing them: "'bless us all—shit!' he shouted, 'I'm trying to say the middle class plus shit, I mean plus revolution, is equal to one big collective dead ass'" (p. 37). He gets some pleasure out of the exhibitionism and the obscenity while casting the fearful anality onto the audience; he protects himself from self-exposure through role playing; but finally he cannot control the responses of this crowd as he can manipulate a reader's response through the calculations of literary rhetoric. The hero purges himself but bewilders and alienates his audience. Later he will recoup his losses by writing up the episode as a comedy. One tends to agree with Richard Poirier's judgment: "Only in writing can Mailer exist in a form that embraces his contradictions. . . . Where Mailer is not, by virtue of the act of writing, able to control a situation, the hidden thrust of his energy is toward the sacrificial waste of himself, toward shit."[12]

Paradoxically, even as Mailer proclaims himself the prophet of "dirt and the dark deliveries of the necessary" (p. 41), he feels a conflicting urge to cleanse himself. If he is foul-mouthed at the Ambassador Theater, he also delights in confessing his bathroom contretemps. The following morning, he thinks, "His exertions of the night before had been perfect for delivering him of some weeks of concentrated rage, perhaps even violence, at a variety of frustrations, he felt cleansed of the kind of hatred which leaves one leaden or tense. . . . Yelling on stage seemed literally to have loosened the screw of the vise" (p. 56). Metaphorically, he has overcome his psychic constipation. Later, as he marches toward the Pentagon, "Mailer knew for the first time why men in the front line of a battle are almost always ready to die: there is a promise of some swift transit—one's soul feels clean. . . ." (p. 113). When he is released from prison on Sunday, he feels shriven: "There was a sweet clean edge to the core of the substance of things. . . . this clean sense of himself. . . . it was not unlike the rare sweet of a clean loving tear not dropped, still held. . . ." (pp. 212–13). Above all, he needs to feel clean in order to overcome "the private conviction that he was getting a little soft, a hint curdled, perhaps an almost invisible rim of corruption was growing around the edges" (p. 73).

III

This analysis of the conflict in the work has perhaps not done sufficient justice to the leavening effect of humor in managing that conflict, for *The Armies of the Night* is fundamentally a comedy. Mailer certainly distances us from his hero's aggression and ambivalence by enabling us to laugh frequently at his contradictions. Moreover, the novel is saturated with various forms of verbal humor—not only the punning, word play, and crude scatology of *Why Are We in Vietnam?* but the whole gamut of sophisticated wit, relying on such devices as offbeat allusions (the mean Marshal with "stone larynx, leather testicles, ice cubes for eyes" [p. 144]); absurd juxtapositions ("he looked on transaction via telephone as Arabs look upon pig" [p. 5]); comic anticlimax ("those young men brave enough, idealistic enough [and doubtless vegetarian enough!] to give their draft cards back to the government" [p. 55]); and abrupt shifts in diction ("his imbroglio with the p°ssarooney" [p. 50]).

Why Are We in Vietnam? was a comic novel peopled with grotesque caricatures. Its plot was slim, more appropriate for a short story, so the novel was spun out through verbal comedy, word play and scatology, much of it directed against the audience. (D. J's harangues remind one of Mailer's obscene performance at the Ambassador Theater.) In contrast, the humor of *The Armies of the Night* depends not only on witty rhetoric but also on believable characters and comic situations. Remembering it, one recalls such low and high comedy scenes as the inebriated Mailer urinating on the floor of the darkened men's room at the Ambassador Theater and later confessing his misdeed to the crowd; or Mailer in his three-piece suit crossing a police line and making a broken-field run like "a banker gone ape" (p. 131) to get himself arrested at the Pentagon; or Mailer exchanging insults with a Nazi in the police van; or the clever Jewish lawyer Hirschkop outsmarting the WASP Commissioner Scaife and getting Mailer released from prison without bail.

The Armies of the Night is even comparable in certain respects to a novel like Fielding's mock-heroic comic epic, *Tom Jones*. Like *Tom Jones*, *Armies* has an urbane, self-conscious narrative persona who makes his digressions part of the pleasure of the story. We collaborate with him as he finds a new form and a new kind of comic hero, and we share his excitement at the newly discovered possibilities of this liberating form. The old-fashioned, formal tone of the narrative provides Mailer a framework to contain the chaos and ambiguity of contemporary events. The hero's farcical adventures are recounted in a supple, often wittily epigrammatic style: "Man might be a fool who peed in the wrong pot, man was also a scrupulous servant of the self-damaging admission" (p. 31).

The comedy in *Armies* also helps to balance the anal sadism of the work. Wit, as Freud suggests in *Jokes and Their Relation to the Unconscious*, can be a means of managing aggression. Freud sees jokes as a form of "developed play"[13] that uses some of the same psychic processes as dreams, such as "condensation, displacement, and indirect representation."[14] Those jokes he calls "tendentious" are subversive, circumventing repression and allowing roundabout expression of hostile impulses or the obscene: "A whole class of obscene jokes allows one to infer the presence of a concealed inclination to exhibitionism in their inventors; aggressive tendentious jokes succeed best in people in whose sexuality a powerful sadistic component is demonstrable. . . ."[15] Such jokes guarantee a reception for invective "which they would never have found in a non-joking form."[16] Aggressive jokes create allies for the teller against the hated person or institution, bribing the hearer with the comic pleasure of a momentary release from inhibition: "Where argument tries to draw the hearer's criticism over on to its side, the joke endeavours to push criticism out of sight."[17]

Most of the jokes in *The Armies of the Night* fit Freud's category of the "tendentious." They are a roundabout means of expressing aggression, whether it is the hero's hostility against himself or against his enemies, and they function in a subversive fashion to short-circuit our critical faculties, using sarcasm and ridicule to make us hate what the hero hates. A good example of such tendentious wit is the hero's attack on Paul Goodman, whom he evidently dislikes because of Goodman's overly liberal attitudes toward sex and his awful writing style. At least these are the ostensible reasons; once one decides to hate someone, anything can serve as a reason.[18]

A look at the jokes about Goodman may give us a clue as to the real source of his aggression against the man. Mailer ridicules Goodman's literary style, saying it "read like LBJ's exercises in Upper Rhetoric (the Rhetoric, Mailer now decided, being located three inches below and back of Erogenous Zone Clitoric)" (p. 98). He also decides that "Goodman looked like the sort of old con who had first gotten into trouble in the YMCA . . ." (p. 29). If we consider these remarks for a moment, we see that Mailer is really casting aspersions on Goodman as a homosexual pervert. He associates him with the evil authority figure, LBJ, and also connects him to the vagina and the anus in the allusions of the first remark. He is able to get away with the attack for two reasons. First, the invective is elegant and roundabout, masked by wit. Second, the jokes are in the mind of the hero, that fictional "Mailer," and not in the mind of the narrator, that other Mailer who is well above the fray and would not stoop to such low blows.

Thus, the achievement of *The Armies of the Night* is not in any dramatic change in Mailer's personality—the same obsessions and ambivalence of his other works persist here, the same system of metaphors recurs—but in the means of approaching that personality, in the *form* of the work. Form is, among other things, a system of defense. Any writer whose work is so charged with anal ambivalence as Mailer's will be particularly concerned with form and structure as a means to counter dangerous tendencies toward chaos and shapelessness. Mailer's twenty-year-long experimentation with form—from omniscience, to first-person, to third-person narration, to essays and reportage, to self-interviews—culminates in *The Armies of the Night*, in whose third-person narration and formal narrator he was able to find a congenial solution to the problem of presenting himself in print, harnessing his ambivalence to make it yield the maximum literary dividends.

The danger that he faced was that, having finally found the most successful form with which to express his warring tendencies, he began to repeat himself. After *The Armies of the Night*, the form began to wear thin, and his one major character, Norman Mailer, was exposed too often, until even the ambivalence became predictable. When the tendency to self-defense overbalances the instinct for advenure, a writer goes stale. In the seventies, Mailer lost some of his major impact as a writer, the ability to shock and startle us. As of this writing, it is ten years since *The Armies of the Night*; we are still awaiting that long-promised epic novel. Perhaps Mailer will again be able to transform himself and find the new form that will jolt us once more.

Notes

1. See Warner Berthoff, "Witness and Testament: Two Contemporary Classics," *New Literary History* 2, No. 2 (Winter 1971), 323: "we read him now with all the interest a witness-bearer deserves whose obsessions have been borne out by the explosion of actual events."

2. See Stanley T. Gutman, *Mankind in Barbary: The Individual and Society in the Novels of Norman Mailer* (Hanover, N.H.: University Press of New England, 1975), p. 179: "The Washington March allows Mailer to observe America at a critical point: growth. . . may lead to a better, more human society; refusal to grow . . . will . . . hasten the impending totalitarianism."

3. Jean Radford, *Norman Mailer: A Critical Study* (New York: Harper and Row, 1975), p. 116.

4. Ibid., p. 117.

5. Melvin Maddocks, "Norm's Ego Is Working Overtime for *You*," *Life*, 10 May 1968, p. 8.

6. Gutman, *Mankind in Barbary*, p. 189: "A sense of division—one could call it ambivalence or schizophrenia—permeates the novel, thematically, in its tone, and its formal construction." See also Mas'ud Zavarzadeh, *The Mythopoeic Reality: The Postwar American Nonfiction Novel* (Urbana: University of Illinois Press, 1976), p. 175: "schizophrenia . . . is not just stated in the book but enacted in its very narrative fabric and point of view."

7. Richard Levine, "When Sam and Sergius Meet," in *Will the Real Norman Mailer Please Stand Up?*, ed. Laura Adams (Port Washington, N.Y.: Kennikat Press, 1974), p. 30.

8. Nevertheless, Mailer's egotism in *The Armies of the Night* still seemed objectionable to some critics. See, for example, Kingsley Widmer, "The Post-Modernist Art of Protest: Kesey and Mailer as American Expressions of Rebellion," *Centennial Review*, 19, No. 3 (Summer 1975), 133: "Mailer's pretentious narrator certainly gets in the way. . . . Bathos slips in. . . . in the exhibitionism and literary aggrandizements."

9. See Gutman, *Mankind in Barbary*, p. 192: "This romantic and egotistical affirmation . . . is perhaps at the core of Mailer's popularity. . . . Because many of his readers are faced with a simultaneous loss of belief and a fear of impending totalitarianism, they find his egotism little short of sublime."

10. Dr. Benjamin Spock, *Baby and Child Care* (rev. 1968; New York: Pocket Books, 1946), pp. 356–57.

11. Norman Mailer, *Cannibals and Christians* (New York: Dial Press, 1966), p. 97. Mailer later regretted that statement and adds a footnote at the bottom of the same page: "Since I did not wish to insult the memory of Wolfe, it would have been happier and perhaps more accurate to have said: like the greatest fifteen-year-old alive."

12. Richard Poirier, *Norman Mailer* (New York: Viking, 1972) pp. 93–94.

13. Sigmund Freud, *Jokes and Their Relation to the Unconscious*, trans. James Strachey (New York: Norton, 1960), p. 119.

14. Ibid., p. 165.

15. Ibid., p. 143.

16. Ibid., p. 103.

17. Ibid., p. 133.

18. Mailer always has difficulty in relating to openly homosexual or bisexual writers, perhaps because of his insecurity about his own manhoood. Should such writers criticize him in print, Mailer responds with savage vituperation. Thus his ambivalence about the sharp-tongued Truman Capote, his uneasy friendship with James Baldwin, his long-standing vendetta against Gore Vidal, and his distaste for Paul Goodman.

Those masterful images because complete
Grew in pure mind, but out of what began?
A mound of refuse or the sweepings of a street,

. . . .

Now that my ladder's gone,
I must lie down where all the ladders start,
In the foul rag-and-bone shop of the heart.
                              Yeats,
                                "The Circus Animals' Desertion"

According to Richard Poirier, the central subject of *Why Are We in Vietnam?* is waste and buggery. "D.J.'s memory is doomed to scatology, and, though he dare not bugger his mate, his mind is obsessed with jokes and images of buggery, of sexual entrances that lead not to the centers of creation but to the center of waste."[1] For Poirier, this obsession helps to explain even the erratic, disjointed form of the narrative. "It can be said that the book is given wholly to interruptions and distractions, though there is no telling from what, unless it be the urge to kill or hump."[2]

Although Poirier's observations about *Vietman* are essentially correct, he does not go far enough. As we have seen, the fantasies evoked in the novel go beyond sodomy; they center on a repeated compulsion, an urge to anally rape and destroy the parents or the love object, to disembowel and excrete upon them (that is, to "waste" them or convert them into waste), and finally to digest the remains. This last act of cannibalism and coprophagia serves to absorb the power of the defeated victim and repossess the expelled love object, and thus to ward off punishment and atone for the anal-sadistic impulses.

Even if these obsessions are only carried out in the novelist's imagination, they seem to have the force of reality. Not only is D.J. caught up in these incestuous, destructive fantasies, but Mailer projects them outward onto the nation, even onto the cosmos. The God that D.J. hears as a voice in the North is "a beast, not a man, and God said, 'Go out and kill—fulfill my will, go and kill'" (*WV*, p. 203). Mailer tries to suggest that America is in Vietnam in order to enact precisely these barbaric rituals, to leave Vietnam "all gutted, shit
207

on, used and blasted" (p. 205), and that the nation commits atrocities not through choice but out of compulsion.

The critic C. T. Samuels complains that "what hovers over Mailer's book is nothing so momentous and public as Vietnam, but rather . . . a private obsession with sodomy. . . . Though scores of people will agree that our government is engaged in unnatural acts with the Vietnamese, I doubt that this is what they have in mind."[3] The same complaint about the novel is voiced by Samuel Hux: "for Mailer, violence is somehow akin to buggery . . . in the quality and intensity of its perversity. . . . Is it always possible to tell when Mailer is commenting from varying distances on the national character and when Mailer is experiencing through fiction an obsession native to his own thought?"[4] According to James Toback, in *Vietnam* "Mailer's development from politics to metapolitics is complete. The world—and especially America—is now viewed as an expression of Mailer's most extreme longings and fantasies."[5]

One could counter these critics by arguing that American involvement in Vietnam did seem to be based on motives that were extrapolitical and almost wholly irrational. The war dragged on and on, and attained the status of a full-blown obsession. American anal-sadism with regard to Vietnam was exhibited by the use of the term *waste*, which came into popular currency as a synonym for murder during the war, by the reference to Vietnam as a "quagmire," and by the pronounced difficulties of the President in setting up a timetable for "phased withdrawal" from the involvement. One could argue as Frederic Jameson does that the force of *Why Are We in Vietnam?* "springs from this coincidence in it of the personal obsession and the historical contradiction."[6]

Nevertheless, the critics do have a valid point when they argue that Mailer seems to be confusing himself with America, projecting his private obsessions onto the national scene. Perhaps Mailer is able to write about these fantasies so powerfully only because of his intense involvement in them; Vietnam happened by fortuitous coincidence to offer him a fruitful opportunity for talking about his own obsessions and his favorite topic—himself. In *The Armies of the Night*, he admits that "the paradox of this obscene unjust war is that it provided him new energy" (*AN*, p. 188).

The objections raised by the critics point toward the central problem, not only of *Vietnam* but of all of Mailer's later work. In *Vietnam*, Mailer reached a temporary dead end in a journey that began in his fiction in "The Time of Her Time." Beginning with "The White Negro," Mailer became increasingly explicit in his essays and reportage about his personal obsessions, and beginning with "The Time of Her Time," the distance between creator and creation in his fiction started to narrow, until the novels seemed to be only an acting out of his private fantasies. Mailer found that, in order to get past this blind alley, he had to back up and make a long detour around the outskirts of the novel.

The deliberate confusion between his body and the body politic, between the forces at work inside Mailer's head and the dynamics of outside, historical reality, understandably frustrated many readers of *An American Dream* and *Why Are We in Vietnam?* In order to achieve that "willing suspension of disbelief" in a novel, an audience needs a protective distance from the author's fantasies that it does not demand from an essay. Mailer, on the contrary, seemed to need more and more direct self-exposure and to rely increasingly on self-exploitation. After *Vietnam*, he abandoned fiction and wrote *The Armies of the Night*, in which he finally found the ideal hero he had been looking for all these years, a hero who incorporated all of his own rich contradictions: himself. Mailer was able to expose directly his own fantasies and simultaneously to distance himself from them, and thus defeat shame. Unlike his previous two novels, *Armies* was enormously popular as well as a critical success. Mailer then spent several years experimenting with this quasi-fictional form, with progressively dwindling results, and he even moved into running for political office and making films, both means by which he could exhibit himself, act out his fantasies in public and have others participate in them much more directly than through the medium of the novel.

Now Mailer can present himself to us openly as an aesthetic creation, an object for contemplation, deliver himself to the public like an elaborate feast, garnished and served up on the platter of art. It is both the supreme sacrifice of the artist and complete narcissism. If art is "regression in the service of the ego," as Ernst Kris claims,[7] Mailer has merely carried the egotism of the artist to its logical conclusion. After more than ten years devoted to other fields, Mailer is still reported to be at work on a long new novel; one wonders whether he can return with any success to the rather oblique rewards of fiction.

To understand the line of development of Mailer's art, it might be useful briefly to compare him with two other writers who were always obsessed by excrement: Swift and Carlyle. This is not to say that Mailer is in the same league with these writers, but merely that some of the unconscious impulses behind their work are similar and tend to result in the use of some of the same literary mechanisms. What these authors have in common is a hyperacute sensitivity to waste, decay, and the unclean—to what is viscerally rejected or, symbolically, called "refuse." Many authors incorporate anal along with other fantasies in their work, but anal fantasies are the primary material in the work of Swift, Carlyle, and Mailer, to the exclusion of almost everything else; they are *obsessional* writers, with the strengths (intensity) and the limitations (repetitiousness) that term implies.

Carlyle was obsessed with *Teufelsdröckh* ("devil's dung") and, like Mailer, had the messianic urge to confront society with its own impurities, to cleanse it of waste and greed, evils that Carlyle saw everywhere. Swift could never recover from his amazement and revulsion at the realization that "Celia sh-ts." Like the typical obsessional described by Fenichel, all three men have or had a high intelligence mixed with superstition, and Mailer, like Carlyle and Swift, is deeply religious and concerned with God and the Devil.[8] Also like Swift and Carlyle, Mailer is a very aggressive writer, who is essentially a preacher and moralist and scathing wit, afflicted with a hyperdeveloped superego. The writing of all three at its best is distinguished by its fierceness and intensity.

Like Swift and Carlyle, Mailer is a "left conservative," a rebel against himself and against his time, possessed by what G. K. Chesterton calls "divine disgust."[9] According to Chesterton, Carlyle's writings "had all the unnatural clearness of visions, but they also had some of the distortions."[10] The same could be said for *An American Dream.*

Mailer has harnessed his own ambivalence to create a rhetoric that moves with wit and gusto between the high flown and the obscene, a rhetoric that is sometimes as fierce and funny as that of Swift or Carlyle. What Mailer cannot master, however, is his overeffusiveness, his tendency to overwrite. Like Carlyle's, Mailer's rhetoric can be powerful and scourging but has a tendency to fall in love with itself, into rant and repetitiousness.

Swift was a mastermind, a deviser of intricate systems who yet mocked system, as in his satire in *Gulliver's Travels* of the overly ingenious inventors of Lagado, who dealt in human excrement. Mailer too is fond of elaborating his own outrageous systems. *Why Are We in Vietnam?* is the most "Swiftian" of Mailer's novels, not only in its savagery, obscenity, and invective but also in its insistent strain of ridicule which extends into self-mockery. D.J. presents versions of Mailer's own pet theories concerning God and the Devil, insanity, cancer, and excrement in parody form.[11] Fenichel writes:

The compulsion neurotic is ambivalent. He is so even toward his

own systems and rules. When he takes side against his dangerous
instinctual impulses, he needs systems and rules as protection.
When he turns against his superego, he also turns against systems
and rules imposed by his superego. He may openly rebel against
them or he may ridicule them by tracing them ad absurdum. [12]

Neither Swift nor Carlyle was really a novelist, although each
drew on the devices of fiction to create homiletics or fables or
satires. The obsessive writer relies on the psychological device
of *projection* and lacks most of the capacity for *introjection*, the
ability to identify imaginatively with someone who is alien to
his emotional framework, which is necessary to the novelist. Swift
and Carlyle are essentially inspired visionaries rather than novelists.
As Chesterton says of Carlyle,

> he had also this quality of the highest visionary artist, that the
> things he had not seen at all he was quite wrong about; I mean
> the things he had not visualized either with the eye of the spirit
> or that of the body. He is always wrong, and even outrageously
> wrong, about anything in which he is not intensely interested. . . .
> He could only be accurate when he was excited. [13]

This might explain why Mailer is at his best when he is writing
about the subject in which he is the most deeply involved: himself
and his own obsessions. As indicated earlier, all of the characters
in *The Naked and the Dead* seemed to boil down into one single
character who was Mailer. Perhaps now we can see why.

As Mailer grew more openly involved with his obsessions in his
later works, his writing became bolder and more powerful, but his
characters shriveled into transparent projections of himself and
his own fantasies. Like the characters in *Gulliver's Travels*, the
personages of *Why Are We in Vietnam?* are walking stereotypes or
mythical creatures, giants and dwarfs, grotesque and palpably
unreal figures out of daydreams and nightmares. As though to
compensate for the increasing thinness of his characters, Mailer
developed an effusive style, a relentless bombardment of words.

Mailer has never been really comfortable with the form of the
novel; he has always leaped away from it into other artistic activities
that offer him more immediate and direct gratifications. Either
his novels come to him rapidly, as in a vision (he admits he wrote
Vietnam in four months) or, more often, he has to force them out
slowly and painfully (see his description of the composition of
Barbary Shore and *The Deer Park* in *Advertisements for Myself*).
Perhaps there is a kind of anal ambivalence in this phenomenon.

Mailer has always envisioned the novel as a harsh and capricious mistress, a "Bitch Goddess" like Deborah in *American Dream*. Sometimes she eludes him for years, and then, for no reason at all, bestows her rewards. "Writing up political events is easy because your plot is ready-made," Mailer said in 1972. "When I work on a novel, I can lose a month just trying to figure out what happens in the next chapter."[14] In other words, he doesn't want to bother any more to mask or invent; he prefers to present his fantasies directly. Since he has abandoned the novel, his work flows freely; he has turned into the most prolific major author in America. But still, he feels guilty; the rewards come too easily. He wants to return to his original harsh taskmistress of the novel.

Ironically, his temperament may be fundamentally nonnovelistic. Posterity may decide that his greatest contribution to literature is in works like *The Armies of the Night*, which lie on the borderline between fact and fiction. Carlyle too liked to write "History as a Novel."

Mailer's obsessions have carried him through five novels, and although he has been able intermittently to illuminate his fantasies with visionary brilliance, transforming them into something rare and strange, he has not been able to provide all the rewards one expects from a great novelist. Perhaps for all their brilliance and intensity, the essential narrowness and repetitiousness of his obsessions set a limit on the possibilities of his achievement in the realm of the novel. In *Vietnam*, Mailer seems to have pushed to the limit and beyond, to a *reductio ad absurdum*. James Toback wonders whether *Vietnam* is "a breakthrough or a breakdown,"[15] and Donald L. Kaufmann speculates that the novel may be Mailer's last, his "footnote to fiction."[16]

It is too soon to say, however, whether Mailer has rung the final changes on his tune. He has already undergone so many transformations; he may astonish us again and produce that "Great American Novel" he has always demanded of himself. Mailer had the first word in this study and now he has the last, this cautionary note:

One should dig deep within oneself to find out his own nature. But you can't dig down too far, or you'll come out your own asshole.[17]

Notes

1. Richard Poirier, *Norman Mailer*, (New York: Viking, 1972) p. 152.

2. Ibid., p. 134.

3. C. T. Samuels, "Mailerrhea," *The Nation*, 23 October 1967, p. 406.

4. Samuel Hux, "Mailer's Dream of Violence," *Minnesota Review* 8 (1968): 502.

5. James Toback, "Norman Mailer Today," *Commentary* (October 1967), p. 75.

6. Frederic Jameson, "The Great American Hunter: or Ideological Content in the Novel" *College English* 34 (November 1972): 195.

7. Ernst Kris, *Psychoanalytic Explorations in Art* (New York: Schocken, 1967), p. 177.

8. See Otto Fenichel, *The Psychoanalytic Theory of Neurosis* (New York: Norton, 1945), pp. 300–301.

9. G. K. Chesterton, in his introduction to *Past and Present* by Thomas Carlyle (1843; rpt. London: Oxford University, 1960), p. vii.

10. Ibid., p. x.

11. See Toback, "Norman Mailer Today," pp. 74, 76.

12. Fenichel, *Neurosis*, p. 286.

13. Chesterton, *Past and Present*, p. xi.

14. Mailer in conversation, Berkeley, California, 24 October 1972.

15. Toback, "Norman Mailer Today," p. 74.

16. Donald L. Kaufmann, "Catch 23: The Mystery of Fact (Norman Mailer's Final Novel?)," *Twentieth Century Literature* 17 (Fall 1971): 256.

17. Mailer, as reported by Leo Braudy in "The Pride of Vulnerability," *Norman Mailer*, ed. Leo Braudy (Englewood Cliffs, N.J.: Prentice Hall, 1972) pp. 10–11.

Bibliography: List of Works Cited

I. Works by Norman Mailer

Mailer, Norman. *Advertisements for Myself*. New York: Putnam's, 1959.
_____. *An American Dream*. New York: Dial, 1964.
_____. "An American Dream." Serialized in *Esquire*, January–August 1964.
_____. *The Armies of the Night*. New York: New American Library, 1968.
_____. *Barbary Shore*. New York: Rinehart, 1951.
_____. *Cannibals and Christians*. New York: The Dial Press, 1966.
_____. *The Deer Park*. New York: G. P. Putnam's Sons, 1955.
_____. *The Deer Park: A Play*. New York: Dial, 1967.
_____. *Existential Errands*. Boston: Little, Brown and Company, 1972.
_____. *Genius and Lust: A Journey Through the Major Writings of Henry Miller*. New York: Grove Press, Inc. 1976.
_____. "Mailer on Marriage and Women." Interview by Buzz Farbar. *Viva*, October, 1973, pp. 75–76, 144–52.
_____. *The Naked and the Dead*. New York: Rinehart, 1948.
_____. *Of a Fire on the Moon*. Boston: Little, Brown and Company, 1970.
_____. *The Presidential Papers*. New York: G. P. Putnam's Sons, 1963.
_____. *The Prisoner of Sex*. Boston: Little, Brown and Company, 1971.
_____. *St George and the Godfather*. New York: New American Library, 1972.
_____. "A Transit to Narcissus." *The New York Review of Books*, 17 May 1973, pp. 3–10.
_____. *Why Are We in Vietnam?* New York: G. P. Putnam's Sons, 1967.

II. Works about Norman Mailer

Adams, Laura. *Existential Battles: The Growth of Norman Mailer*. Athens, Ohio: Ohio University, 1976.
_____. ed. *Will the Real Norman Mailer Please Stand Up?* Port Washington, N.Y.: Kennikat, 1974.
Aldridge, John W. *After the Lost Generation*. New York: McGraw-Hill, 1956.
_____. "The Energy of New Success." In *Norman Mailer: A Collection of Critical Essays*. Edited by Leo Braudy. Englewood Cliffs, N.J.: Prentice-Hall, 1972.
_____. "From Vietnam to Obscenity." In *Norman Mailer: The Man and His Work*. Edited by Robert F. Lucid. Boston: Little, Brown and Company, 1971.

_____. "Perfect Absurd Figure of a Mighty, Absurd Crusade." *Saturday Review*, 13 November 1971, pp. 45–46, 48–49, 72.

Alter, Robert. "Norman Mailer." In *The Politics of Twentieth-Century Novelists*. Edited by George A. Panichas. New York: Thomas Y. Crowell Co., Inc., 1974.

Alvarez, A. "Norman X." *Spectator*, 7 May 1965, p. 603.

Baldwin, James. "The Black Boy Looks at the White Boy." In *Norman Mailer: A Collection of Critical Essays*. Edited by Leo Braudy. Englewood Cliffs, N.J.: Prentice-Hall, 1972.

Bersani, Leo. "The Interpretation of Dreams." *Partisan Review* 32 (Fall 1965): 603–8.

Berthoff, Warner. "Witness and Testament: Two Contemporary Classics." *New Literary History* 2 (Winter 1971): 311–27.

Boyers, Robert. "Attitudes toward Sex in American 'High Culture.'" *Annals of the American Academy of Political and Social Sciences*, No. 376 (March 1968), pp. 36–52.

Braudy, Leo, ed. *Norman Mailer: A Collection of Critical Essays*. Englewood Cliffs, N.J.: Prentice-Hall, 1972.

_____. "Norman Mailer: The Pride of Vulnerability." In *Norman Mailer: A Collection of Critical Essays*. Edited by Leo Braudy. Englewood Cliffs, N.J.: Prentice-Hall, 1972.

Breit, Harvey. "Talk with Norman Mailer." *New York Times Book Review*, 3 June 1951, p. 20.

Burg, David F. "The Hero of *The Naked and the Dead*." *Modern Fiction Studies* 17 (1971): 387–401.

Burgess, Anthony. *The Novel Now*. New York: Norton, 1967.

Busch, Frederick. "The Whale as Shaggy Dog: Melville and 'The Man Who Studied Yoga.'" *Modern Fiction Studies* 19, No. 2 (Summer 1973): 193–206.

Bufithis, Philip. *Norman Mailer*. New York: Frederick Ungar Publishing Co., 1978.

Cecil, L. Moffitt. "The Passing of Arthur in Norman Mailer's *Barbary Shore*." *Research Studies* (Washington State University) 39, No. 1 (March 1971): 54–58.

Cook, Bruce. "Norman Mailer: The Temptation to Power." *Renascence* 14 (Summer 1962): 206–15, 222.

DeMott, Benjamin. "Docket No. 15883." *American Scholar* 30 (Spring 1961): 232–37.

Eisinger, Chester E. *Fiction of the Forties*. Chicago: University of Chicago Press, 1963.

Ellmann, Mary. *Thinking about Women*. New York: Harvest, 1968.

Evans, Timothy. "Boiling the Archetypal Pot: Norman Mailer's *American Dream.*" *Southwest Review* 60 (Spring 1975): 159–70.

Fiedler, Leslie. "The Breakthrough: The American Jewish Novelist and the Fictional Image of the Jew." *Midstream* 4 (Winter 1958): 15–35.

————. "Master of Dreams." *Partisan Review* 34 (Summer 1967): 353–54.

————. "The New Mutants." *Partisan Review* 32 (Fall 1965): 505–25.

————. *Waiting for the End.* New York: Dell Publishing Co., Inc., 1964.

Flaherty, Joe. *Managing Mailer.* New York: Coward-McCann, 1969.

Gross, Theodore L. *The Heroic Ideal in American Literature.* New York: The Free Press, 1971.

Gutman, Stanley T. *Mankind in Barbary: The Individual and Society in the Novels of Norman Mailer.* Hanover, N.H.: University Press of New England, 1975.

Hassan, Ihab. *Radical Innocence: Studies in the Contemporary American Novel.* New York: Harper and Row, 1961.

Hux, Samuel. "Mailer's Dream of Violence." *Minnesota Review* 8 (1968): 152–57.

Jameson, Frederic. "The Great American Hunter; or, Ideological Content in the Novel." *College English* 34 (November 1972): 180–97.

Kaufmann, Donald L. "Catch 23: The Mystery of Fact (Norman Mailer's Final Novel?)." *Twentieth Century Literature* 17 (Fall 1971): 247–56.

————. *Norman Mailer: The Countdown.* Carbondale, Ill.: Southern Illinois University Press, 1969.

Kazin, Alfred. "The Alone Generation." In *Recent American Fiction: Some Critical Views.* Edited by Joseph J. Waldmeir. Boston: Houghton Mifflin Company, 1963.

Langbaum, Robert. "Mailer's New Style." *The Modern Spirit: Essays on the Continuity of Nineteenth and Twentieth-Century Literature,* pp. 147–63. New York: Oxford University Press, Inc., 1970.

Lawler, Robert W. "Norman Mailer: The Connection of New Circuits." Ph.D. diss., Claremont, 1969.

Leeds, Barry H. *The Structured Vision of Norman Mailer.* New York: New York University Press, 1969.

Levine, Richard. "When Sam and Sergius Meet." In *Will the Real Norman Mailer Please Stand Up?* Edited by Laura Adams. Port Washington, N.Y.: Kennikat Press, 1974.

Lucid, Robert F., ed. *Norman Mailer: The Man and His Work.* Boston: Little, Brown and Company, 1971.

Maddocks, Melvin. "Norm's Ego is Working Overtime for *You.*" *Life,* 10 May 1968, p. 8.

Marcus, Steven. "An Interview with Norman Mailer." In *Norman Mailer: A Collection of Critical Essays.* Edited by Leo Braudy. Englewood Cliffs, N.J.: Prentice-Hall, 1972.

Middlebrook, Jonathan. *Mailer and the Times of His Time*. San Francisco: Bay Books, 1976.

Millett, Kate. *Sexual Politics*. Garden City: Doubleday and Co., Inc., 1970.

Muste, John M. "Norman Mailer and John Dos Passos: The Question of Influence." *Modern Fiction Studies* 17 (1971): 361–74.

Podhoretz, Norman. "Norman Mailer: The Embattled Vision." In *Norman Mailer: The Man and His Work*. Edited by Robert F. Lucid. Boston: Little, Brown and Company, 1971.

Poirier, Richard. "Morbid-Mindedness." In *Norman Mailer: The Man and His Work*. Edited by Robert F. Lucid. Boston: Little, Brown and Company, 1971.

_____. *Norman Mailer*. New York: The Viking Press, 1972.

_____. "Ups and Downs of Mailer." In *Norman Mailer: A Collection of Critical Essays*. Edited by Leo Braudy. Englewood Cliffs, N.J.: Prentice-Hall, 1972.

Prigozy, Ruth. "The Liberal Novelist in the McCarthy Era." *Twentieth Century Literature* 25, No. 3 (October 1975): 253–64.

Radford, Jean. *Norman Mailer: A Critical Study*. New York: Barnes and Nobel Books, 1975.

Ramsey, Roger. "Current and Recurrent: The Vietnam Novel." *Modern Fiction Studies* 17 (1971): 415–31.

Rosenthal, Melvyn. "The American Writer and His Society: The Response to Estrangement in the Works of Nathaniel Hawthorne, Randolph Bourne, Edmund Wilson, Norman Mailer, and Saul Bellow." Ph.D. diss., Connecticut, 1968.

Samuels, C. T. "Mailerrhea." *Nation*, 23 October 1967, pp. 405–6.

Schrader, George A. "Norman Mailer and the Despair of Defiance." *Yale Review* 51 (December 1961): 267–80.

Schroth, Raymond A. "Mailer and His Gods." *Commonweal*, 29 May 1969, pp. 226–29.

Schulz, Max. F. "Mailer's Divine Comedy." *Radical Sophistication: Studies in Contemporary Jewish-American Novelists*. Athens, Ohio: Ohio University Press, 1969.

Shaw, Peter. "The Tough Guy Intellectual." *Critical Quarterly* 8 (Spring 1966): 13–28.

Silverstein, Howard. "Norman Mailer: The Family Romance and the Oedipal Fantasy." *American Imago* 34, No. 3 (Fall 1977): 277–86.

Solotaroff, Robert. *Down Mailer's Way*. Urbana, Ill.: University of Illinois, 1974.

Stark, John. "*Barbary Shore*: The Basis of Mailer's Best Work." *Modern Fiction Studies* 17 (1971): 403–8.

Steiner, George. "Naked But Not Dead." *Encounter* (December 1961), pp. 67–70.

Tanner, Tony. "In the Lion's Den." *Partisan Review* 34 (Summer 1967): 467.

————. "On the Parapet: A Study of the Novels of Norman Mailer." *Critical Quarterly* 12 (1970): 153–76.

Toback, James. "Norman Mailer Today." *Commentary* (October 1967), pp. 68–76.

Trilling, Diana. "The Moral Radicalism of Norman Mailer." In *Norman Mailer: The Man and His Work.* Edited by Robert F. Lucid. Boston: Little, Brown and Company, 1971.

Wagenheim, Allen J. "Square's Progress: *An American Dream.*" *Critique* 10 (1967): 45–68.

Widmer, Kingsley. "The Post-Modernist Art of Protest: Kesey and Mailer as American Expressions of Rebellion." *Centennial Review* 19, No. 3 (Summer 1975): 121–35.

Witt, Grace. "The Bad Man as Hipster: Norman Mailer's Use of the Frontier Metaphor." *Western American Literature* 4 (Fall 1969): 203–17.

Zavarzadeh, Mas'ud. *The Mythopoeic Reality: The Postwar American Nonfiction Novel.* Urbana, Ill.: University of Illinois, 1976.

III. Psychoanalytic Works

Abraham, Karl. "Contributions to the Theory of Anal Character." In *An Outline of Psychoanalysis,* rev. ed. Edited by Clara Thompson; Milton Mazer; and Earl Wittenberg. New York: Modern Library, 1955.

————. *Selected Papers of Karl Abraham.* London: Hogarth Press, 1949.

Erikson, Erik H. *Childhood and Society.* 2d. ed., rev. New York: Norton, 1963.

Fenichel, Otto. *The Psychoanalytic Theory of Neurosis.* New York: Norton, 1945.

Freud, Anna. *The Writings of Anna Freud.* Vol. 5. New York: International Universities Press, 1969.

Freud, Sigmund. *Character and Culture.* Edited by Philip Rieff. New York: Collier, 1963.

————. *A General Introduction to Psychoanalysis.* New York: Washington Square, 1965.

————. *Jokes and Their Relation to the Unconscious.* Translated by James Strachey. New York: Norton, 1960.

————. *On Creativity and the Unconscious.* Edited by Benjamin Nelson. New York: Harper & Row, 1958.

————. *Sexuality and the Psychology of Love.* Edited by Philip Rieff. New York: Collier, 1963.

————. *Three Essays on the Theory of Sexuality.* Edited and translated by James Strachey. New York: Avon, 1962.

Gardner, Howard. *The Arts and Human Development*. New York: John Wiley & Sons, Inc., 1973.

Klein, Melanie. *Contributions to Psychoanalysis*. London: Hogarth Press, 1948.

———. *The Psychoanalysis of Children*. London: Hogarth Press, 1959.

Kline, Paul. *Fact and Fantasy in Freudian Theory*. London: Methuen, 1972.

Kris, Ernst. *Psychoanalytic Explorations in Art*. New York: Schocken Books, Inc., 1967.

Laing, R. D. *The Politics of Experience*. New York: Ballantine Books, Inc., 1967.

Paris, Bernard J. *A Psychological Approach to Fiction: Studies in Thackeray, Stendhal, George Eliot, Dostoyevsky, and Conrad*. Bloomington, Ind.: Indiana University Press, 1974.

Phillips, William, ed. *Art and Psychoanalysis*. Cleveland: World Publishing Co., 1967.

Rank, Otto. *The Myth of the Birth of the Hero and Other Writings*. New York: Vintage, 1959.

Reich, Wilhelm. *Character Analysis*. Translated by Theodore P. Wolfe. New York: Farrar Strauss, 1949.

———. *The Function of the Orgasm*. Translated by Theodore P. Wolfe. 1942. Reprint New York: Bantam, 1967.

———. *The Mass Psychology of Fascism*. Translated by Theodore P. Wolfe. New York: Orgone Institute Press, 1946.

Robinson, Paul A. *The Freudian Left: Wilhelm Reich, Geza Roheim, Herbert Marcuse*. New York: Harper, 1969.

Rycroft, Charles. *Wilhelm Reich*. New York: The Viking Press, 1971.

Spock, Dr. Benjamin. *Baby and Child Care*. Rev. ed. New York: Pocket Books, 1968.

Index

Abraham, Karl, 25, 164, 183

Acrophobia. *See* Falling, fear of

Advertisements for Myself (Mailer), 13, 25, 33, 39, 44, 55, 192; role of artist in, 35; self-mythologizing in, 188; style of, 113, 131; themes of, 84

"Advertisements for Myself on the Way Out" (Mailer), 188

Alcoholism, 157

Aldridge, John W.: on *An American Dream*, 136, 137, 149; on *The Naked and the Dead*, 61; on *Why Are We in Vietnam?*, 55, 179, 180, 181

Alvarez, A., 159

American Dream, An (Mailer), 130–71; alcoholism in, 157; as allegory, 51, 149, 165; anal ambivalence in, 136, 137, 140, 166; anal journey in, 137–38; anal rape in, 125, 151–52; anal-sadism in, 26, 125, 126, 160; androgyny in, 151, 154, 155–56, 161; authority figure in, 141, 154, 157; anatomy in, 140, 141, 168; balance in, 139–40, 158; birth like death in, 134, 142–43; bitch goddess in, 84, 124, 147–49; breast imagery in, 142; cancer in, 46, 154–55, 159, 162–63, 173, 181; cannibalism in, 149; castration in, 143, 145, 146, 161; compared to *The Armies of the Night*, 132; compared to *Barbary Shore*, 141, 153; compared to *The Deer Park*, 103, 105, 141, 153, 157, 167; compared to a Dickens novel, 138, 153; compared to "The Man Who Studied Yoga," 87; compared to *The Naked and the Dead*, 129–36, 137, 142, 152, 158, 169, 172, 174, 180–81; compared to "The Time of Her Time," 114–15, 119; compared to *Why Are We in Vietnam?*, 148, 172–74, 175–76, 180, 181, 183–84; condensation in, 14, 133–34; control in, 139, 158, 173; counterphobia in, 152, 156, 161; deus ex machina in, 105; as dream, 13, 14, 132, 134, 140, 153; fairy tale in, 125, 133, 134, 138, 149, 153; falling, fear, of in, 152, 159, 162–63, 164–65; fantasy in, 132, 133; father figure in, 103, 107, 133, 138, 140–46 passim, 150, 158–67, passim; first-person narration in, 131–33, 149; God and Devil in, 47, 51, 125, 136–37, 138, 139, 151, 160, 161, 163, 164, 165, 168; greed in, 199; history in, 133; homosexuality in, 135–36, 137, 141, 143–44, 151, 158, 160, 161; id in, 132, 140, 163, 164; impotence in, 135, 155, 165; incest in, 140, 146, 147, 161, 162–63, 164; initiation ritual in, 134, 141; isolated hero in, 135; and R. D. Laing, 48; Mailer's fantasies in, 136, 142, 188, 208–9; as monodrama, 154, 159, 165, 169; moon in, 16, 146–47, 159; mother figure in, 140, 141, 146–49, 153, 155–56, 161, 166, 168; murder in, 141–50; myth in, 14, 133, 137, 149, 153; obsession neurosis in, 138, 139, 140, 147, 148, 162–63, 164; as Oedipal drama, 138–39, 140, 147; oral-sadism in, 82, 134, 148–49; orgasm in, 149–150, 152; as overdetermined, 163–64; paranoia in, 76, 133, 135, 136, 153, 154, 165–66; psychosis in, 140; power in, 131, 135, 168; rage in, 149, 165; and Reich, 46–47; sense of smell in, 148; shame in, 149, 157; son figure in, 18, 140–41, 143, 168; suicide in, 135, 140, 141, 154, 162; as vision, 210; vomiting in, 46, 53 n. 26, 150; war in, 157, 163, 169; womb imagery in, 90, 155. *See also* Rojack, Stephen

"American Dream, The," 13, 17, 168

American Mischief (Lelchuk), 43

Anaka, Mount (in *The Naked and the Dead*), 32, 63, 135, 187, 198

Anal: character, 25, 71, 125; eroticism, 23, 24, 57, 111, 153; fixation, 34, 59, 90, 140, 154; orientation, 55; phase, 22; rape, 24, 65–66, 81, 113, 120, 125, 126, 151–52; regression, 62, 64; retention, 36, 144; urethral, 126–27. *See also* Abraham, Karl; Anal ambivalence; Anality; Anal-phallic; Anal sadism; Autonomy; Erickson, Erik; Fenichel, Otto; Freud, Sigmund; Klein, Melanie; Obsession neurosis; Paranoia; Shame

Anal ambivalence: in *An American Dream*, 136–37, 140, 166; in *The Armies of the Night*, 186, 192, 198, 199, 200, 202, 205; in *The Deer Park*, 111, 199; and form, 205, Freud on, 23, 24; of Mailer, 22, 59–60, 186, 189, 198, 205; in "The Man Who Studied Yoga," 94; in "The Time of Her Time," 118–20. *See also* Anal; Anality; Anal-phallic; Anal sadism; Autonomy; Obsession neurosis; Paranoia; Shame

Anality: Abraham on, 25; and cancer, 154–55, 173, 181; and castration, 67;

221